C000177817

Assessment of Learners with Dyslexic-Type Difficulties

Sylvia Phillips

Kathleen Kelly

& Liz Symes

Angeles | London | New Delhi
gapore | Washington DC

Los Angeles | London | New Delhi
Singapore | Washington DC

SAGE Publications Ltd
1 Oliver's Yard
55 City Road
London EC1Y 1SP

SAGE Publications Inc.
2455 Teller Road
Thousand Oaks, California 91320

SAGE Publications India Pvt Ltd
B 1/I 1 Mohan Cooperative Industrial Area
Mathura Road
New Delhi 110 044

SAGE Publications Asia-Pacific Pte Ltd
3 Church Street
#10-04 Samsung Hub
Singapore 049483

Editor: Jude Bowen
Assistant editor: Monira Begum
Production editor: Nicola Marshall
Copyeditor: Elaine Leek
Proofreader: Emily Ayers
Indexer: Author
Marketing manager: Lorna Patkai
Cover design: Wendy Scott
Typeset by: C&M Digitals (P) Ltd, Chennai, India
Printed and bound by CPI Group (UK) Ltd,
Croydon, CR0 4YY

Library of Congress Control Number: 2012955969

British Library Cataloguing in Publication data

A catalogue record for this book is available from
the British Library

ISBN 978-1-4462-6022-7
ISBN 978-1-4462-6023-4

Assessment of Learners with Dyslexic-Type Difficulties

Education at SAGE

SAGE is a leading international publisher of journals, books, and electronic media for academic, educational, and professional markets.

Our education publishing includes:

- accessible and comprehensive texts for aspiring education professionals and practitioners looking to further their careers through continuing professional development

- inspirational advice and guidance for the classroom

- authoritative state of the art reference from the leading authors in the field

Find out more at: **www.sagepub.co.uk/education**

CONTENTS

ABOUT THE AUTHORS

Sylvia Phillips

Sylvia Phillips, BA, DASE, MEd (SEN), AMBDA, began her career as a teacher of English in secondary schools where she first became interested in why some learners had severe literacy difficulties. She later joined Manchester Metropolitan University where she was a Principal Lecturer, Head of SEN, and then Head of Continuing Professional Development. At MMU she developed the first courses for specialist dyslexia teachers at both undergraduate and postgraduate levels. During her time there, she also continued to work in primary, secondary and special schools, both with teachers and directly with pupils. She developed and taught on SEN courses for teachers in the UK and was the UK partner (with Italy, Belgium and Spain) developing and teaching EU courses on 'Inclusion and SEN' for European educationalists. She has served on the Accreditation Board of the British Dyslexia Association and has also been involved in several dyslexia research projects. She is currently course leader of the specialist dyslexia teachers' course at Glyndŵr University, Wales. She has co-authored *Putting the Code to Work* (Primary and Secondary editions, 1998, MMU – MET Publications), *Inspection and Beyond* (1997, Pearson), *Management Skills for SEN co-ordinators* (1999, Falmer Press), and *A Multi-sensory Teaching System for Reading* (1998, MMU Publishing), a fully scripted set of materials for teaching small groups of pupils with dyslexia. She is the co-author of Kelly and Phillips (2011) *Teaching Literacy to Learners with Dyslexia: A Multi-sensory Approach*. Sylvia's other main areas of interest lie in 'learner voice', pupils' social, emotional and behavioural difficulties, and supporting teachers undertaking enquiries into their practice.

Kathleen Kelly

Dr Kathleen Kelly, PhD, MA (SEN), Dip TESL, AMBDA, is a senior lecturer at Manchester Metropolitan University, in the Centre for Inclusion and Special Educational Needs. She is Programme Leader for the MA in Specific Learning Difficulties and has presented papers at a number of international conferences in this area. For several years she has taught courses on specific learning difficulties (dyslexia) to undergraduates as part of the initial teacher training programme in addition to postgraduate awards. She has considerable experience in delivering courses to meet the criteria set out by the British Dyslexia Association for Approved Teacher Status (ATS) and is Associate Member of the British Dyslexia Association (AMBDA). Kathleen has taught a wide range of learners with dyslexia, from children as young as four years to those at Key Stage 5. She has worked in both mainstream and special schools, for language support and learning support services, as a SENCO in a primary school, and as Head of Sixth Form in a special school. She has many years' experience of supporting multilingual children with special educational needs (including specific learning difficulties). Multilingualism and dyslexia is a particular area of interest and her doctorate was also in this area. She is the co-author of Kelly and Phillips (2011) *Teaching Literacy to Learners with Dyslexia: A Multisensory Approach*.

Liz Symes

Liz Symes, BA French and Spanish, PGCE, DipSpLD, AMBDA, is a senior lecturer at Manchester Metropolitan University in the Centre for Inclusion and Special Educational Needs. She was a primary school teacher in Trafford and Manchester for 17 years and in her last school was SENCO and Deputy Headteacher. At MMU she works in initial teacher education on both undergraduate and postgraduate programmes. She has developed a unit on the undergraduate ITT programme with a SEN and inclusion focus and leads a specialism on the same programme in Specific Learning Difficulties. This specialism has been accredited by the British Dyslexia Association and enables successful students to apply for the BDA award of Accredited Teacher Status (ATS ITT). For the last four years she has led an initiative to develop opportunities for undergraduate students to pursue and develop their interest in working with children with special educational needs through optional extended placements in special schools. She is currently a member of the Accreditation Board of the British Dyslexia Association.

ACKNOWLEDGEMENTS

The authors would like to thank the following:

The Department for Education for permission to include 'The Simple View of Reading' from (Rose, 2006) *Independent Review of the Teaching of Reading*, Appendix 1: 77.17. London: HMSO.

Dr. Lindsay Peer, CBE, for contributing her personal view of the role of an educational psychologist, for Chapter 21, and Diana Sutton, specialist teacher, for providing the original report on which the report in Chapter 20 is based.

We would also like to acknowledge some of the many people who have contributed to our professional development as tutors involved in teaching in the field of dyslexia and other learning difficulties. These include:

- colleagues who have shared ideas;
- teachers and other practitioners taking courses with us;
- the many learners with dyslexia and dyslexic-type difficulties we have taught who have helped us to improve our practice in assessment and teaching.

Special thanks are due to Professor R. Burden of Exeter University and Chair of the BDA Accreditation Board, who kindly read several chapters in draft form. His comments, suggestions and support have been invaluable.

Finally, we would like to thank our partners, Mike, Derek and David, for their patience and support during the writing of this book.

LIST OF FIGURES AND TABLES

Figures

Tables

DOWNLOADABLE MATERIALS

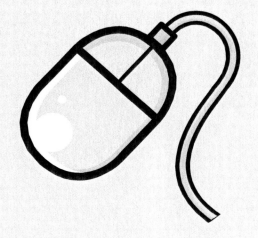

This book is supported by online resources that can be downloaded from www.sagepub.co.uk/phillipskelly&symes for use in your setting. A full list of the resources is available below:

Figure 19.3   Example of pro forma for ILP
Figure 20.1   Assessment report pro forma

Table 4.1   Example of a semi-structured observation schedule
Table 4.2   Example of an event sampling observation schedule
Table 4.3   Checklist for identification of pupils who may have dyslexia
Table 5.2   Attitudes to English lessons (secondary school pupils)
Table 6.5   Example of a miscue analysis record form based on the DfES (2003) guidance booklet
Table 7.1   Diagnostic spelling assessment record
Table 8.1   Observation of handwriting: record sheet
Table 8.2   Assessment of handwriting: record sheet

Appendices

INTRODUCTION

Concern is often expressed about the numbers of learners who have great difficulty developing literacy and numeracy skills – particularly literacy because of its increasing role in accessing the curriculum as learners proceed through school. Teachers themselves are conscious of the fact that although their teaching leads to the *majority* of children successfully learning to read (as the latest figures from the Department for Education [DfE, December 2012] show), a significant minority do not. A major issue for teachers, therefore, is to feel competent in identifying and assessing learners' difficulties in ways that help them to devise appropriate interventions. This implies a need to be able to identify specific aspects of difficulty and recognise individual differences.

This book has been written to provide a practical handbook for teachers seeking guidance on how to identify and assess learners who present difficulties acquiring literacy and numeracy, with an emphasis on literacy because of the necessity to 'read to learn'. There is an assumption that these learners have experienced 'good teaching' yet not reached the standards expected for their age. (It is not about assessing 'readiness' or preparation for literacy/numeracy teaching.) There is also an assumption that many learners appear to cope within the average (and above) range in non-literacy-based lessons/subject areas and that there are no serious physical/medical reasons for their difficulties. Some of these learners may have a specific learning difficulty (dyslexia) whereas others may have more general learning difficulties. The observable *charac-teristics* of their reading/spelling (and numeracy where applicable) difficulties are, however, very similar. For that reason, we call them 'dyslexic-type' difficulties. In the USA, there is now a tendency to use the generic term 'reading disabilities' to describe the difficulties of children and people who have a particular difficulty acquiring reading skills. This term includes those with dyslexia (see *inter alia* Shaywitz et al., 2008, and Jennings et al., 2009).

We are also concerned that many pupils from minority ethnic groups, pupils for whom English is an additional language (EAL) and many white indigenous children, because of social, cultural and linguistic backgrounds, may have dyslexia, but, for a variety of reasons, it goes undetected. In Parts II and III of this book, which deal with the assessment process, we have included specific reference to some of the issues arising from each chapter in relation to cultural and linguistic diversity. Particular attention is paid to issues of assessment of learners with EAL. The fact that these issues are placed at the end of each chapter does not imply that they are an afterthought. Rather, we want to draw attention to some of the possible reasons as to why children with dyslexia may not be easily identified in some groups.

We hope that the book will be useful for *all* teachers (including those on initial teacher training courses) who wish to know more about identifying and assessing learning difficulties in primary and secondary schools. It provides guidance about how to devise, score and interpret teacher-made assessments in addition to how to select and use standardised tests. The book will, however, be of particular value to SENCOs and specialist teachers in the field. It has been designed also to be used as a standard text on assessment for all teachers, including those training to be specialist teachers of learners with dyslexia at both Approved Teacher Status (ATS) and Associate Member of the British Dyslexia Association (AMBDA) levels, where it would support a training course.

The book draws on the authors' considerable experience of teaching learners with literacy and numeracy difficulties in primary and secondary schools in addition to training initial teacher-training students, qualified teachers and other educational practitioners to assess and teach children with general and specific learning difficulties. Ideas and examples in this book have also been used successfully on SENCO-training courses and specialist courses on dyslexia.

 The accompanying website contains additional materials, references and photocopiable materials that are available to download at: www.sagepub.co.uk/phillipskelly&symes

References

DfE (2012) Department for Education website. www.education.gov.uk/schools/performance – *Teacher Assessment Tab* (accessed 13 December, 2012).

Jennings, J.H., Schudt, J. and Lerner, J.W. (2009) *Reading Problems: Assessment and Teaching Strategies*, 6th edn. Boston: Pearson Education.

Shaywitz, S.E., Morris, R. and Shaywitz, B.A. (2008) 'The education of dyslexic children from childhood to early adulthood', *Annual Review of Psychology*, 59: 451–75.

PART I

DYSLEXIC-TYPE DIFFICULTIES AND ASSESSMENT: SETTING THE CONTEXT

The first three chapters of the book provide an overview of the need to identify and assess the learning difficulties associated with dyslexia. Attention is drawn to the fact that many learners present similar characteristics and will benefit from detailed assessment of their strengths and weaknesses in order to teach and support them more appropriately so that they may be successful in school. The first chapter provides a brief overview of the nature of dyslexia together with theories of causation. This is used as the basis for proposing the areas of assessment. The second chapter summarises some of the main purposes and types of assessment and proposes a model for the assessment process. This model forms the basis for the rest of the book and applies to a process that may depend wholly on informal or formal assessment – or, more usually, involve a combination of both. Finally, the third chapter summarises the main aspects of legislation and policy that affect the assessment of children and young people experiencing difficulties in learning.

At the time of writing there are plans for substantial reform in the area of special educational needs. A new Code of Practice for Special Educational Needs is to be published in 2014. We are conscious, therefore, that there may be some changes which will affect current provision. However, we believe there will still be a need for teachers to be able to have the knowledge and skills to identify learners with dyslexia and dyslexic-type difficulties appropriately so that they may benefit appropriately from education.

CHAPTER 1

DYSLEXIC-TYPE DIFFICULTIES: IMPLICATIONS FOR ASSESSMENT

Chapter Overview

This chapter will enable the reader to:

- understand the relationship between general and specific learning difficulties/ dyslexia;
- consider theories and research which inform the identification and assessment of literacy and numeracy difficulties in order to develop appropriate intervention.

Although the latest figures on pupils' progress at Key Stage 2 (DfE, 2012) showed an increase in attainments in English and mathematics from 74% in 2011 to 79% in 2012, this gives no cause for complacency. A detailed breakdown shows that 11% of pupils did not make expected progress in English and 13% in mathematics. This chapter considers a range of difficulties in literacy and numeracy experienced by these learners, who include pupils with specific learning difficulty (dyslexia) and those who experience general learning difficulties. We have used the term 'dyslexic-type difficulties' as an umbrella term to describe the many common characteristics they present. However, we argue that it is both possible and important to distinguish between learners with dyslexia and those with more general difficulties in order to determine appropriate intervention and support. The chapter focuses on considering and justifying which characteristics and skills should and can be assessed by teachers. The emphasis is on literacy because of the increasing need to 'read to learn' as a child progresses through school.

Any pupil who is experiencing difficulties in learning (i.e. not making the same progress as most of his/her peers) should not only be closely monitored but their needs should be identified and assessed so that intervention can be put in place before those difficulties become entrenched. It is essential also that assessment identifies not only strengths but also potential barriers to learning. This is true for both literacy and mathematics, as Chinn (2011) points out. Difficulties in mathematics and numeracy are only briefly mentioned here but expanded on in two dedicated chapters in Parts II and III of this book.

Characteristics of Difficulties in Literacy and Numeracy

Difficulties in literacy

Literacy difficulties are typically characterised by poor decoding skills resulting in slow and often inaccurate reading which may lead to poor reading comprehension. There is much overlap between the difficulties in decoding often noted in learners with dyslexia (for example poor letter-sound knowledge, omission of letters or syllables when reading, losing place in reading, difficulty in skimming and scanning texts for information) and those experienced by other learners with literacy difficulties. It is a fact that many children present similar characteristics and difficulties but their underlying needs may be very different and therefore require different forms of intervention.

Rose (2006) in his review of literacy teaching in England advised the adoption of the Simple View of Reading (SVoR) model (Gough and Tunmer, 1986) as a framework for the development of literacy. This model is discussed further in Chapter 6. It emphasises that 'Reading' implies reading for meaning, i.e. reading comprehension, which is the product of two dimensions: decoding skills and language/listening comprehension. This is useful in offering an explanation of some of the differences among learners with reading difficulties, accounting for 'good' or skilled readers (with good decoding skills and language comprehension) and suggesting three broad groups of 'poor' readers:

- those with poor decoding skills but good language comprehension who can understand a text if it is read to them (most learners with dyslexia are in this group);
- those who can decode, i.e. read the text aloud, but without understanding (sometimes this is found in learners with English as an Additional Language (EAL), especially in the early stages of English language acquisition; it can sometimes be observed in children with autistic spectrum conditions and those with severe learning difficulties; it may be observed also in some learners who have weaknesses in both dimensions but whose decoding skills have improved by targeted teaching although their comprehension remains poor);
- those who have both poor decoding skills and poor language comprehension (they often have other learning difficulties).

It is important to recognise that the model suggests that each dimension represents a range from good to poor and therefore there will be a variety of individual differences. However, it provides a clear framework for assessing two aspects of reading difficulties, as discussed in Chapter 6. It points also to a need to assess listening/language comprehension as well as reading comprehension.

Difficulties in numeracy

If we apply a similar framework to the development of numeracy skills, we can examine possible strengths and difficulties in mathematics. Mathematical ability could be seen as a product of:

- computational skills (number fact knowledge, speed of working, sequential skills) and
- conceptual understanding (ability to reason, see relationships and generalise).

This suggests:

- some learners may have relatively good conceptual understanding but weaknesses in computational skills due to difficulty learning and retrieving number facts, slow processing speed or confusion with directionality (learners with dyslexia may exhibit this profile); if they have a flexible approach to mathematics, they may be able to develop strategies to support weak number fact knowledge;
- some may have poor conceptual understanding but may master the four basic rules even if they are unsure of their application;
- some others may have poor conceptual understanding (this includes children with dyscalculia and those with general learning difficulties) and may also struggle with computation.

Who are the learners who experience difficulties?

Those most 'at risk' (in England) are children who start school with:

- limited exposure to the English language – this includes many children where English is not spoken in the home (and for whom English is an Additional Language) but it also includes a high proportion of children whose first language is English but who have had a limited range of experiences and opportunities to learn to use a wide range of English expressions, often resulting in poor oral language skills and, in particular, a lack of knowledge and understanding of much of the vocabulary of school;
- poor phonological awareness and letter knowledge (this will include many learners with dyslexia but also others with general learning difficulties);
- little experience of exposure to the printed word, books or the purpose of reading;
- the possibility of having inherited dyslexia (Pennington, 2011);
- a 'specific learning difficulty', which often co-exists with dyslexia and/or leads to literacy difficulties, e.g. dyspraxia (Developmental Co-ordination Disorder), autistic spectrum conditions including Asperger's Syndrome, and Attention Deficit (Hyperactivity) Disorder (ADHD).

Many of the children presenting these 'risk factors' also have more general learning difficulties, but some may have dyslexia or dyslexic-type difficulties.

Can we differentiate between 'poor readers' who have dyslexia and those who do not?

'Discrepancy theory' has traditionally been used to distinguish between specific and general learning difficulties. This suggested that where a learner's reading age is significantly below that predicted by their chronological age and 'IQ' score (general intelligence/ability) the child could be considered to have dyslexia, i.e. a specific learning difficulty. By comparison, learners with reading difficulties whose reading attainment could be accounted for by below-average scores of ability would be seen as having general difficulties.

Discrepancy theory has been criticised on a number of grounds including:

- the impact dyslexia itself may have on verbal ability (which may depress 'ability'/ IQ scores reducing the 'ability'/IQ-attainment gap) so that some children may therefore not be identified although they have dyslexia (MacBlain et al., 2005);
- the fact that learners of all abilities may have dyslexia but it is harder to demonstrate a 'discrepancy' if measured ability is below average;

- the fact that the behavioural characteristics of learners with reading difficulties with high and low ability/intelligence scores are similar, so that the need to distinguish between them is redundant (Stuebing et al., 2002).

Moreover, Snowling (2000) points out that some children with dyslexia display more difficulty with spelling and writing than with reading and may be overlooked if a discrepancy between IQ and reading only is looked for. She also pointed out that children who do not practise reading might show a discrepancy but not be dyslexic. Earlier, Stanovich (1996: 161) argued that a number of studies indicate that the processes involved in decoding (including phonological segmentation and reading non-words) are similar for poor readers regardless of intelligence, and asked:

> Why is a low IQ child with demonstrated speech segmentation problems, with poor word recognition skills and hence reading comprehension, not dyslexic?

Current definitions of dyslexia have moved away from the discrepancy model to one that considers differences in cognitive processing (Singleton, 2003). However, the debate continues as to whether *any* learner with the same processing difficulties and uneven learning profiles should therefore be identified as having dyslexia.

Defining Dyslexia

Many definitions exist, but the current definition adopted by the British Dyslexia Association is that of the Rose Report (2009: 30), which suggested the following:

- dyslexia is a learning difficulty that primarily affects the skills involved in accurate and fluent word reading and spelling;
- characteristic features of dyslexia are difficulties in phonological awareness, verbal memory and verbal processing speed;
- dyslexia occurs across a range of intellectual abilities;
- it is best thought of as a continuum, not a distinct category, and there are no clear cut-off points;
- co-occurring difficulties may be seen in aspects of language, motor co-ordination, mental calculation, concentration and personal organisation, but they are not, by themselves, markers of dyslexia;
- a good indication of the severity and persistence of dyslexic difficulties can be gained by examining how the individual responds or has responded to well-founded intervention.

With the addition that:

> In addition to these characteristics, the BDA acknowledges the visual processing difficulties that some individuals with dyslexia can experience, and points out that dyslexic readers can show a combination of abilities and difficulties that affect the learning process. Some also have strengths in other areas, such as design, problem solving, creative skills, interactive skills and oral skills. (www.bdadyslexia.org.uk)

The emphasis on phonological processing skills implies that this should form the core of any assessment for dyslexia. However, the BDA's additional paragraph is important for drawing attention to the fact that some people with dyslexia have visual processing difficulties. The current definition acknowledges that dyslexia can occur across a range of intellectual abilities and suggests that an indication of severity can be seen by how a learner responds to intervention, although it could be argued that this approach relies on the learner failing at school before the severity of their needs is recognised. Co-occurring difficulties are also noted and these should be assessed as well as phonological processing skills.

The underpinning reasons for such difficulties are many and varied and some may be beyond the control of teachers. What we know, however, is that whatever the reasons for the difficulties, in literacy in particular, the effects on the learner can be profound. Even as a very young child, failure to learn to read successfully may lead to low self-esteem and increasing inability to access the full curriculum and keep up with teachers' expectations. Indeed relationships with peers may be impaired and, in many cases, children with literacy difficulties have been susceptible to bullying. All too often, a consequence is that learners with difficulties begin to use avoidance strategies and/or misbehaviour. In some cases, they themselves may begin to bully others as a means of gaining 'prestige'. Others may present the behaviour known as 'learned helplessness' where they may give up *trying* to learn because 'I know I can't do it'.

Early intervention is important. As children grow older, they are expected to 'read to learn'. Many learners enter secondary school with very low levels of literacy and are unable to cope with the demands of literacy-based subjects. They may know how to use the Internet to access information but cannot read or understand the information given.

What Should We Assess?

In this chapter we focus particularly on the assessment of literacy because of its impact on all learning. The main sources for determining what to assess are:

- models of reading and spelling processes;
- models of reading and spelling development (descriptive);
- research into the nature and causes of literacy difficulties, particularly those associated with dyslexia.

What do models of reading and spelling processes suggest we assess?

The Simple View of Reading model has already been discussed. Two other models of reading which can inform assessment are the Dual-Route of Reading (Coltheart, 2005) and the connectionist or 'triangle' model developed by Seidenberg and McClelland in 1989 (Adams, 1990; Seidenberg, 2005).

The Dual-Route of Reading suggested two pathways:

- a direct, lexical route, which uses visual memory for automatic recognition of familiar words;
- an indirect, phonological processing route, which is important for decoding unfamiliar words.

An impairment or weakness in either pathway would affect ability to 'read'/decode words.

Similarly, the connectionist model points to interactions between visual and phonological strategies and 'meanings' of words. There is, perhaps, greater explicit reference to the importance of context in a text in this model. Both models can also form the basis of a model of spelling. A more detailed summary of these models and their application can be found in Chapters 4 (reading) and 5 (spelling) in Kelly and Phillips (2011). The value of these models is that they point to the need to assess not just the surface characteristics of literacy difficulties but also underlying cognitive processing skills, including visual and auditory perception, memory, phonological awareness and their application to and knowledge of grapheme-phoneme correspondence. The dual-route model points to the need also to investigate a learner's ability to read non-words that are phonetically regular (e.g. grib) as this can reflect phonological processing skills. About 80% of learners with dyslexia have some degree of phonological deficit and about 20% have a visual processing difficulty, although some have both.

How can models of reading and spelling development inform assessment?

Some models of reading and spelling, particularly those of Ehri, Frith and Gentry, provide developmental frameworks that can be used for assessing literacy. These are discussed in Part II (where full references are provided) because they are particularly useful in informal assessment. They also remind us that the nature of learning and learning difficulties can change over time. Many learners with dyslexia, for example, present characteristics that are 'typical' in the literacy development of very young children (such as confusing 'b' and 'd' in spelling at a much later age than is observed in 'normal' development). Similarly, learners with dyslexia may, with good teaching, improve their decoding skills in reading and where they have good language comprehension, their reading comprehension will be good. For many, however, spelling remains a difficulty and often is their major problem at secondary school.

Early assessment and intervention is necessary for all learners who fail to acquire early literacy skills, whatever the cause, because children who find reading difficult are less likely to *want* to read. The result is likely to be that they get less practice and increasingly fall behind their peers. Stanovich (1986) refers to this as the Matthew effect because the gap between good and poor readers widens.

How do theories of causation inform assessment?

Morton and Frith (1995) suggested that using a causal modelling framework is helpful in analysing theories of psychological and learning behaviours such as dyslexia. They identify three 'levels' of theories of causation and emphasise the interaction at all levels with the environment. This can be depicted as in Figure 1.1.

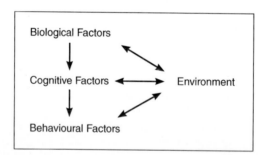

Figure 1.1   Summary of Morton and Frith's causal framework model

Kelly and Phillips (2011) provide a fuller description of theories of causation, which are summarised below.

Biological factors

There is evidence that dyslexia is a genetic, neurobiological condition. The relevance for teachers' assessments is that knowledge that parents/siblings have dyslexia can mean that the learner is 'at risk' of having inherited it (Pennington and Olson, 2005). However, it does not mean that the child *will* have dyslexia and even where early signs of dyslexic characteristics (e.g. phonological difficulties) have been identified in the children of parents with dyslexia, some do not develop literacy difficulties (Snowling et al., 2007). Snowling suggests that perhaps this is because the parents consciously adopt strategies to foster their child's reading development. However, the issue of 'dyslexia in the family' often comes up in parental interviews and it is an area worth exploring as part of the assessment process, together with information about compensatory or preventative strategies and support provided at home.

Cognitive factors

The term 'cognitive processing' refers to the psychological processes involved in learning, such as phonological processing, memory, auditory and visual processing, and speed of processing information. Research has suggested a number of cognitive processing deficits that might be responsible for dyslexia and which can be assessed. One of the most researched areas is that of phonological processing deficits (Snowling, 2000; Vellutino et al., 2004). Difficulty in phonological processing is seen as a core deficit. Difficulties in distinguishing sounds in words (blending, segmenting, and manipulating sounds) and in acquiring the alphabetic principle (knowing that letters/graphemes represent sounds/phonemes) are early indicators of later literacy difficulties. Other areas of difficulty in phonological processing include limited verbal short-term memory, problems in rapid naming (the ability to name objects at speed) and poor verbal repetition ability (the ability to repeat a multisyllabic word orally without error). Snowling (2000) attributed these to difficulty in 'phonological representations' or the way that the brain codes sounds and words. In addition, she suggested that phonological coding deficits are responsible for short-term memory difficulties and that inefficient verbal rehearsal strategies may result in information being lost during transfer from short- to long-term memory. This offers an explanation for difficulties in remembering long or complex instructions, relaying messages correctly and recalling names or events out of sequence.

Learners with dyslexia appear to have problems in storage and retrieval of information. Gathercole and Packiam-Alloway (2008) attribute these difficulties to problems in working memory capacity, the part of memory that holds on to information until it is transferred from short-term to long-term memory. They argue that the amount of information that can be held in working memory is limited and if a learner is given information that exceeds their memory capacity, some of that information will be forgotten. They point out that not all children of the same age have the same working memory capacity. Another explanation for difficulty is that something distracts us and prevents us from attending to information in working memory (e.g. a noisy background) and information gets lost. A third possible explanation is an inability to switch attention from one activity to another. If this is more difficult for some learners then it may lead to loss of information in activities such as mental calculations where it is necessary to switch attention frequently from the calculation (manipulation of the numbers, e.g. as in rounding up) to the items being stored (the numbers to be calculated, e.g. '273–97'). Similarly, working memory affects reading and spelling. One implication is that assessing verbal short-term memory (the ability to recall a string of verbal information immediately after it is given) is not sufficient; we also need to assess working memory.

Das (2009) maintains that in assessing cognitive processes we should move beyond phonological coding to that of sequencing. In particular, the learner's ability to sequence both sounds and letters within words and words within sentences should be considered. Stein (2001, 2008) further suggests that learners with dyslexia have impaired visual and auditory processing. Difficulty in processing rapidly changing auditory stimuli (such as speech) can compromise phonological awareness and memory storage and result in slower work rate (Tallal, 2007; Valeo, 2008). Difficulties in visual processing can result in visual stress and sensory integration problems when trying to read (Everatt, 2002; White et al., 2006), where letters appear to blur or move about, creating difficulty in determining the order of letters in words and hence lack of reading fluency. Signs of visual stress may include headaches, eye strain, tracking difficulties, words or lines omitted when reading or copying text, difficulty remembering what has been read and poor concentration (Jordan, 2006). Such problems may be found in learners with dyspraxia (Developmental Co-ordination Disorder – DCD) and poor concentration is a feature also of Attention Deficit (Hyperactivity) Disorder (ADHD), both of which can co-exist with dyslexia. (Formal assessment of visual processing difficulties is normally carried out by an optometrist/ ophthalmologist.)

Slow processing speed resulting in problems in integrating and synchronising different forms of information has also been considered as a possible cause of dyslexia (Breznitz, 2008). Fawcett and Nicolson (2008) propose that learners with dyslexia might have particular difficulties when a task or activity requires the co-ordination of different brain regions, as in *reading aloud* (where eye-movements, speech and cognitive processes such as word recognition and retrieval must be co-ordinated), *spelling* (in which cognitive processes such as analysing speech sounds in words and identifying the letters that represent those sounds must be co-ordinated) and *writing* (where eye and hand movements and cognitive processes such as organisation of ideas, sequencing of words, and retrieval of spellings must be co-ordinated). They attribute such difficulties to a lack of automatic skill development, resulting not only in literacy difficulties but also problems in multi-tasking and poor motor planning and appearing clumsy and unco-ordinated. (Some would see such motor difficulties as indicators of DCD.)

Behavioural factors

These are the behaviours or characteristics of difficulties observed in the classroom and that first alert teachers to look more closely at a learner's difficulties. There will be particular difficulties in decoding, i.e. in reading words aloud (word recognition), and reading is likely to be slow, laboured and lack fluency. Spelling is often inconsistent with a similar lack of knowledge of how sounds are represented by letters, i.e. poor knowledge of grapheme-phoneme correspondence. These characteristics form the basis of observations and assessments carried out by teachers, as described in Part II of this book, and inform the selection of formal tests, as detailed in Part III.

Even before school, a child may be late in developing some speech patterns, say syllables (in some words) in the wrong order, display difficulty in remembering two-part instructions and have poor ability to detect rhyme. This may be accompanied by co-ordination difficulties, such as learning to ride a bicycle, or poor self-help skills, e.g. dressing. Information about these difficulties may be obtained when talking to or during interviews with parents. Difficulties are compounded as learners grow older and more demands are made of these skills at secondary school.

Environmental factors

The Morton and Frith model is particularly useful for reminding teachers of the impact of *interaction* between any 'within-child' aspect and the environment. All too often, however, research into learning difficulties has concentrated only on the way the home environment affects learning. There are many studies that show the benefits of homes where there are positive attitudes towards learning (e.g. Snowling et al., 2007), books to read and where adults and others regularly read and where visits to different places to extend children's experiences and vocabulary take place (Jennings et al., 2009). At the time of writing, these aspects of 'parenting skills' are being actively debated (Field, 2012).

The relationship between social class, poverty and educational achievement is well established. Recent surveys in England, like those in the USA, show that children from lower socio-economic groups are more likely to underachieve than those from higher groups. The educational level of parents is also a significant factor. Issues of gender, ethnicity, culture and language add to the complexity of understanding how to 'Create a fairer educational system' (Dyson et al., 2010). A recent review of the literature is provided by Perry and Francis (2010) and the case for early intervention to raise standards, particularly in literacy and numeracy, has been argued for more than forty years and recently reiterated by Gross and others (Gross, 2008).

All too often, however, knowledge of this relationship is used as an 'explanation' for children's low educational achievement. Schools can and *do* make a difference through their teaching and learning strategies and by ensuring children have opportunities to benefit from experiences such as school visits, creative approaches to technology, and after-school clubs. They also find ways of working with parents/carers. It is vital to remember that many of the children from disadvantaged homes may have dyslexia. This fact is sometimes overlooked when people look only at a relationship between low achievement and social disadvantage! It is, therefore, important to consider the environment at school and whether this raises barriers to learning for some children and young people. (Some would argue this is more fruitful as teachers have more control over what happens there.) Recent moves to make schools more dyslexia-friendly have made schools more 'learning-friendly' for all pupils. However, in undertaking assessments teachers need to consider aspects such as the levels of reading required by some of the texts/worksheets that they use, the vocabulary used in school and the arrangements for giving additional support for those experiencing difficulty. One aspect is the 'balance' between direct teaching of reading/spelling/numeracy to those with difficulties and 'supporting' learners, particularly those with reading difficulties, by having an assistant read 'to or for' them. Whilst this gives access to the wider curriculum and enables those with good listening/language comprehension skills, *too much* support can be seen as 'propping up' rather than helping the learner to become an independent reader. Reid (2009) emphasises the importance of understanding the demands of the curriculum and the effect that a mismatch between this and learning needs, together with time pressures, excessive noise levels, lack of appropriate aids and unrealistic expectations, can have on a learner with dyslexia.

The attitudes and expectations of teachers are very important in giving a sense of the possibility of achievement to those struggling with learning. Their attitude to those with difficulties will be conveyed not only to the learners but also their peers, thereby potentially giving rise to negative social interactions amongst learners. Asking questions of the learner and teachers/TAs in addition to direct observation in a range of lessons should all be part of the identification and assessment process.

Many learners will experience some of the difficulties described in this chapter. It is important to note that isolated difficulties may be experienced by most children and therefore teachers and TAs need to look for clusters of difficulties using checklists or observation as part of the initial identification process. However, clusters of difficulties may also be found in children with other types of learning difficulties (e.g. general learning difficulties) and some of the co-occurring difficulties mentioned in the Rose (2009) definition can overlap with other specific learning difficulties. It is important, therefore, to be aware that having identified one specific learning difficulty does not rule out the possibility of the existence of others.

Summary

The complex nature of dyslexia requires a comprehensive assessment on which to base intervention. This chapter has provided a rationale for determining the areas to be taken into account when assessing learners presenting dyslexic-type difficulties. We summarise these in Table 1.1, using the Morton and Frith framework because this includes both observable characteristics and the need to explore some of the underlying cognitive processes. It also ensures that we consider which of a learner's experiences to date, including their school experiences, may have helped them or exacerbated their difficulties. Our model also values the contributions of learners and parents.

Table 1.1   What should we assess when investigating dyslexic-type difficulties?

Behavioural					External Factors
Reading	**Spelling**	**Writing**	**Numeracy**	**General**	Learning environment: Dyslexia friendly Teaching and learning styles Resources Distractions/ noise levels Teacher/pupil relationship Parental support Attendance at school Social/ emotional: Self-esteem Anxiety Stress Lack of confidence
Word recognition/ decoding: g–p correspondence Single word reading (regular and irregular) Non-word reading Passage reading Reading rate Comprehension	Free writing: g–p correspondence Regular words Irregular words Spelling rules	Letter formation Speed Punctuation Grammar Organisation Presentation in copying and free writing	Basic numeracy Mental maths Maths symbols Maths language Word problems Cognitive learning style	Articulation Sequencing Organisation Fine/gross motor Concentration Copying skills Attitude to learning Language/ Listening Comprehension Cognitive learning style	
Cognitive					
Memory: Short-term memory Working memory	Phonological Awareness: Blending Segmenting Manipulation	Reasoning Ability: Verbal Non-verbal	Processing Skills: Auditory Visual (including scotopic sensitivity) Speed of processing (including rapid naming)		
Biological					
Family history (parent voice) *Usually obtained in interviews*					

Points for Discussion

- Do you think there is a need to distinguish between learners with dyslexia and those presenting similar literacy difficulties but who have general learning difficulties? Why?
- What assessment procedures are currently used in your school to identify dyslexic-type difficulties?

Further Reading

Kelly, K. and Phillips, S. (2011) *Teaching Literacy to Learners with Dyslexia*. London: SAGE.
A discussion of the theories of causation of dyslexia can be found in Chapter 1 of this book.
Reid, G. (2009) *Dyslexia: A Practitioner's Handbook*, 4th edn. London: Wiley.
An excellent practical overview of many aspects of assessment and intervention for dyslexia.

References

Adams, M.J. (1990) *Beginning to Read: Thinking and Learning about Print*. Cambridge, MA: MIT Press.

Breznitz, Z. (2008) 'The origin of dyslexia: the asynchrony phenomenon', in G. Reid, A.J. Fawcett, F. Manis and L.S. Seigel (eds.), *The SAGE Handbook of Dyslexia*. London: SAGE. pp. 12–29.

British Dyslexia Association (2011) www.bdadyslexia.org.uk.

Chinn, S. (2011) *The Trouble with Maths*, 2nd edn. London: Routledge.

Coltheart, M. (2005) 'Modelling reading: the dual-route approach', in M.J. Snowling and C. Hulme (ed.), *The Science of Reading: A Handbook*. Oxford: Blackwell. pp. 6–23.

Das, J.P. (2009) *Reading Difficulties and Dyslexia*. London: SAGE.

DfE (Department for Education) (2012) *Pupils' progress at Key Stage 2*. www.education.gov.uk/schools/performance

Dyson, A., Goldrick, S., Jones, L. and Kerr, K. (2010) *Equity in Education: Creating a Fairer System*. University of Manchester for the European Agency for Development in Education.

Everatt, J. (2002) 'Visual processes', in G. Reid and J. Wearmouth (eds), *Dyslexia and Literacy: Theory and Practice*. Chichester: Wiley. pp. 85–98.

Fawcett, A.J. and Nicolson, R.I. (2008) 'Dyslexia and the cerebellum', in G. Reid, A.J. Fawcett, F. Manis and L.S. Siegel (eds), *The SAGE Handbook of Dyslexia*. London: SAGE. pp. 77–98.

Field, F. (2012) 'We need a new dynamic poverty measure'. www.frankfield.com/latest-news/articles/news.aspx?p=102450.

Gathercole, S.E. and Packiam-Alloway, T. (2008) *Working Memory and Learning*. London: SAGE.

Gough, P.B. and Tunmer, W.E. (1986) 'Decoding, reading and reading disability', *Remedial and Special Education*, 7: 6–10.

Gross, J. (2008) *Getting in Early: Primary Schools and Early Intervention*. London: The Centre for Social Justice.

Jennings, J.H., Schudt-Caldwell, J. and Lerner, J.W. (2009) *Reading Problems: Assessment and Teaching Strategies*, 6th edn. Boston: Pearson Education.

Jordan, I. (2006) *How a Teacher can Recognise, Assess and Screen for Visual Dyslexia, Visual Dyspraxia and Other Vision Linked Stress*. Available from IanJordan@visual-dyslexia.com

Kelly, K. and Phillips, S. (2011) *Teaching Literacy to Learners with Dyslexia*. London: SAGE.

MacBlain, S., Hassard, K. and MacBlain, F. (2005) 'Dyslexia: the ethics of assessment', *Academic Exchange Quarterly*, 9 (1).

Morton, J. and Frith, U. (1995) 'Causal modelling: a structural approach to developmental psychopathology', in D. Cicchetti and D.J. Cohen (eds), *Manual of Developmental Psychopathology*. New York: Wiley. pp. 357–90.

Pennington, B. F. and Olson, R.K. (2005) 'Genetics of Dyslexia', in Snowling, M.J. and Hulme, C. (Eds), *The Science of Reading: A Handbook*. Oxford: Blackwell. pp. 453–72.

Pennington, B.F. (2011) *Using Genetics and Neuropsychology to Understand Dyslexia and its Co-morbidities*. BDA Conference, Harrogate, 3rd June 2011.

Perry, E. and Francis, B. (2010) *The Social Class Gap for Educational Achievement*. London: RSA.

Reid, G. (2009) *Dyslexia*. London: SAGE.

Rose, J. (2006) *An Independent Review of the Teaching of Early Reading*. London: Department for Education and Skills.

Rose, J. (2009) *Identifying and Teaching Children and Young People with Dyslexia and Literacy Difficulties*. London: Department for Children, Schools and Families.

Seidenberg, M.S. (2005) 'Connectionist models of word reading', *Current Directions in Psychological Science*, 14: 238–42.

Singleton, C. (2003) 'Advice on learning activities and differentiated teaching for pupils with dyslexia who may have specific cognitive weaknesses', Fact Sheet 19, Lucid, www.lucid-research.com.

Snowling, M.J. (2000) *Dyslexia*, 2nd ed. Chichester: Wiley–Blackwell.

Snowling, M.J., Muter, V. and Carroll, J. (2007) 'Outcomes in adolescence of children at family-risk of dyslexia', *Journal of Child Psychology and Psychiatry*, 48: 609–18.

Stanovich, K.E. (1986) 'Matthew effects in reading: some consequences of individual differences in the acquisition of literacy', *Reading Research Quarterly, 26*: 7–29

Stanovich, K.E. (1996) 'Towards a more inclusive definition of dyslexia', *Dyslexia*, 2: 154–66.

Stein, J. (2001) 'The magnocellular theory of developmental dyslexia', *Dyslexia*, 7: 12–36.

Stein, J. (2008) 'The neurobiological basis of dyslexia', in G. Reid, A.J. Fawcett, F. Manis and L. Siegel (eds), *The SAGE Handbook of Dyslexia*. London: SAGE. pp. 53–76.

Stuebing, K.K, Fletcher, J.M., LeDoux, J.M., Reid Lyon, G., Shaywitz, S.E. and Shaywitz, B.A. (2002) 'Validity of IQ-discrepancy classifications of reading disabilities: a meta-analysis', *American Education Research Journal*, 30: 469–518.

Tallal, P. (2007) 'Experimental studies of language impairments: from research to remediation'. http://en.scientificcommons.org (accessed May 2012); also available at: www.santafe.edu/media/

Valeo, T. (2008) 'Dyslexia studies catch neuroplasticity at work: The Dana Foundation', www.dana.org. (accessed May 2012).

Vellutino, F.R., Fletcher, J.M., Snowling, M.J. and Scanlon, D.M. (2004) 'Specific reading disability (dyslexia): what have we learned in the past four decades?', *Journal of Child Psychology and Psychiatry*, 45: 2–40.

White, S., Milne, E., Rosen, S., Hansen, P., Swettenham, J., Frith, U. and Ramus, F. (2006) 'The role of sensorimotor impairments in dyslexia: a multiple case study of dyslexic children', *Developmental Science*, 9: 237–69.

CHAPTER 2

PURPOSES AND FORMS OF ASSESSMENT

Chapter Overview

This chapter will enable the reader to:

- further their understanding of the purposes of assessment in the education of learners with dyslexic-type difficulties;
- further their awareness of different types of assessment procedures;
- appreciate the significance of assessment as a process.

Assessment is a systematic process or procedure for collecting information about specific characteristics or behaviours which can lead to action that facilitates successful learning. Assessment should be seen as an essential part of teaching. Tests are one method of assessment but a range of other procedures can be used, such as interviews, observations and analysis of the learner's performance in the curriculum, e.g. writing, spelling, reading and mathematics.

A test is a procedure in which an individual's behaviour is obtained and evaluated. It is a sample of behaviour at a particular point in time and it is therefore important that the sample is as representative of the behaviour being evaluated as possible. It can involve quantification of a learner's achievements (e.g. the percentage of errors a child makes in reading a text) and/or qualitative evaluation (e.g. describing the strategies a child uses in reading).

Purposes of Assessment

Assessment can be used for a range of purposes. The main ones are:

1   To inform decisions about:

- level of attainment;
- placement, e.g. in a particular class or group of children;
- need for additional support or counselling;
- need to refer for further assessment.

2   To identify strengths and difficulties (some may say, to make a 'diagnosis'), in order to:

- make recommendations about appropriate teaching;
- to set individualised targets and develop a specific teaching programme;
- to 'diagnose' specific learning difficulties/dyslexia;
- produce an assessment for the Disabled Student Allowance (DSA) in Further and Higher Education;
- justify a request for access arrangements/examination concessions.

3   To monitor and evaluate progress in order to determine:

- rate of successful learning;
- if the level and amount of support is appropriate;
- whether to change targets and teaching methods;
- the need to refer for further assessment including outside specialists.

4   To make policy decisions at both local authority and school level, e.g. allocation of resources.

5   To predict future success, e.g. academic grades and career guidance.

6   To conduct research into, e.g., the nature and characteristics of dyslexia; standardisation of tests; the underlying processes of reading.

All these purposes for assessment are relevant to learners with dyslexia, although this book is largely concerned with the first three, particularly with identifying dyslexic-type difficulties in order to devise appropriate intervention and support. Often this can lead to a formal 'diagnosis' of dyslexia, especially when standardised tests have been used. Two major criticisms are sometimes levelled at this use of assessment.

First, the term 'diagnosis' can be seen as a medical term, implying that the difficulty lies within the child and the 'medical' model ignores the major contribution of the environment in both producing and exacerbating difficulties. The 'social' model, which was a reaction to the medical model, drew attention to the fact that learning difficulties and disabilities are caused by the way that society is organised. These models present a dichotomy that is over-simplistic (Shakespeare and Watson, 2002). We advocate the use of an 'Interactional' Model of SEN (for a discussion of an interactional analysis see Frederickson and Cline, 2009), which acknowledges that there may be some underlying difficulties or disabilities within a child but also recognises the importance of environmental factors and the interaction between the two. This approach was echoed in the SEN Code of Practice (DfES, 2001: 44, para. 5.6):

> The assessment process should always be fourfold. It should focus on the child's learning characteristics, the learning environment that the school is providing for the child, the task and the teaching style. It should be recognised that some difficulties in learning may be caused or exacerbated by the school's learning environment or adult/child relationships. This means looking carefully at such matters as classroom organisation, teaching materials, teaching style and differentiation in order to decide how these can be developed so that the child is enabled to learn effectively.

This approach underpins the model of assessment recommended later in this chapter.

Secondly, a 'label' may have a negative impact on the expectations of both the person given the 'label' and the person giving it. In particular, this can result in the possible lowering of self-esteem. Interestingly, in our experience, many learners with literacy difficulties who are then 'diagnosed' as dyslexic find the term positive as it helps them to understand their difficulties and actually raises self-esteem, as expressed by both parents and children in Riddick's study (2010). Riddick (2010: 82) notes that 20 of the 22 parents interviewed described themselves as 'relieved' when they were told that their child was dyslexic. Two examples of parents' reactions are given below:

> 'Oh, God, such a relief! It was the first time he wasn't lazy, wasn't stupid. It wasn't his fault.'

> 'Really I was quite relieved to know, because it's an explanation. I think you're disappointed for them, aren't you, and a bit anxious about what it means.'

The children's views of the label 'dyslexia' were also collected. They were asked, 'Didn't you resent being called dyslexic because it made you feel different?' Riddick

(2010: 83) reports that 21 out of the 22 children were positive about the label 'dyslexia'. For example:

> 'I'm glad I'm called dyslexic rather than lazy.'

> 'I'm not branded as thick now.'

> 'I quite like it. I used to wonder why I couldn't keep up.'

> 'I'd rather know that I've got dyslexia than think I was an idiot.'

> 'It's quite helpful. It's better to get it sorted out.'

Although the sample size is quite small, it points to the perceived helpfulness of this particular label in understanding a child's difficulties. The study also found children in the two schools that were most supportive of the concept of dyslexia were comfortable with others knowing they were dyslexic and in using the term in public.

It might be argued that having a particular difficulty or label can set in motion a particular course of action regardless of individual need, as it can involve thinking of children by a category first and as an individual second. For this reason, we prefer to use the term 'learner with dyslexia' rather than 'dyslexic learner'.

A further criticism of diagnostic assessment relates to the fact that performance in any test or assessment procedure, because it is a 'snapshot' of behaviours at a particular time and in a particular situation, may not be typical of a learner and this could lead to misidentification and inappropriate action.

Types of Assessment

All teachers tend to use assessment as part of the normal teaching cycle. They set targets for learning, teach the learner, and monitor progress by assessing them informally. This process enables them to evaluate the effectiveness of their own teaching. The teaching-assessment cycle, therefore, can be used to give feedback to learners, parents and teachers. Such assessment is often called 'formative' as it takes place during a teaching programme where teaching can be readily adapted in response to learners' progress (assessment carried out at the end of a teaching programme is referred to as 'summative' assessment). This model indicates where learners are experiencing difficulties but is not sufficient to describe the assessment required to identify and detail the nature of learning difficulties in ways which can lead to specific forms of intervention for individual learners. Assessment is a process that requires certain knowledge and skills. These include:

- the ability to develop assessment procedures and use these systematically (referred to here as informal or curriculum based approaches), and;
- the ability to select relevant standardised tests (these are often referred to as 'formal' procedures).

Teachers need to be able to:

- use both approaches appropriately;
- administer, score and interpret without personal bias.

Tests can be developed for use by groups or individuals. Group tests are usually quick to administer, easy to score, and indicate differences in performance within a group. They usually require the use of pen and paper and normally involve some reading. Group tests are useful in schools to monitor standards and can be used to screen learners in order to identify those with difficulties who can then be assessed using individual procedures.

Individual tests, on the other hand, require a 1:1 situation, very often take longer to give and longer to score and interpret but provide more in-depth information from which to plan appropriate teaching which is why the emphasis in this book is on *individual assessment*.

Tests are usually described as norm-referenced (standardised), criterion-referenced or informal. Norm-referenced tests are designed to compare an individual's perfor-mance to a specified population – usually other learners of the same age. They can be used to identify strengths and weaknesses, summatively at the end of a programme, but can be used to monitor progress during the programme (see Part III for more detail of the use of norm-referenced tests). Criterion-referenced tests evaluate a learner's attainment or progress against a set of previously determined standards. These could be either published or teacher-made, such as using a checklist for dyslexia or a list of frequently used words (as suggested in Chapter 6).

Ipsative assessment is used to compare a learner's performance with their own previous performance rather than their peers, and may be normative, criterion-referenced or informal (teacher-devised). We have used 'informal' testing to include the use of teacher-made, curriculum-based assessment. This may involve teachers devising criterion-based tests, e.g. phonics skills, or systematically analysing strengths and difficulties in work produced by a learner, e.g. in mathematics or written assignments. The value of observation in both early identification and throughout the assessment process is stressed (see Chapter 4).

All of these approaches can be used in carrying out an assessment. The views of others should also be sought in order to obtain as full a picture of the learner as pos-sible. This will include contributions from the learners themselves, parents/carers and teachers as indicated in Figure 2.1. Gathering information from others can involve a range of methods as discussed in Chapter 5. We propose the following model of the assessment process.

This model outlines an assessment process starting from the time a learner is first observed to have a difficulty or has been identified through screening. It then suggests stages (or actions to be taken), including acknowledging that it might be necessary to refer for external professional advice and support. Where there is no specialist within a school this may require consulting a specialist teacher. Assessment in school may be

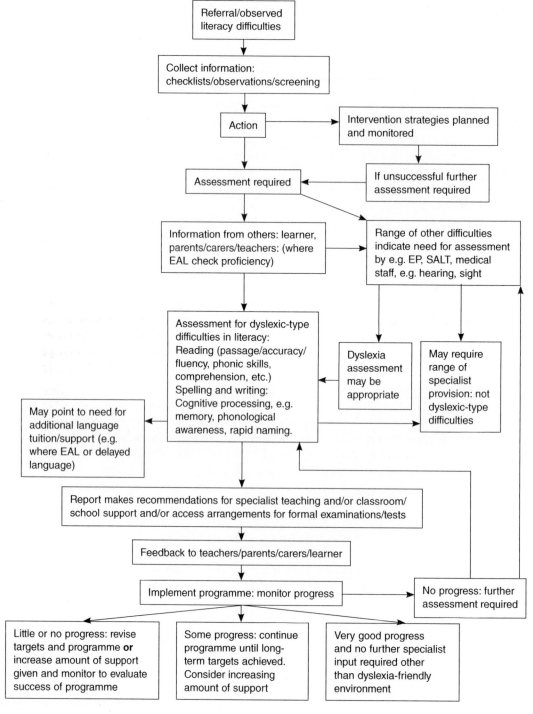

Figure 2.1   Model for assessment of dyslexic-type difficulties

based on the use of informal or formal methods or a combination of both. The assessment should lead to recommendations for teaching or classroom/school support (or access arrangements where applicable). The model draws attention to the fact that where intervention is necessary, progress should be monitored. It proposes that where no progress is made, further assessment may be required either by a specialist in dyslexia, or (if other information comes to be known suggesting there may be other or, additional difficulties) other specialist professionals. The model also draws attention to the fact that where a programme is very successful there may be no need for further specialist input as long as the learner is in a dyslexia-friendly environment. However, in some cases there may still be a need to continue a programme because there has been some, but insufficient, progress to enable the learner to cope independently. In this case, it may also be useful to consider increasing the amount or frequency of support. Where very little progress is made but dyslexia is still seen as a major cause of difficulty then there should be some revision of both targets and programme, or the amount of support should be increased and progress monitored more closely.

Summary

After outlining some of the main purposes of assessment, this chapter has proposed a sequential model of the assessment process that can be used for evaluating dyslexic-type difficulties in ways which would lead to appropriate action to meet an individual learner's needs. In doing so, it has also defined some of the terminology in common use in the literature on assessment.

Points for Discussion

- Consider the use of assessment in your school. Find out the main purposes for which it is used and identify the types of assessments used for each purpose.
- Compare the policies and practices of assessment of dyslexic-type difficulties in your school to the model of assessment in this chapter.
- Who currently carries out assessment of literacy and numeracy difficulties in your school? What is your role in this?

Further Reading

Pierangelo, R. and Giuliano, G.A. (2008) *Assessment in Special Education: A Practical Approach*, 3rd edn. Upper Saddle River, NJ: Pearson.

An American text which considers the use of a variety of forms of assessment both formal and informal in assessing learners with special educational needs in the USA.

Reynolds, C.R., Livingston, R.B. and Willson, V. (2009) *Measurement and Assessment in Education*, 2nd edn. Upper Saddle River, NJ: Pearson.

A comprehensive introduction to the use of formal and informal assessment in education with good explanations of the terminology used.

References

DfES (Department for Education and Skills) (2001) *Special Educational Needs Code of Practice*. London: HMSO.

Frederickson, N. and Cline, T. (2009) *Special Educational Needs, Inclusion and Diversity*, 2nd edn. Maidenhead: Open University Press.

Riddick, B. (2010) *Living with Dyslexia*, 2nd edn. London: David Fulton.

Shakespeare, T. and Watson, N. (2002) 'The social model of disability: an outdated ideology?', *Research in Social Science and Disability*. 2: 9–28.

CHAPTER 3

LEGISLATION, POLICY AND PRACTICE

Chapter Overview

This chapter will enable the reader to become familiar with:

- the legislation concerning SEN and disability particularly in relation to assessment and human rights;
- national policies for related practice.

The London 2012 Paralympics with its theme of 'enlightenment' made us all reflect on how far we have come in recent decades in relation to human rights issues and the inclusion of children with disabilities and/or special educational needs. Whilst sporting events have been instrumental in bringing disability to the attention of the world, legislation has played a major part in bringing about the changes in practice that have occurred in education. This chapter discusses some of the key legislation from the past two decades that led to the Equality Act of 2010.

Historical Context

The Salamanca Agreement

In June 1994, 300 participants representing 92 governments and 25 international organisations met in Salamanca, Spain, to consider the 'fundamental policy shifts required to promote the approach of inclusive education' and to enable schools to meet the needs of all children, especially those with special educational needs. The British Government signed up to the Salamanca agreement (UNESCO, 1994) which states that every child has a right to education and that those with special educational needs must have access to 'regular schools which should accommodate them within a child centred pedagogy capable of meeting their needs' (p. viii). It also stated that mainstream schools with an inclusive approach were the 'most effective means of combating discriminatory attitudes, creating welcoming communities, building an inclusive society and achieving education for all' (p. ix). The framework proclaimed that every person with a disability has the right to express their wishes with regard to their education, as far as this can be ascertained. It highlighted the inherent right of parents to be consulted on the form of education that best suited the needs of their children. Whilst acknowledging the value of specialist resources and skills available in special schools or units, the framework proposes that if these are placed within a mainstream school then they can provide more suitable support for the small number of children who cannot benefit from being in the mainstream classroom or school. It points out that 'inclusion and participation are essential to human dignity and to the enjoyment and exercise of human rights' (p. 11). The agreement formed the foundation for much of the legislation that followed. In the same year that the agreement was signed, the first Code of Practice (DfES, 1994) was issued that gave schools guidance on how to meet the needs of children with a disability or a special educational need.

Code of Practice (1994) and SEN Code of Practice (2001)

In England the 1993 Education Act placed a duty on the Secretary of State to issue a Code of Practice and the right to amend it from time to time. The 1994 Code recommended a staged approach to meeting the needs of children with special educational needs. It distinguished between a disability and a special educational need, using the term 'special educational need' to refer to children with learning difficulties or disabilities that make it harder for them to learn or access education than most children of the same age. These difficulties may be long term or of a temporary nature. Disability has a legal definition and refers to a physical or sensory impairment, a learning difficulty, a medical condition or illness that has a *substantial long-term adverse effect* on the daily life of the individual. A person may have a disability but not have a special educational need and vice versa (dyslexia is considered to be both a special educational need and a disability). Adhering to the principles of the Salamanca Agreement the Code recommended that child and parents should be involved in the decisions made about the child's education.

The 1993 Education Act was instrumental in increasing the rights of children with special educational needs and their parents. Under this Act parents had the right to appeal decisions relating to the provision made for children with special educational needs to a Special Educational Needs Tribunal. Grounds for appeal were that either:

the Local Education Authority:

- refused to make a formal assessment;
- refused to issue a statement;

or parents were unhappy with:

- the description of their child's needs as described in the statement;
- the description of the type of special educational provision;
- the school named;
- the fact that the statement is not maintained;
- a refusal to reassess (if the LEA has not made a new assessment for at least 6 months).

A time frame of up to 26 weeks was given for the processes involved. Previously parents had to appeal directly to the Secretary of State (under the 1981 Education Act) and a response could take up to two years. Hence the setting up of tribunals was seen by parents as a major step forward.

The rights and duties contained in the 1993 Education Act were consolidated in the 1996 Education Act and further guidance provided on how LEAs and other bodies involved could fulfil their statutory duties towards children with Special Educational Needs in the revised SEN Code of Practice (DfES, 2001). The 1996 Education Act (Section 316) placed a duty on LEAs to educate children with special educational needs in mainstream schools whether or not they had a statement. However, in the case of those who had a statement, they should be placed in a mainstream school unless it was incompatible with the wishes of the parents or the 'provision of efficient education for other children'. The 2001 Code gave clearer guidance on the writing of Individual Education Plans (IEPs), the kind of evidence required for statutory assessment and the flexible arrangements that should be made by schools in meeting the needs of children with a SEN. The strategies suggested offered some guidance in implementing the National Curriculum Inclusion Policy (DfEE,1999: revised DfE, 2011b) which says that teachers must take into account the type and extent of a pupil's learning difficulty in carrying out assessment and in curriculum planning, setting suitable learning challenges, responding to diverse needs and overcoming potential barriers to assessment and learning. In curriculum planning they should allow appropriate lengths of time to complete the task, opportunities to develop the necessary skills for practical elements, and identify any aspects or targets that may cause specific difficulty for an individual. Where appropriate, pupils should be provided with access to specialist equipment or approaches, to alternative or adapted activities that are consistent with the guidance provided in the SEN Code. These documents placed a much greater responsibility on teachers to meet the needs of children with SEN within a mainstream setting.

Not only was there an increased emphasis on children and parents' rights in relation to the assessment process but also in relation to their access to information held about a child. Teachers need to be aware that any information held by the school must be made available for parents to see, under the Data Protection Act 1998, and that information cannot be disclosed, altered, disseminated or destroyed without their knowledge, and where possible, their permission.

Disability Legislation

In 2001 a legal duty was placed on schools to meet the needs of children with disabilities in the Special Educational Needs Disability Act (SENDA).

SENDA (2001)

SENDA (2001) Part 2 placed new duties on schools and LEAs to outlaw disability discrimination. It made schools responsible for ensuring that disabled pupils were treated not less favourably (without justification) in both their physical and curricular access to education and for preparing accessibility plans that were to be available for inspection by Ofsted. The Act made it unlawful for schools to discriminate against a disabled child in the arrangements it made for determining admission to the school and in the education or associated services provided (SENDA Part 2, chapter 1, 28A). It required schools to make 'reasonable adjustments' for children with a disability. The duties were anticipatory, that is schools and other education providers had to think ahead and consider what they may need to do before problems arose. Examples of reasonable adjustments for learners with dyslexia might include access to a computer and voice-activated software for dictating assignments or speech-text software that reads texts, e-mails or webpages to the learner, and a reader or scribe in examinations. SENDA gave a wide range of legal rights to children with disabilities for the first time, rights that were strengthened by the Disability Discrimination Act (DDA) 2005.

DDA (2005)

The DDA (2005) amended the earlier Disability Discrimination Act of 1995 and introduced the Disability Equality Duty (DDA, 2005, Part 5A) for 'public authorities' including schools, colleges and universities. The Disability Equality Duty set out:

1   A general duty to promote disability equality.
2   A specific duty that includes a requirement to prepare and publish a disability equality scheme showing how the school is meeting its general duty.

The general duty required schools to:

- promote equality of opportunity between disabled people and other people;
- eliminate discrimination;
- eliminate harassment related to disability;
- promote positive attitudes towards people with disabilities;
- encourage participation of disabled people in public life;
- take steps to meet disabled people's needs, even if it requires more favourable treatment.

The Disability Equality Scheme should set out:

- the arrangements for gathering information on the effect of the school's policies on:
  o the recruitment, development and retention of employees with disabilities;
  o the educational opportunities available to and the achievements of pupils with disabilities;
- the arrangements for using information to support the review of the school's 'action plan' and to inform subsequent schemes.

The Disability Discrimination Act applied not only to pupils in schools but also to members of staff with a disability and to parents and other users with disabilities. It required schools to be proactive in collecting relevant information and promoting equality. An example of this might be for schools to contact parents of children with disabilities who do not regularly attend parents' evenings to find out if there is a problem that the school could resolve (such as providing a crèche for the children while parents talk to teachers). The DDA (2005) has now been superseded by the Equality Act of 2010.

The Equality Act (2010)

The Equality Act 2010 provides a single source on discrimination law covering:

- age;
- disability;

- gender reassignment;
- marriage and civil partnership;
- pregnancy and maternity;
- race;
- religion or beliefs;
- sex;
- sexual orientation.

(Chapter 15, Part 1, 1:4)

The above are referred to as 'protected characteristics' in the 2010 Act. An implication for education is that it is unlawful for schools to discriminate against, harass or victimise a pupil or potential pupil with a protected characteristic (with the exception of 'age' and 'marriage and civil partnership' as these characteristics do not apply):

- in relation to admissions;
- in the way it provides education for pupils;
- in the way it provides access to any benefit, facility or service;
- by excluding a pupil or subjecting them to any other detriment.

(Chapter 15, Part 6, ch. 1)

Much of the legislation relating to schools remains the same as it did previously, particularly in relation to disability discrimination. The Act defines a disability as relating to someone who '(a) has mental or physical impairment and (b) the impairment has a substantial and long term adverse effect on the person's ability to carry out normal day-to-day activities' (Chapter 15, Part 2, 1:6). Certain medical conditions such as cancer, HIV infection and multiple sclerosis are considered to be disabilities (see Schedule 1, Part 1, 6:6).

Direct discrimination

The Equality Act (2010) distinguishes between 'direct' and 'indirect' discrimination; both are unlawful. Direct discrimination arising from disability is defined in Chapter 15, Part 2, 2:15 as follows:

A person (A) discriminates against a disabled person (B) if:

(a) A treats B unfavourably because of something arising in consequence of B's disability, and;

(b) A cannot show that the treatment is a proportionate means of achieving a legitimate aim.

(This does not apply if A shows that A did not know, and could not reasonably have been expected to know, that B had the disability).

In other words, direct discrimination occurs if one person treats another less favourably because of a protected characteristic, than they treat, or would treat, other people. An example of this would be if a school refuses to admit a child because of a special educational need.

Indirect discrimination

Indirect discrimination is also defined in the Act (Chapter 15, Part 2, 2:19) and relates to applying a 'provision, criterion, or practice' which is discriminatory in relation to their protected characteristic (for example, if a school only provides details of important school events in printed format to learners with dyslexia or parents with dyslexia).

The 2010 Equality Act highlights the need for schools to be proactive in making reasonable adjustments. It states that they have a duty to make reasonable adjustment where:

1   a provision, criterion or practice puts a disabled person at substantial disadvantage;
2   a physical feature puts a disabled person at a substantial disadvantage;
3   a disabled person would, but for the provision of an auxiliary aid, be put at a substantial disadvantage.

Schools must comply with the first and third requirement (the second is already part of the school plan) and have a duty to take such steps as are necessary to avoid the disadvantage. The duty to provide auxiliary aids and services is not due to come into effect however, until 2014, following consultation on implementation and approach. Colleges and universities must comply with the first, second and third requirements. If the first or third requirement relates to the provision of information then establishments must take steps to ensure that information is provided in an accessible format. Not to make the necessary reasonable adjustments could result in 'indirect discrimination' which is unlawful.

Harassment

Unlawful behaviour covered by the Act also includes harassment and victimisation. Harassment is defined in Chapter 15, Part 2, 2:26 of the Equality Act 2010. It is 'unwanted conduct related to a relevant protected characteristic'. Unwanted conduct is 'conduct which has the effect or purpose of creating an intimidating, hostile, degrading, humiliating or offensive environment'. This covers behaviour such as bullying but potentially extends to action which intentionally or unintentionally causes offence or intimidates a person with a protected characteristic, e.g. making derogatory comments about a person's spelling ability or the presentation of written work, or asking a learner with dyslexia to read aloud in front of peers without checking with them that they are happy to do so. If a teacher belittles a child because of a disability, this could lead to prosecution for unlawful harassment.

Victimisation

Victimisation is where a person is treated less favourably because they have done something which is a protected act. This includes bringing proceedings for discrimination under this Act, making allegations of discrimination, giving evidence for another person who is bringing proceedings under the Act or anything that is done under or in connection with the Act. This is to ensure that people do not avoid making a complaint or giving evidence because of fear of retaliation. However, giving false evidence or information is not protected, nor is an allegation that is made in bad faith.

Schools are still required under the 2010 Equality Act to have an accessibility strategy for improving the access of learners with disabilities and this must be in writing (Schedule 10). The accessibility plan should increase the learner's ability to participate in the school curriculum, increase the extent to which they can take advantage of education and benefits, facilities and services, and improve the delivery of information to disabled pupils. The act states that in preparing an accessibility plan the responsible body must have regard to the need to allocate adequate resources to implement the plan. Accessibility plans should be kept under review and revised as necessary.

SEND Tribunal

Schedule 17 of the 2010 Equality Act sets out 'disabled pupils: enforcement' – the right to take disputes to a Special Educational Needs and Disability Tribunal (for schools in England this is now a 'first-tier tribunal'). A claim that a responsible body has contravened Chapter 1 of Part 6 (Education) because of a pupil's disability may be made to the tribunal by a parent within six months of the date when the conduct occurred. If the tribunal finds that a contravention has occurred, it has the power to 'make an order as it thinks fit' with a view to reducing the adverse effect on the person making the claim but it cannot order payment of compensation. In addition to disability discrimination, this tribunal still deals with appeals against SEN decisions as described on p.29. This role may change under the legislation of 2014.

SEN Green Paper (2011)

In March 2011 the SEN Green Paper (DfE, 2011a) 'Support and Aspiration: A new approach to special educational need and disability' set out proposals for educational reform and a plan for a four-month consultation phase from September 2011. Reports from LAs involved in piloting the proposed changes were due in December 2012 in preparation for a new bill in January 2013 but in response to requests for a longer period of time for pathfinders to trial these changes, the government has now extended the schemes until 2014. In October 2012, Steven Kingdom, Deputy Director SEND at the Department for Education, announced at a Westminster Briefing, that a new Code of Practice will be published in 2014 and should be implemented from September, 2014.

The key elements of the 2011 SEN Green Paper are summarised below:

1 **Early Identification and Assessment**
   The government proposes a single agency approach to assessment with early checks for children involving health, education and social care. Statements of Special

Educational Need are to be replaced by 'Education, Health and Care Plans' (EHC) for 0–25-year-olds. These are to be available locally through the LA 'local offer'.

2 **Parental Control**
Parents of children with an EHC plan can express a preference for any state-funded or special school, including academies and free schools. This does not guarantee a place, however. Parents can have a personal budget, a payment in lieu of services provided by the school.

3 **Learning and Achieving**
It is proposed that a single category of SEN replace 'School Action' and 'School Action Plus' and that a new measure be introduced into school performance tables to measure the progress of low attainers.

4 **Preparing for Adulthood**
The Education, Health and Care Plan will cover young adults up to the age of 25 and will extend beyond school into FE.

5 **Services Working Together**
The reforms bring a requirement for services to work together to identify the needs of children with SEN. The SEN Green Paper proposes making mediation compulsory before going to a SEND tribunal.

At the time of writing these are still proposals. In any changes made to the provision of children and young people with special educational needs, a major concern must be that the protection of children's and parents' rights in the current system are continued under the new Act and that parents are reassured that any changes will bring better provision for their children. It is also important that there is no delay in resolving any conflict that may arise and that appropriate time limits are set. These issues were raised through the consultation process and are currently being addressed by the Parliamentary Under-Secretary of State with responsibility for special educational needs and disability.

Summary

This chapter provides an overview of key legislative framework for considering provision for special educational needs, particularly in relation to assessment. It acknowledges that at the time of writing education reforms are imminent and that a new Code of Practice will be introduced in 2014.

Points for Discussion

- Evaluate practices in your workplace in relation to possible 'indirect discrimination'.
- What policies and practices are in place in your school to ensure that children and parents of children with literacy difficulties are aware of their rights in relation to assessment for special educational needs?
- How might the proposed education reforms affect the identification of children with SEN?

Further Reading

Equality and Human Rights Commission (2012) *Public Sector Equality Guidance for Schools in England.* Available at www.equalityhumanrights.com

Offers guidance for schools with short case studies illustrating some of the implications for practice.

Saunders, K. and Cochran, K. (2012) *Dyslexia Friendly Schools Good Practice Guide.* Bracknell: British Dyslexia Association.

This book contains contributions from a range of schools and authorities showing how schools can be made more dyslexia-friendly. It provides a good guide to making appropriate reasonable adjustments and maximising opportunities for achievement of learners with dyslexia.

References

Data Protection Act 1998. London: HMSO; also available at www.legislation.gov.uk

DfE (Department for Education) (1994) *Code of Practice on the Identification and Assessment of Special Educational Needs.* London: HMSO.

DfE (Department for Education) (2011a) *Support and Aspiration: A New Approach to Special Educational Needs and Disability.* www.education.gov.uk/publications

DfE (Department for Education) (2011b) *Including All Learners: Learning Challenges.* 30 November, 2011: www.education.gov.uk/schools/teachingandlearning/curriculum/b00199686/inclusion/challenges

DfEE (Department for Education and Employment) (1999) *The National Curriculum: Handbook for Primary Teachers in England.* London: HMSO.

DfES (Department for Education and Skills) (2001) *Special Educational Needs Code of Practice.* London: HMSO.

Disability Discrimination Act 2005. London: HMSO.

Education Act 1993. London: HMSO.

Education Act 1996. London: HMSO; also available at www.legislation.gov.uk

The Equality Act 2010. London: HMSO.

Kingdom, S. (2012) *The Government's Plan for SEND.* Westminster Briefing, 23 October, The Commonwealth Club, London.

Special Educational Needs Disability Act (SENDA) 2001. London: HMSO.

UNESCO (1994) *The Salamanca Statement and Framework for Action on Special Needs Education.* Salamanca, Spain, June 7–10, 1994.

PART II

INFORMAL APPROACHES TO ASSESSMENT

This part of the book considers informal approaches that all teachers may use to identify specific strengths and difficulties. The first two chapters, whilst using informal approaches, are concerned also with the first stages of any assessment process, as suggested in the model proposed in Chapter 2 of this book. The power and use of observation and scrutiny of learners' performance in the curriculum are highly significant aspects of assessment. They throw light on learning in different contexts and can identify consistent behaviours compared with context-specific attainments. The following chapter suggests how people other than the teacher who is undertaking assessment can make important contributions to the process, bringing different information and perspectives. Central to this are the contributions of parents and, importantly, *the learner*. The methods and content of both these chapters can (and should) be used even when conducting formal assessment. Without the information these approaches yield, no assessment is complete.

The remaining chapters in Part II consider, in some detail, a range of informal approaches to assessing dyslexic-type difficulties, with an emphasis on literacy because this is fundamental to so much learning in school. Examples of informal, teacher-made assessment procedures are offered, which teachers can use or adapt as they wish. In many cases they are based on materials used in the normal curriculum and can therefore also be described as curriculum-based.

CHAPTER 4

INFORMAL APPROACHES: IDENTIFICATION AND SCREENING

Chapter Overview

This chapter will enable the reader to:

- understand the need to be proactive in identifying learners with dyslexic-type difficulties as early as possible;
- use informal assessment methods as part of the process of identifying and screening for dyslexia.

The first stage of the assessment process is to identify those children who are not making satisfactory progress and who present dyslexic-type difficulties. Rose (2009: 42) commented that 'It is generally agreed that the earlier dyslexic difficulties are identified the better are the chances of putting children on the road to success.' Where children's difficulties are not identified early a pattern of failure may set in that can lead to low self-esteem, to learned helplessness, the development of avoidance strategies (particularly in literacy-related subjects) or even a dislike of school. The SEN Code of Practice (DfES, 2001) proposed that a critical factor for successful implementation of the fundamental principles of meeting special educational needs is that 'LEAs, schools and settings work together to ensure that any child's special educational need are identified early' (DfES, 2001: 4). However, evidence presented to the Rose Report and research undertaken by Riddick (2010) report the frustration and disillusionment of parents over the length of time taken for their child's difficulties to be identified and formally assessed. The view of respondent M (Rose, 2009: 42) is representative of the experiences of many parents:

> 'Things just hit rock bottom. I was forever either on the phone to her teacher or the Head trying to get someone to come and assess her for her reading problems. It went on for ages; the school said there was a waiting list, she didn't have a problem, I needed to get her diagnosed by someone myself and on and on it went.'

Although concerns about an individual are often initially raised by a teacher or parent, schools need to adopt a systematic procedure for identification by screening groups of learners, usually using a formal method as described in Chapter 13. This should be carried out regularly from the early years of schooling. However, whether or not formal screening is used in the school, teachers should be proactive in identifying individual learners who appear to have unexpected difficulties in some areas of the curriculum, especially literacy acquisition. They need to be able to use informal methods such as those described below.

Issues of Early Identification

Although at the time of writing changes to definitions of SEN and special educational provision are being suggested in the DfE Report (May, 2012) 'Support and Aspiration: A New Approach to Special Educational Needs and Disability Progress and Next Steps' (the response to the consultation on the SEN and Disability Green Paper of 2011) there remains a strong emphasis on early identification and better integration of services.

The term 'early identification' encompasses both the need to identify dyslexic-type difficulties in the early years and also the need for teachers to respond quickly to learners who appear to be at risk of 'having dyslexia' at any age of schooling. The younger the child is when this happens the more likely it is that the support given will be similar to approaches being used with children of the same age, e.g. the use of synthetic phonics and teaching of letter–sound correspondence. However, the older the child, the greater the difference between intervention (the additional support needed) and their normal curriculum, which further compounds low self-esteem.

One issue revolves around the age at which dyslexia can be identified and assessed. The Rose Report (2009) advocates that teachers should identify children making poor progress compared to their peers despite receiving good quality Wave 1 teaching. This implies that identification cannot take place until around the age of six or seven. However, he does suggest that the Early Years Foundation Stage should pay more attention to monitoring children's language development and identifying emerging difficulties in language and literacy. We believe that this monitoring should take place continuously comparing progress in literacy with that in other curriculum subjects, particularly those not reliant on reading and writing.

There are others who make a case for early screening in the pre-school years, e.g. Crombie et al. (2004), Crombie (2012), the BDA (who have produced checklists for pre-school up to adult), Muter, Hulme and Snowling (1997) and Fawcett and Nicolson (2004). Whilst such approaches are usually welcomed by teachers and parents, it is important to recognise that screening at this very young age can lead to children showing positive indicators of dyslexia who are later found not to have dyslexia (these are known as 'false positives'). In the same way, some children may not show such indicators but later are identified as being 'dyslexic' (a 'false negative' finding). The younger the child, the greater the chance of over- or under-identification simply because young children develop at very different rates and also have very different home experiences or respond to school in different ways. On the whole, early identification is useful if it is taken as an indicator of children 'at risk' requiring supportive intervention and close monitoring rather than giving a diagnosis (or label) of dyslexia.

A further issue appears to be that more boys than girls (about 4:1) are identified as being dyslexic during the school years (Shaywitz et al. 2008; Singleton, 1999) whereas in Higher Education more girls than boys are identified as dyslexic for the first time. One theory proposed for this is that boys may have presented more challenging behaviours to teachers in school, resulting in psychological assessment where their dyslexic-type difficulties were discovered. It is important therefore not to assume that dyslexic-type difficulties are more commonly found in boys.

Informal Approaches to Identification

Informal approaches can be used as part of formative assessment to identify signs of progress and areas of weakness, prior to further detailed assessment that targets specific areas. They should be used where a teacher is concerned about a learner's progress, or where a concern has been raised by a parent. In schools where a formal system of screening is in place, they may be used to gather more information about a learner who has been identified as 'at risk' or where, for some reason, there has been no formal screening of that particular learner.

The most common approaches used by teachers are:

- observations;
- checklists;
- published informal screening tests.

Observation

Purpose

A teacher's observation skills – what she/he sees and hears – are important in both assessment and teaching. The purpose of observation is to obtain as much information as possible about how an individual learns: their strengths, difficulties and learning strategies. Most texts on the use of observation as a form of assessment tend to be about the assessment of very young children (e.g. Hobart et al., 2009; Riddall-Leech, 2008; Sharman et al., 2007 [which now includes up to 16-year-olds]). This is because young children develop and change very quickly, so that it is important to capture their growth and development regularly and over time. It is also the case that whilst certain 'milestones' of 'typical' behaviours can be identified, it is more difficult to devise appropriate standardised tests. Other texts on observation tend to emphasise the use of observation in research (e.g. Bell, 2010; Gray, 2009; Hopkins, 2008; Punch, 2009). Whilst they draw attention to the same categorisation of types of observation, it is important to recognise that they are writing from different perspectives. Observation will involve recording what is seen and heard. It is important that whoever is observing should record what is seen (or heard) and not 'interpret' the observed behaviour. Possible interpretations can be made *after* analysing an observation. An example is that we should not record 'daydreaming' when what we have observed is that 'pupil directs gaze at ceiling/window' rather than doing the set task.

In order to identify dyslexic-type difficulties, observations should be undertaken in a variety of settings and at different times of day. This will yield more detailed and reliable information than is provided by a formal screening test which is just a 'snapshot' of an individual's performance on one particular occasion.

A further value of observation is that it provides 'a reality check' – in that it enables us to provide *evidence* about a learner's performance/behaviours which, as Gray (2009: 396) points out, goes 'beyond a person's opinions and attitudes' that may have been expressed as a teacher's or parent's/carer's concern, or even 'ticked' on a checklist, as described later in this chapter.

Types of Observation

Observation can be structured (such as event sampling, time sampling and duration sampling) or unstructured (e.g. field notes). Usually observation will be carried out by a TA or a teacher other than the one taking the lesson. This is not only more practical but also means the learner is observed in the normal lesson.

Structured observation

Structured observation includes the use of a schedule specifying characteristics that should be observed or the times when observation should be carried out. A major criticism of the use of structured observation is that it is very subjective because the aspects of behaviour to be observed are predetermined. This may mean that other aspects, which may be significant, are ignored. However, whether these are events or decisions about contexts, the fact that a set of behaviours/characteristics is used as the basis for observation or that a specific context is specified, is useful for identification because the *purpose* is to discover whether or not a child is experiencing particular difficulties. If a teacher draws up an observation schedule for use in a school, then there will be some consistency amongst users (whether teachers or TAs) in terms of what and how they record their observations. (This consistency is also a feature of checklists and published screening instruments, such as those described below.)

There are three main types of structured observation which can be used in the identification of learners with literacy difficulties.

1. Time sampling

This involves observing what is happening at regular time intervals, e.g. every five minutes during a literacy lesson or every half-hour during the day. Where a TA or teacher is observing a lesson taught by another teacher the intervals can be shorter, e.g. every two minutes during a literacy lesson or every five minutes during the day. The time interval will depend on the context and period over which the observation is to be made.

The purpose of this approach is to try to discover what strategies/approaches to learning are frequently used by the targeted learner. It would therefore be appropriate to use if a teacher expresses a general concern about learning/attitude to learning. One disadvantage is that some very significant features of a learner's behaviour are not noted simply because they do not occur 'at the moment' of observation. Sometimes, however, this method may be employed when a teacher has been asked to complete a checklist but is unsure about how 'typical' some of the listed behaviours are for the learner.

2. Event sampling

This involves devising a schedule listing the behaviour considered to be characteristic of dyslexic-type difficulties that can be observed in a particular situation and recording each occurrence.

This approach can be useful when used in different subjects, to compare engagement and strengths in, e.g., literacy-based lessons with performance in, say, art, design and technology, science. Within English/literacy lessons, there can be comparisons between specific skills, e.g. use of oral language and written work.

3. Duration sampling

This form of observation is used to find out how long a learner spends on a targeted activity, e.g. writing stories/a written assignment, where the observer uses a stopwatch to time aspects such as 'time before starting to write', each 'period' of writing and 'time not writing' (bearing in mind that this could be very productive 'thinking' time). Does the targeted learner take longer to start to do a written task than, for example, starting a painting or making a model?

Whilst the three forms of observation described above are often used by teachers when researching behaviours in their classrooms, we believe they have limited use in identifying learners with dyslexia and can be time-consuming compared with other methods of identification.

Unstructured observation: field notes

This form of observation requires an observer to make notes about what they observe as it occurs. Whilst this appears to be less subjective than structured observation, in fact it is likely that an observer is perhaps unconsciously selective in what they choose to write about. These observation notes are then analysed to see if particular patterns occur.

Two main uses of field notes are:

- if a teacher/TA is asked to complete a checklist and realises she/he is not familiar with some of the general statements, the checklist can be put to one side and observations made, prior to completing a checklist;
- in secondary schools where 'pupil shadowing' (or 'pupil pursuit') may be undertaken to compare behaviours in different subject areas with different teachers.

Semi-structured observations

We consider that the use of semi-structured observation is a very effective way of identifying learners with dyslexic-type difficulties. This involves drawing up a schedule that determines areas to be observed – i.e. a form of structured field notes. This ensures key aspects are considered, and even when observations are carried out by different observers there are broad criteria (based on the characteristics of dyslexia) to form a basis for comparison. We consider this the most useful approach (see Table 4.1).

A semi-structured schedule must consider the information required:

- the context of learning should be noted, e.g. the time of day, subject or lesson, interactions with teachers and other learners, noise levels and distractions;
- the nature of the tasks, e.g. input and required output, amount of support given and/or sought, resources available/used;
- detailed account of how the learner responds to the task, e.g. what they said and did, strategies used and how effective they are, (such as finger pointing in reading);
- learner's performance/output, e.g. methods of recording (writing, model making, etc.);

Table 4.1   Example of a semi-structured observation schedule

OBSERVATION	
Name:	**Date of birth:**
Date of observation:	**Time:**
Lesson/Subject:	

Teacher input: *(e.g. note clarity of instructions, whether modelled/examples given, nature of task set, any reading involved)*

What the learner is expected to do: *(e.g. whether output prescribed/open ended, type of product, method of recording)*

Support given: *(e.g. amount, type, resources)*

Learner's interactions with teacher, TA, other learners:

Learner's response to task: *(e.g. what learner said/did, concentration, strategies, following instructions; evidence of learning – answering questions/output)*

Summary of strengths/difficulties *(including any indications of a dyslexic nature)*

Photocopiable
Assessment of Learners with Dyslexic-Type Difficulties © Sylvia Phillips, Kathleen Kelly and Liz Symes, 2013 (SAGE).

- amount of work produced;
- level of participation in discussion or answering questions;
- indicators of the characteristics of dyslexia.

This can form the basis for further investigation, including more targeted observation as in the example given for event sampling in Table 4.2, which examines the ability to follow instructions in class.

General points about observation

The value of observing in a number of different lessons or subjects in order to reveal whether there are differences across the curriculum should be clear. Discrepancies between observations can be analysed to clarify the nature of the difficulty. They may, for example, indicate a specific learning difficulty or point to inconsistencies related to differences in the learning context or be the product of both. An event sample may be used to gather more detailed information for a targeted area than a checklist or more general observation schedule. In the example given in Table 4.2 the level of complexity of instructions given can be analysed, as can information about speed of processing information. Where a learner has produced work as part of a lesson this can be annotated to give additional useful information, e.g. in the case of written work a note could be made as to whether it was supported by an assistant, if a word bank or dictionary was used, whether spellings of words were provided by a teacher or another learner.

Observation is also useful to see whether or where a behaviour or difficulty reported by a parent/carer or member of school staff occurs. In addition to being used for screening purposes, observational data can be collected to monitor a learner's progress or gather information prior to a review meeting.

Information from analysis of samples of work

A further example of the use of observation is to examine samples of a learner's work. Those that will be most revealing in terms of dyslexic-type difficulties are reading, writing and spelling. Detailed analyses of these would form part of informal assessment as described in Chapters 6, 7 and 8, but at this stage of screening certain indicators could be looked for. In reading, these might be difficulties in decoding, losing place in reading, lack of fluency, and poor phonic skills at an age where learners have had access to good teaching of reading. In written work there would be difficulties in spelling and applying phonic rules, possibly transposition of letters in words, orientation errors might be common, and often poorly formed handwriting. (A checklist can be useful here.) Samples of work may also indicate difficulties in sequencing and/or memory (e.g. words omitted when copying; numbers in wrong order in maths; omitting a stage when describing a process).

Table 4.2   Example of an event sampling observation schedule

OBSERVATION
Name: **Date of birth:**
Date of observation: **Time:**
Task: Following instructions given orally by a teacher to a class.
Lesson/Subject:
Note of instructions given *(a note should be made of each instruction given and a letter or number or code can be given to each one)*
Type of response *(a tick or mark is used to record frequency; reference should be made to the appropriate instruction using the coding noted above)*
1. **Asks for instruction to be repeated**
2. **Responds appropriately**
3. **Carries out part of instruction**
4. **Long pause before carries out instruction**
5. **Observes other pupils and follows their lead**
6. **Misinterprets the instruction** *(does something different)*
7. **Starts to follow instruction then asks for instruction to be repeated**
8. **'Appears' confused/puzzled**
9. **No response**
10. **Impolite or non-compliant response/refusal**
Teacher's response if the learner does not respond appropriately or immediately:

Photocopiable
Assessment of Learners with Dyslexic-Type Difficulties © Sylvia Phillips, Kathleen Kelly and Liz Symes, 2013 (SAGE).

Checklists

Purpose

The purpose of a checklist is to identify whether a learner's difficulties are characteristic of dyslexia. A list of common indicators is provided and the teacher (or parent) notes those typical of the learner, e.g. transposition of letters (beard for bread, saw for was), poor grapheme–phoneme correspondence in reading.

In addition to reading, spelling and writing, a checklist would normally include aspects of phonological processing, speed of processing, sequencing, memory, visual/motor skills, and organisational skills. Some will include mathematics to reveal whether there is a discrepancy between literacy and numeracy and also because some learners experience difficulties in both areas. It is important to relate characteristics to a learner's chronological and developmental age as some of these behaviours may be of a temporary nature, e.g. incorrect orientation of letters in the early stages of learning to write. The British Dyslexia Association (BDA) has produced checklists at pre-school, primary, secondary and adult levels, which may be found at www.bdadyslexia.org.uk. Checklists can be used either as part of a systematic screening policy or to obtain further information about an individual learner when a concern has been raised.

Checklists as part of systematic screening

Systematic use of checklists for screening normally occurs only at primary level. A teacher could complete a checklist for all the children in the class to identify those for whom further investigation may be necessary, e.g. through observation or use of a more formal screener. This is normally carried out when children have been at school for half a term so that a teacher is fairly confident that she/he has enough knowledge of a child's learning. Where a teacher is unable to complete part of a checklist for a particular child they should set it aside while gathering further information.

Using checklists with individual learners

Where a concern has been voiced by a teacher or parent about an individual, a checklist is a quick means of clarifying the extent to which the learner presents dyslexic-type difficulties. In a primary school this could be carried out by a teacher or teaching assistant. In a secondary school a checklist can be given to each member of staff who teaches that learner and the results collated to see if there is any agreement about indicators of dyslexia. In these instances it may also be useful to give a checklist to a parent to see if there are any aspects that they have observed at home.

Table 4.3   Checklist for identification of pupils who may have dyslexia

<table>
<tr><td colspan="3" align="center">**CHECKLIST**
For Identification of Pupils
who may have Dyslexia

(NB: This is a rapid screen and a high score does NOT mean that the pupil is dyslexic)</td></tr>
<tr><td colspan="3">**Name:**
Date of birth: Chronological age:</td></tr>
<tr><td colspan="3">**Background:**
Family history of dyslexia: Yes / No   Known hearing loss: Yes / No
Home language English: Yes / No   Late to start talking: Yes / No
Had speech / language therapy before starting school: Yes / No</td></tr>
<tr><td>**Area**</td><td>**Characteristics/behaviours**</td><td>**Tick if observed**</td></tr>
<tr><td>General/ organisational</td><td><ul><li>Often appears not to have the right things/equipment for a task</li><li>Slow to process instructions</li><li>Difficulty following more than one instruction at a time</li><li>Poor concentration skills</li><li>Difficulties in sequencing, e.g. getting dressed or carrying out tasks in the right order</li><li>Often forgets to bring things, e.g. dinner money/PE or games kit/ notes from home</li><li>Doesn't remember concepts from one lesson to the next</li><li>Difficulty in word finding (although may have a good spoken vocabulary)</li></ul></td><td></td></tr>
<tr><td>Concept of time</td><td><ul><li>Often confused about time of day</li><li>Problems adapting to changes of routine (likes structure and ability to predict routines)</li><li>May refer to time/days awkwardly (e.g. 'the day before what it is today' rather than 'yesterday')</li></ul></td><td></td></tr>
<tr><td>Literacy / reading</td><td><ul><li>Reluctant to read</li><li>Doesn't read for pleasure</li><li>Loses place frequently (e.g. one line to the next line)</li><li>Poor grapheme–phoneme correspondence</li><li>Confuses visually similar words</li><li>Reverses/confuses position of letters (e.g. was/saw)</li><li>Reverses/inverts letters (e.g. b/d, n/u)</li><li>Omits words</li><li>Doesn't recognise common high-frequency words</li><li>Sounds out words</li><li>Processes visual information slowly (affecting fluency/pace)</li><li>'Barking' at print/lacks expression</li><li>Comprehension may be better than reading fluency implies</li><li>Doesn't understand what has been read as concentrating on decoding</li></ul></td><td></td></tr>
</table>

(Continued)

Table 4.3   (Continued)

Area	Characteristics/behaviours	Tick if observed
Writing	• Difficulties in organising/structuring written work • Difficulties in sequencing • Restricts written vocabulary and ideas because of awareness of organisational and spelling difficulties • Content doesn't reflect oral ability • Many crossings out • Written work often not completed • Reluctant to write • Writes slowly • May show confusion of tenses and words (because of problems with time, name finding and sequencing) • Poor handwriting • Reversals / inversions of letters (b/d. m/w, p/q) • Writing poorly spaced • Letter formation lacks consistency of shape and size • Difficulties copying from the board • Spelling shows poor grapheme–phoneme correspondence • Transposition/omission of letters	
Maths / numeracy	• Difficulties in mental maths work • Problem remembering maths tables • Difficulties setting work down logically • Confuses/reverses visually similar numbers (e.g. 6/9, 3/5) • Reading difficulties hinder understanding of questions although may understand the 'maths'	
Attitude to learning / classroom tasks	• Participates in oral work more enthusiastically than work requiring reading/writing • May employ avoidance strategies rather than begin a writing/reading activity • Low self-esteem with regard to school work • May develop challenging behaviours/become the class-clown • May become withdrawn • May observe what other pupils do before starting work (Stott's view of an 'observational learner') because hasn't fully understood instructions (May be interpreted as 'copying')	
Other associated aspects	• May have poor gross/fine motor skills • Poor pen/pencil grip • Confuses left and right • May be excessively tired by activities (because of extra effort involved) • Performs unevenly from day to day	
Strengths Identify any areas (general/subject specific) where there is evidence of average/ high ability/ knowledge/skills		

Photocopiable

A checklist should not be based on a single observation but should reflect the behaviours of the learner generally. An interesting question about the use of checklists is 'how many items have to be ticked to decide if the child is at risk of dyslexia?' It is very difficult to try to quantify this but if clusters of difficulties are found then more detailed information may be required before making this decision. There are two aspects to this. One is that, subject to availability, a formal screener for dyslexia could be used which might pick up underlying processing difficulties. Secondly, there could be further observation using a schedule as described earlier, together with informal or formal assessment of their work as discussed in the following chapters. It is also important that follow-up observation takes into account the different contexts in which learning occurs, since it may be that aspects of these may contribute to the difficulties.

An example of a checklist we have found useful is provided as Table 4.3. It includes an opportunity to make additional positive comments, as one criticism of many checklists is that they tend to emphasise negatives because of their purpose to help identify areas of weakness. We recommend that, when asking teachers/parents to complete any checklist, you encourage them to make practical comments on:

- the learner's strengths, e.g. oral skills/vocabulary, lateral thinking/unusual ideas, strategies used, subjects they perform well in;
- unexpected discrepancies, e.g. lots of ideas but cannot organise them, good oral language but poor written work, performance in different subjects.

Published Informal Screening Tests

A number of informal procedures are available on-line, including those from local authorities. Many of these provide resources to enable teachers to assess areas of cognitive processing that present difficulties for learners with dyslexia through a series of tasks and activities. Very often there is no indication of a threshold for determining the 'at risk' level. One published resource which claims to do this is the 'Ann Arbor Group Screening Test' (Phillips and Leonard, 2005) for age 4.5 years through to adults. This is a set of criterion-referenced assessments whose purpose is to screen whole year groups to identify dyslexic-type difficulties for further investigation at ages 4.5–7.0, 7.0–8.0, 8.0–9.0, 11.0–12.0, 13.0 and post-16. These are pencil and paper tests that can be administered to a group, a whole class or an individual and are timed tests taking about 25 minutes. The instructions are scripted. The tests require learners to read the questions and instructions (with the exception of 4.5–7.0 year olds) and they are given two minutes to read the test and raise questions. (The teacher can read instructions for any child who has difficulty in reading them.) The learners are told that the aim is to see how quickly they can complete all parts of the test. Instructions for scoring are given in the manual and a percentage cut-off point is given to identify those 'at risk' of dyslexia.

The tests give useful information about visual discrimination, basic numeracy, sequencing and fine motor skills in addition to writing and spelling. A disadvantage of these tests is that they are very strictly timed and many learners will not complete all subtests. Indeed, the authors state that 'trials have proved that children who suffer from specific learning difficulties will take more than twice as long to complete the tests than those who do not experience any learning difficulties' (Phillips and Leonard, 2005: 2). Those who do not complete the test score zero for any items not attempted, and as the percentage is calculated on the total number of marks possible, their percentage is likely to be low, producing an 'at risk' score. This would be compatible with the theory of slow processing speed and lack of automaticity but means that there may be no information about some of the skills involved in incomplete or non-attempted subtests. In some cases the non-attempted subtests could be areas of strength (which if completed would change the percentage score). If a teacher wishes to obtain this information to use diagnostically they can give additional time (contrary to the manual's instructions) to complete the subtests but must not score any items not completed after the time limit.

Points to look for in choosing an informal screening test

- Can be used with groups and also individuals;
- Easy to administer and score;
- Provides cut-off point to indicate those 'at risk';
- Gives patterns of strengths and weaknesses (useful diagnostically).

Issues of Cultural and Linguistic Diversity

The area of identifying dyslexic-type difficulties in very young children is contentious because children develop and change very quickly between 0 and 5 years old. Their early home experiences, including language and early literacy skills, also vary considerably before attending school. These points have often been raised by teachers concerned about any form of very early assessment of 'difficulties'. The issue of early identification is particularly significant in the case of learners from minority ethnic groups and particularly for those children for whom English is an additional language (children with EAL). A major problem in identifying dyslexia in multilingual learners is the fact that many of the indicators of dyslexia occur as part of the normal acquisition of EAL in its early stages. Examples of these are:

- reversals of letters or words in reading and written work may reflect the script of the first language (L1), e.g. Urdu, so the learner sometimes reads right to left. It may, on the other hand, simply reflect lack of knowledge of letter order, e.g. 'hw' instead of 'wh';

- omissions of the definite and indefinite article may occur because they do not exist in some languages;
- consonant confusion, e.g. between voiced and unvoiced consonants (p/b), because the two forms do not exist in some languages; some letters may be confused because they do not exist in L1, e.g. j/g by Italian speakers because there is no 'j' in Italian.

More examples of how first-phase language factors could affect literacy development resulting in behaviours resembling the characteristics of dyslexia can be found in Kelly and Phillips (2012). It is clear that using dyslexia checklists (such as those from the BDA) may result in over-identification of dyslexia in the early stages of English language acquisition. Cummins (1984, 2000) distinguished between the early stages of English language acquisition when language for social situations and 'Basic Interpersonal Communication Skills' (BICS) are learned and the later stages of 'Cognitive and Academic Language Proficiency' (CALP). He suggested that the early stage usually takes about two years to acquire but that the later stages may take many more years to learn and use. There are clear implications of the need for cognitive and academic language for full diagnostic assessment of dyslexia, which is discussed in Part III of this book.

However, the principle of the need for early identification of dyslexic-type difficulties is still important for children learning EAL. Currently there is a tendency for them to be under-identified as having specific learning difficulties. Observation skills and analysis of work should be used, particularly to compare development and progress with peers. The curriculum content and teaching can be observed to see whether they are giving rise to difficulties for the learner. It is also important to ensure that children's use of English – their vocabulary and understanding of the structures of the English language – are being extended.

Where a learner appears to experience great difficulty in learning to read (and spell) despite having acquired basic spoken English, then it may be useful to consider him or her to be 'at risk' of dyslexia, particularly if there is a discrepancy between literacy skills and performance in other areas of the curriculum. If it is known that they are also experiencing literacy difficulties in L1 then it may indicate underlying dyslexic-type difficulties, although because of the orthography of L1 they may be proficient in literacy in their first language but have specific difficulty in English. A fuller discussion of some of the issues of linguistic diversity and assessment of dyslexia can be found in Kelly and Phillips (2011).

Children from black ethnic groups, including black British children born in the UK, also tend to be under-identified in the statistics on learners with dyslexia, although they are often identified when they reach university. The reasons for this are not always clear, (see *inter alia* Richardson and Wydell 2003, and Richardson, 2007).

Summary

This chapter argues that early identification of dyslexic-type difficulties is essential to prevent a pattern of failure setting in and so that appropriate intervention and support can be given as soon as possible. It suggests that schools should be proactive in establishing formal procedures for identification and screening. However, informal methods can play an important part in this, particularly the use of observation, checklists and screening tests to identify learners 'at risk' of dyslexia. Whatever method is chosen, sufficient information is needed in order to determine what further assessment is required. Observation can be a first step in the identification process or used to supplement information gleaned from other screening procedures. Although caution should be exercised in interpreting the performance of learners with EAL, this should not prevent informal assessment of their needs.

Points for Discussion

- Discuss the main issues in the early identification of dyslexia in relation to your working context.
- To what extent does observation underpin all forms of early identification?

Follow-up Activities

1 Use a BDA checklist or the one provided to assess the characteristics of two different learners about whom you have concerns. To what extent does that checklist raise questions about the possibility of dyslexic-type difficulties?
2 Complete a dyslexia checklist for a learner giving cause for concern and also ask a colleague who works (or has worked recently) with that learner to complete one independently. Compare the results and discuss any differences. Why might there be differences?

Further Reading

Gross, J. (Ed.) (2008) *Getting in Early: Primary Schools and Early Intervention*. London: The Smith Institute and Centre for Social Justice.

This text makes a case for early identification and intervention in order to improve national literacy standards.

Kelly, K. and Phillips, S. (2012) 'Identifying dyslexia of learners with English as an Additional Language', in J. Everatt (ed.), *Dyslexia, Languages and Multilingualism*. Bracknell: British Dyslexia Association. pp. 55–71.

This contains a fuller discussion of the issues involved in identifying dyslexia in learners with EAL.

References

Bell, J. (2010) *Doing Your Research Project: A Guide for First Time Researchers in Education, Health and Social Science*, 5th edn. Maidenhead: Open University Press.

Crombie, M. (2012) 'Literacy', in L. Peer and G. Reid (eds), *Special Educational Needs: A Guide for Inclusive Practice*. London: SAGE. pp. 141–53.

Crombie, M., Knight, D. and Reid, G. (2004) 'Dyslexia-early identification and early intervention', in G. Reid and A. Fawcett, (eds), *Dyslexia in Context – Research, Policy and Practice*. London: Whurr. pp. 203–16.

Cummins, J. (1984) *Bilingual Education and Special Education: Issues in Assessment and Pedagogy*. Clevedon: Multilingual Matters.

Cummins, J. (2000) *Language, Power and Pedagogy: Bilingual Children in the Crossfire*. Clevedon: Multilingual Matters.

DfE (Department for Education) (2012) *Support and Aspiration: A New Approach to Special Educational Needs and Disability – Progress and Next Steps*. London: DfE.

DfES (Department for Education and Skills) (2001) *Special Educational Needs Code of Practice*. London: HMSO.

Fawcett, A.J. and Nicolson, R.I. (2004) 'Dyslexia: the role of the cerebellum', in G. Reid and A.J. Fawcett (eds), *Dyslexia in Context: Research, Policy and Practice*. London: Whurr. pp. 25–47.

Gray, D.E. (2009) *Doing Research in the Real World*, 3rd edn. London: SAGE.

Hobart, C., Frankel, J. and Walker, M (2009) *A Practical Guide to Child Observation and Assessment*, 4th edn. Cheltenham: Nelson Thornes.

Hopkins, D. (2008) *A Teacher's Guide to Classroom Research*, 4th edn. Maidenhead: Open University Press.

Kelly, K. and Phillips, S. (2011) *Teaching Literacy to Learners with Dyslexia: A Multi-sensory Approach*. London: SAGE.

Kelly, K. and Phillips, S. (2012) 'Identifying dyslexia of learners with English as an Additional Language', in J. Everatt, *Dyslexia, Languages and Multilingualism*. Bracknell: BDA. pp. 55–71.

Muter, V., Hulme, C. and Snowling, M. (1997) *The Phonological Abilities Test*. London: Psychological Corporation.

Phillips, M. and Leonard, M.A. (2005) *Group Screening Test*. Belford, Northumberland: Ann Arbor Publishers.

Punch, K.F. (2009) *Introduction to Research Methods in Education*. London: SAGE.

Richardson, B. (ed.) (2007) *Tell It Like It Is: How Our Schools Fail Black Children*, 2nd edn. London: Bookmarks/Trentham Books.

Richardson, J.T.E. and Wydell, T.N. (2003) 'The representation of students with dyslexia in UK Higher Education', *Reading and Writing*, 16: 475–503.

Riddall-Leech, S. (2008) *How to Observe Children*, 2nd edn. London: Heinemann.

Riddick, B. (2010) *Living with Dyslexia*, 2nd edn. Abingdon: Routledge.

Rose, J. (2009) *Identifying and Teaching Children and Young People with Dyslexia and Literacy Difficulties*. London: Department for Children, Schools and Families.

Sharman, C., Cross, W. and Vennis, D. (2007) *Observing Children and Young People*, 4th edn. London: Continuum.

Shaywitz, S.E., Morris, R. and Shaywitz, B.A. (2008) 'The education of dyslexic children from childhood to young adulthood', *Annual Review of Psychology*, 59: 451–75.

Singleton, C. (1999) *Dyslexia in Higher Education: Policy, Provision and Practice*. Report of the National Working Party on Dyslexia in Higher Education. Hull, UK: University of Hull.

CHAPTER 5

GATHERING INFORMATION FROM OTHERS

Chapter Overview

This chapter enables readers to:

- appreciate the contributions to the assessment process made by the learner, parents and other school staff;
- consider how they might obtain their views;
- use the resultant information to help shape a plan of intervention.

As soon as a learner's difficulties have been recognised it is important to collect as much relevant information as possible about that learner. This not only implies further assessment by the teacher but also gathering information from other sources. Scrutiny of school records may be a first step (although sometimes these can include inaccurate or dated information), but it is important to involve 'significant others' in the assessment process. These are (*inter alia*):

- the learners themselves;
- parents/carers;
- other teachers/TAs/professionals who may have current (or very recent) knowledge of the learner.

The approaches suggested in this chapter are appropriate whether the assessment process will be based on informal or formal assessments.

Discovering the views of others supports the adoption of a social or interactional model of learning difficulties (see Chapter 2) before (or simultaneously) exploring an individual's difficulties. The views of others help to build a more holistic picture of the learner, their strengths as well as difficulties in different situations. It is important at this stage, to recognise the importance of the environment (school and home) in affecting learning. Not only does this offer more information about any difficulties but points to 'differences' in learning in different settings and can suggest how the environment can be adapted to promote more successful learning.

The Views of the Learner

The active participation of the learner as a contributor to the assessment process (rather than the 'object' being assessed) is vital if the process and any subsequent intervention is to be a positive experience, enhancing self-esteem rather than leading or adding to a feeling or sense of failure. It is the child or young person who has the clearest view of what challenges them most and gives rise to difficulties in learning situations. Moreover, as discussed in Chapter 3, involvement in this process is a right of the child.

Pupil participation should start at the beginning of the assessment and continue throughout, including making decisions about any special tuition or grouping, drawing up targets and individual learning plans (ILPs). For example, a study of the views of learners aged 10–11 and 13–14 with statements for moderate learning difficulties showed that in mainstream schools they preferred support through withdrawal rather than in class (Norwich and Kelly, 2004). Seeking the views of the child and 'taking them into account' is a fundamental principle of the SEN Code of Practice (DfES, 2001: 7, para. 1.5). 'Taking account' of the views does not, of course, mean that their views or preferences will necessarily be followed. However, it does imply they should be not only elicited but also appreciated so that if they are not carried out, appropriate explanations will be provided. Many adults (including many parents and teachers) are concerned about the extent to which a child's view should be taken into consideration or acted upon, particularly if the child is very young or has a cognitive or emotional difficulty. They support their concern by referring to the word 'capable' and the reference to 'age and maturity' in Article 12 of the Convention of the Rights of the Child.

However, seeking children's views as part of the assessment process was an approach used by many teachers and psychologists long before it became an aspect of the Rights of the Child. It has been part of the writers' regular practice with *all* learners, not just those with dyslexic-type difficulties. In this we were influenced by the American psychologist George Kelly who developed Personal Construct Theory (PCT) in 1955, working with both adults and children (see Kelly, 1991). He suggested, somewhat ironically, that, 'If you want to know what is wrong with someone, ask him (sic) – he might tell you', as she/he is the person experiencing a difficulty. Kelly's approach was developed extensively in the UK in both research and education in the 1970s and 1980s, e.g. Bannister and Fransella (1986). Tom Ravenette, an educational psychologist working in Newham, East London, made extensive use of the approach using 'informal talks' with learners and methods where they could write or draw to express their feelings or just 'talk' about them (Ravenette, 1977, 1999, 2003). An excellent discussion of the use of drawing to investigate children's self-image can be found in Bell and Bell (2008). Talking to learners or using other means of communication will reveal their personal feelings and response to situations rather than reflect an adult's preconceived ideas. The methods and language used must, of course, be appropriate to the individual child, to ensure their understanding. One key to the use of PCT is to give an opportunity to produce a 'bi-polar construct'. Thus if we want to know what they believe helps them to learn, we also want to know what hinders them. For young children we might ask them to draw five pictures where they are 'happy' in school and one where they are not. (It has sometimes been the case that we have been told, 'I can't think of five happy times – can it be four sad/unhappy and one happy?') Informal talks, interviews, questionnaires, drawings can all be used to elicit views. Readers who are interested in exploring this approach should refer to a recent, practical text by Burnham (2008).

Where learners are used to participating in decision-making in school (which is increasingly the case because of the emphasis on 'learner-voice') they will be accustomed to offering their views and opinions. However, in many cases they may also have seen no resulting action or been involved in limited decision-making. As one student said, 'We have a School Council and we could choose what colour to paint the benches in the playground but we couldn't talk about what maths lessons are like'.

When learners are being asked for their views as part of the process of assessing 'apparent' difficulties even where they have had positive experiences of pupil participation it is likely that they may well feel very apprehensive and this could affect how 'freely' they express their views. It is important, therefore, that there is a trusting relationship between the learner and the adult eliciting their views. Although some would argue that this adult should be an 'impartial' person – or professional who does not work in the school, we consider that the most appropriate adult is a teacher or TA well-known to the learner. This should give confidence that the adult has authority within the school to ensure the learner's contributions are properly considered and also avoid the possible further anxiety of the learner because an 'expert' has been involved.

Informing the learner about the proposed assessment

The purpose of any assessment must be made clear to the learner, who should also know how their views will contribute to the assessment and intervention process. They should understand that not everything they may say will produce the action they request, but that it will be considered and discussed with them. They should know how any information they give will be used and they also need to know who else (roles/names) will be consulted and how those persons' contributions to assessment will be used. The role of the teacher involved (whether class teacher, Special Educational Needs Co-ordinator [SENCO] or other) should be clarified to the learner. If the learner is clear about the process and purpose of the assessment, there is also less risk of issues such as naming specific teachers/TAs being raised, although they will be asked to indicate subjects and teaching methods which help them and those which they find problematic. Nevertheless, anyone involved in talking to individual children needs to be aware of the possibilities of a child wishing to 'confide' about personal likes/dislikes and deal with these professionally. Moreover, in some cases, a child may disclose information relating to safeguarding issues – and the adult must follow their school's (LA's) guidelines should this occur.

The methods described below for eliciting the views of others as part of the assessment process can all be used with children and very young people but even when self-inventories or questionnaires are used, we suggest that 'talking' with a child, in an informal (though possibly structured) manner, should be the first step.

Learners' contributions to the assessment process

The emphasis is on the environment and its effects on learning.

1   Information about 'self-as-learner':

   ○ likes and dislikes about school and learning, subjects and types of activity (e.g. lessons/homework which involve talking/reading/writing);
   ○ emotional responses to particular activities (e.g. withdrawal/avoidance/rejection);
   ○ self-concept as learner (e.g. self-evaluation/what teachers think about 'me' as learner; what is hard/easy? where do I achieve, how/why?). This aspect may be covered by giving a questionnaire as suggested later.

In all cases the question, 'why' should be asked.

2 What makes a 'good teacher' for the learner? (and not a good teacher?). Names are not asked for or recorded if given. Pupils can say what helps them to learn. Why? (e.g. How do I like to learn?)
3 Friendships/peer groups at school: basis for friendships.
4 Information about experiences out of school:

  o likes/dislikes out of school, hobbies and interests; use of spare time (reading/ computer games/pets etc.);
  o what the learner does with family members/friends (where appropriate). This may include reading to others/being read to by parents/carers etc.

All the above information can further understanding about:

- making school/classrooms more 'learner-friendly' for the individual, including providing advice to school staff;
- any areas that should be built on as strengths;
- areas for assessment/observation to clarify detail or 'accuracy' of the learner's perceptions;
- information about motivation to learn in different areas and, in particular, the aspects of literacy where they would like help;
- learning support preferences (withdrawal/in-class/1:1, small group-based);
- interests to build on in intervention, e.g. games or an interest (football/love of animals), or as 'clue words' in devising an individual programme for spelling or reading, e.g. 'oa' as in 'goal', 'i-e' as in linesman, rather than *unrelated* memory aids, which may work well for younger children, e.g. /d/ for dog, /a/ for apple etc.;
- learner's views about involvement of parents/carers in an intervention programme.

The Views of Parents/Carers

As highlighted in Chapter 3, parents are integral to the assessment process, and must be kept involved, informed and feel supported. It is often a parent who is the first to identify a concern about learning and a teacher or SENCO then follows this up through observation and screening, including examining the learner's work and obtaining the views of anyone teaching that learner. This process means that the parents' views are seen to be respected. Although there is a body of literature which suggests that many parents have had to 'fight' to have their concerns about their child's difficulties acknowledged and action taken, the situation should be improving as schools and staff are increasingly aware of the nature of dyslexic-type difficulties. Cases such as those quoted in the Rose Report (Rose, 2009) and Riddick (2010) and that described by Peer (in Peer and Reid, 2012), which were commonly reported in the past, should now be rare. The Lamb Report (Lamb, 2009) suggested the experiences of parents of children with SEN varied, but pointed to parental satisfaction when they felt fully involved in both assessment and decision-making processes. Whether a concern is raised by a parent or teacher, parents are a major source of information and can make a vital contribution to information about a learner (as Buswell-Griffiths et al., 2004 found in the case of parents of learners with dyslexia).

Schools vary as to *when* they inform parents that a learner may have a learning difficulty. Some prefer to wait until after they have undertaken observations and evaluated the learner's literacy skills and learning situations and have confirmed that there *is* a difficulty. This is because they do not wish to 'worry' (or alarm) parents before they have more knowledge of the child. Indeed, sometimes it may be that there is only temporary lack of progress rather than a long-term difficulty. Others seek information from parents at an early stage whilst emphasising this is a 'concern' where a parent's knowledge may help to throw light on the situation. Whenever the school decides to contact parents, it is more appropriate to have a meeting rather than send a formal letter/text. The meeting should be purposeful but informal so that the parents feel comfortable discussing the issues with school staff. Such meetings may be followed up by asking parents to complete a questionnaire or checklist but it is important that any meeting or interview does not appear like an inquisition. Parents should be made aware of the purpose of assessment and be informed of the next steps to be taken, the areas to be assessed and the possible alternatives for intervention. This should be recorded in 'parent-friendly' terms and it would be good practice to let the parents have a copy of this in writing. They also need to be aware that written records will be made and who will be party to any information they give. There must be ample opportunity for parents to raise any questions they have about the assessment process and have these professionally addressed.

Parents'/carers' contributions to the assessment process

Medical information
This should include family medical information, but only pertinent information should be sought and the teacher must be able to justify any question asked of a parent. (Parents often – particularly when they have a good relationship with a teacher, or feel 'relieved' to find a teacher showing a genuine concern about their child – reveal far more personal/domestic information than is necessary or useful for the assessment and this should not be written in a report unless the parent wishes.)

Areas to be considered include:

- any known physical/medical problems and early medical history of the child which could have affected early development of language and cognitive skills;
- any hearing/sight difficulties (tests and dates to be noted);

- achievement of early developmental milestones;
- knowledge of any similar difficulties within the family.

Information about the child at home

It is important to keep the *child* as the focus rather than the family home circumstances. Areas to be considered might take the following format:

- Always start with 'open' questions – 'What's she/he like at home? What would you like to tell me about (*name of child*)?
- Does the learner talk about school at home – and what does she/he say?
- If homework is set, does the learner settle to do it willingly or need persuasion? Is parental support asked for/given? Is the behaviour different depending on the subject area/alternative activities available on certain evenings?
- What are the learner's interests/hobbies? Does she/he read for pleasure? Do siblings read? (if appropriate?) Use of computer? For what? Games – what sort?
- What are the learner's friendships in and out of school?
- If private tuition is being (or has been) given, when and what type?

Parents' concerns about the child

These might relate to cognitive/educational progress and achievements and/or social and emotional aspects:

- What areas would the parents like teachers to assess?
- What help/provision would they like for their child?
- What support could/would they be able to give at home?
- What information would they like from the school?

Two-way dialogue is important here so that parents are aware of what the school can offer – very often this is not known by parents. One parent quoted in the Lamb Report (Lamb, 2009) summed up a situation which is surely shared by many: 'I don't know what I don't know.' Involvement raises parental confidence in the school and gives them a voice. Meetings with parents can also establish the sort of role they can play in any subsequent intervention. It is important (as the SEN Code cautions) not to hold stereotyped assumptions about parents.

Meeting with the parents

Meetings with parents (informal interviews) are the best way of developing a partnership, rather than asking them to complete questionnaires and checklists, although these could be used to 'follow up' a meeting. In the USA such meetings are often called a 'parent–teacher conference' to emphasise dialogue. Although the meeting should be conducted in positive, jargon-free terms, it is important to keep it focused and purposeful.

The following structure has been used successfully:

1   Plan ahead

    ○ Write down the purpose of the meeting and note the information you will give
      to the parent(s) and what you require from them.
    ○ Decide if you can manage this in the time available – what will you do if you
      can't/don't?
    ○ Prepare samples of the learner's work to show the parents – this may involve
      written work, examples of strengths as well as difficulties.
    ○ Where the main issue is reading, it is often useful to show the parents a
      book at the child's current reading level and one which the child might be
      expected to be able to read for their chronological age. It is easier to have
      examples rather than talk in abstract terms or quote 'figures' for reading
      ages etc.

2   The meeting

    ○ The setting should, where possible, be 'informal' rather than 'across a desk'
      and should be out of the hearing of others. A good start can be made by
      having refreshments available and making the use of positive (but genuine)
      statements.
    ○ Establish how you and the parents will address each other.
    ○ Make sure there will be no interruptions during the meeting.
    ○ Discuss strengths before difficulties but be clear what both these are, drawing
      attention to the examples of work.

3   Views of parents

    ○ Ask them for comments on the work you have shown them. Also ask, 'What's
      she/he like at home?' Explore their views and the areas listed earlier in this
      chapter.
    ○ Find out what they would like to happen and what they would like you/the
      school to do.

4   Action plan

    ○ Agree what will happen next, including action by the school and how/when
      you will meet again.

5   Record

    ○ It is useful to keep a written, dated and signed report of the meeting (a pro forma
      can be drawn up based on the above points) and parents should be given/sent
      a copy. This is important for charting the action taken by the school and also for

parents who then know that some action will ensue. (It is also useful because some parents feel emotionally upset about the child and this can affect their ability to recall what was actually said at the meeting.)

o Interviewing and counselling techniques should be employed by a sympathetic teacher to ensure the spirit of partnership is generated and parents feel they have been *heard* and have not merely attended a meeting the outcome of which was pre-determined.

Views from Other Staff

In order to find out as much information as possible about a learner, the opinions of all school staff who know him/her should be sought. In primary schools or early years settings, this may be previous teachers, TAs and Key Workers. In secondary schools, it should include all the teachers/TAs currently working with the learner. Whilst this information can be gathered through meetings, it is more practical to use a short questionnaire or checklist. Very often, a checklist such as that described in the previous chapter is used. It is useful to add a request for the subject area and type of lesson organisation to be included, and for comments on any strengths of the learner. The SENCO or teacher conducting the assessment should give a deadline for responses, and follow up any non-returns.

Staff members' contributions to the assessment process

The focus is on looking for consistencies (or inconsistencies) in behaviours in different situations in order to determine the need for and nature of further assessments. Information is needed on a learner's behaviours in particular learning situations and the demands these situations make on them, helping to produce a profile of their learning experiences. It will, therefore, highlight whether there are specific difficulties. However, it should not be assumed that if there is low achievement in all areas this is because a learner has 'limited ability'. Further exploration of their difficulties is then required, including consideration of their attitudes to and motivation for learning. It may also be worth 'mapping' the learner's attendance and 'late' records onto this information.

At the same time, there may be a need to investigate the way the curriculum and teaching methods give rise to difficulties, e.g. through language and/or concepts introduced and pace of lessons. It is particularly important to examine the extent to which lessons make too many demands on a learner's literacy skills, and any other indicators of dyslexic-type difficulties such as slow processing of information and (particularly short-term) memory capacity. We suggest that information can be obtained from staff either through the use of short meetings (group meetings are held in some schools to share views on a targeted learner) or by asking staff to complete a short questionnaire or checklist (e.g. appropriate BDA checklist). This requires less time and tends to be the most effective method in secondary schools.

Methods for gathering the views of others

The three main methods are:

- interviews;
- questionnaires/inventories;
- checklists (see previous chapter).

Interviews

The advantage of an interview is that it is personal, provides time for listening and valuing the views of those involved (e.g. both the interviewer(s) and interviewee(s)) and can be more flexible than a questionnaire which addresses only areas targeted by the teacher. Interviews allow aspects to be considered in depth and help to establish (or maintain) good relationships.

There are two main forms:

- structured – where a predetermined set of questions is asked (although they do not have to be followed in a rigid order);
- semi/unstructured – no predetermined questions but discussion of areas considered important by both interviewer and interviewee.

Suggestions for topics/questions have been made above. We consider that a semi-structured interview is the most appropriate method for obtaining information. This ensures that the areas targeted by the teacher are discussed but also provides opportunities for interviewees to raise *their* agendas/topics. The teacher (interviewer) prepares a list of topics/areas where information would be useful but starts from a general statement and does not pursue the list in a specific order. This allows the meeting to adopt a conversational tone and facilitates two-way communication. If a particular topic arises in conversation, any question relating to that topic that appears later on the agenda can be ignored. By allowing the interviewee to identify and raise their own concerns the procedure is likely to be more valued by them, whether learner, parent or professional colleague. An example of how to draw on and extend the view of the interviewee is that if a significant difficulty and/or behaviour is identified, it is often useful to ask, 'When is it not like that?'

Questionnaires/Inventories

These may be used as a means of gathering information in the case of learners, parents and other staff although we consider they should be used only as *additional* sources of information in the case of learners and parents. They take a written form, either in terms of a paper and pen exercise or presented on a computer. Thus one implication is that whoever is asked to complete a questionnaire must either be able to read or have the questions read to them. Questionnaires will usually ask for views on aspects of learning and the learner or parent is asked to say how 'typical' this is of the learner or to answer questions that are open-ended, e.g. Name three things that help you (your child) to learn. How do they help? What do good teachers of boys/girls like you do? In the case of questionnaires for parents, they might also include: What are your child's hobbies or interests? How do they learn about them? Does your child enjoy school? Does she/he enjoy some days/lessons more than others? What makes you think this?

Questionnaires should only be given to parents as an 'option' for further information and the fact that some parents may have literacy/language difficulties and/or be apprehensive about putting anything in writing should be considered before using this approach.

Learners, on the other hand, often enjoy completing questionnaires or self-rating inventories either before or after talking to the teacher. A self-rating inventory will include a set of statements and the learner is asked to say which are 'like me' or 'not like me'. They can also be used to find out about attitudes to learning – or aspects of the curriculum.

Content and type of response required can be adjusted to the age and maturity of the child. Sometimes inventories or questionnaires obtain more honest responses than face-to-face interviews where a learner is trying to 'please' a teacher. A further advantage is that inventories can be given to whole classes so that they can reveal the extent to which the targeted learner is similar to or different from others. In some cases, a teacher/TA may read each statement in turn and the learner(s) be given time to respond. A good example of a self-report inventory, for learners aged 9–16 is the 'Myself as Learner Scale', which is reasonably short, easy to administer and score, and, importantly, can be given to whole classes, which means that teachers can obtain useful information about a number of peers at the same time (Burden, 2012). This inventory has also been used in the research into the self-concept of learners with dyslexia. Two examples of inventories for learners are given in Tables 5.1 and 5.2.

Sometimes open-ended questions can be included in questionnaires/inventories, e.g. 'The best thing about English lessons is ...' and 'The worst thing about English lessons is ...'. These should be limited in number when given to learners who have difficulties in writing and spelling. Sometimes, of course, particularly when given to whole classes, such inventories provide an evaluation of the content and styles of lessons rather than information about a learner! However, they provide a basis for further

Table 5.1 Attitudes to literacy lessons (Key Stage 1 children)

Example 1: For children in Year 1	
Things we do in literacy	😀 😮 ☹️
Phonics	😀 😮 ☹️
Singing songs	😀 😮 ☹️
Reading words	😀 😮 ☹️
Reading a book	😀 😮 ☹️
Drawing pictures	😀 😮 ☹️
Listening to stories	😀 😮 ☹️
Writing stories	😀 😮 ☹️
Practising handwriting	😀 😮 ☹️

The teacher explains the meaning of the faces and each time an item is read, asks the child(ren) to circle or tick the one that shows how they feel.

Table 5.2   Attitudes to English lessons (secondary school pupils)

	Example 2: Opinions about English lessons (Year 8)			
	Statement	Agree	Sometimes	Disagree
1	I am good at writing essays and assignments			
2	English lessons are interesting			
3	I find spelling hard			
4	Drama is the best part of English			
5	Class discussions are interesting			
6	The work in English is too easy			
7	The teacher helps when I find things difficult			
8	English lessons should be longer			
9	I would like more discussions in English			
10	English is boring			
11	There is too much writing in English lessons			
12	The best part of English lessons is reading books			

Photocopiable

Assessment of Learners with Dyslexic-Type Difficulties © Sylvia Phillips, Kathleen Kelly and Liz Symes, 2013 (SAGE).

discussion and assessment. An example of a questionnaire for mathematics can be found in Chapter 11.

Other related approaches to finding information about a learner might include asking them to look at a list of interests/out of school activities and put them in rank order.

Open-ended questions are often better than giving a list as they allow for a personal response. Stephen, a 15-year-old student with severe literacy difficulties, was known in school as a 'football fanatic' not interested in anything else. When asked to list his favourite hobbies in order of preference he listed 'collecting foreign coins, particularly from Greece, pre-Euro', with second favourite, 'walking the neighbour's dog' (unpaid) while 'watching football' was third. In discussion, it was discovered that his mother was Greek and relatives sometimes came to stay, bringing the coins, which he described enthusiastically, and he could speak, but not read, some Greek words. He did not share the first two interests with his peers 'because they would laugh'.

Such an open-ended inventory might read:

1   The three things I like best in school are:
2   The three things I do not like in school are:
3   The three things I like doing out of school are:
4   My favourite is ...

Issues of Cultural and Linguistic Diversity

The varying social and educational backgrounds of all children and their families must be acknowledged in any of the proposed approaches to gathering information from learners and parents. There are additional issues to be considered in the case of children for whom English is not a first language (or the main language at home) and many of these also come from religious and cultural backgrounds that might affect their contributions to the assessment process. The advice given in the SEN Code of Practice (para. 2.6) about working with *all* parents that 'There should be no presumption about what parents can or cannot do to support their children's learning' and the need to avoid 'stereotypic views of parents' is particularly true when assessing the possible special educational needs of children with EAL.

Communication is likely to be a major difficulty and this may be related to proficiency in English. Interview questions (or wording of any procedure used) should be adjusted accordingly. However, this may still put additional pressure on some children who may be extremely embarrassed and anxious about talking about any difficulties. Care should also be taken not to use jargon, or where specific terminology is used, to give practical examples and explanations. (This aspect should be considered for *all* parents, as many English-speaking parents will not have this knowledge.)

There is often great reluctance to admit to any difficulty if there is a home culture of high expectation of high academic achievement. A desire to conform and respect teachers may also exacerbate this. (Whilst this can apply to *all* children, teachers report that it is particularly a feature they have observed in many children from minority ethnic groups where they believe there are high expectations of academic success.)

This issue can affect parental participation. In some cultures there may be an unwillingness to admit to any disability or learning difficulty. Care must therefore be taken to ensure that meetings are supportive and emphasise the need to find ways of bringing about successful learning, rather than focusing on what the learner *cannot* do. This is good practice for all parents! In many cases, schools make use of translation services to provide information about special educational provision in their school and also provide information about the legislative framework. Interpreters can be used in meetings, where necessary, both to clarify the dialogue between teachers and parents, and also to explain some of the terminology in written documents. It is particularly important to try to have an interpreter who understands the education system to do this. Some schools are fortunate in having members of staff who are able to interpret, but in schools where there are many home languages, it is unlikely that there will be sufficient multilingual staff. Interpreters can also be used when talking to children, but the need for this is less common as any learner being assessed should have sufficient proficiency in English to cope with social situations (see Chapter 4).

Parents should be informed about the form that the assessment will take and know that any assessment will be in English. It is useful if they can provide information about the child's proficiency in their 'home' language, their use of English out of school, as well as the information requested from all parents. Some parents do not fully appreciate why questions about the child at home are of any concern to the school and may see this as intrusive. This is a 'cultural' difference which requires early, clear explanation. Similarly, some see the teacher as 'expert', and believe that as parents they have nothing of educational value to contribute.

In some cases, it may be only a father who attends a meeting – this can be for cultural/religious reasons but, more often, it is because the father is the more fluent speaker of English.

Although there are often language barriers to communication, in general the same information is sought as of any parents and learners and where a school adopts caring, positive and supportive approaches to parents generally, then the language and cultural differences are understood and 'not an issue', certainly not a problem.

Some parents, regardless of linguistic and cultural background, know very little about what support they can expect for a child with a learning difficulty while others know a lot. Good practice for *all* parents should, therefore, accommodate and support a range of individual differences among parents.

Summary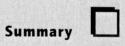

This chapter has suggested how the views of learners, parents and other staff can be collected and evaluated in the light of other information about the learner. Each participant makes a significant contribution and in each case, there should be some feedback to show how that information will be used. In the case of school staff, this should include suggestions about how the learner can currently be best supported. It is important not to spend too long a period collecting the information so that the full assessment process can be conducted quickly in order to reflect learning at a particular time. Information about the interests, hobbies and attitudes of the learner has been emphasised so that it is not regarded purely as 'chat' to maintain good relationships between assessor and learner. It throws light on the learner's perception of self and may point to strategies the teacher can use in any intervention, whether this relates to support in lessons, making classrooms more learning-friendly or drawing on interests in devising activities for direct teaching. It is, of course, important that meetings/interviews with learners and parents are not seen as 'one-off' occasions at an early stage of the assessment process but signal a beginning of continuing communication about outcomes of assessment and intervention.

Follow-up Activities

1 Examine your school's prospectus and other materials that inform parents about what the school does to maintain good relationships with parents, with particular reference to its provision for learners with SEN. In the light of this chapter, how might it affect a parent's willingness to share concerns about their child's learning?
2 Devise a short self-report inventory to discover the attitudes to school and learning of a small group of pupils. Consider what information you will seek.

Points for Discussion

- Discuss some of the information you would seek from colleagues about the performance of learners in their lessons, and the ways in which you might use this information.
- Discuss how you may make recommendations to colleagues about improving curriculum access for a learner who experiences particular difficulties in their lessons. Consider issues of professional sensitivity as well as the learner's needs, and also what it is realistic for a class or subject teacher to do.

Further Reading

Burden, R. (2008) 'Dyslexia and self concept', in G. Reid, A. Fawcett, F. Manis and L. Siegel (eds), *The SAGE Handbook of Dyslexia*. London: SAGE. pp. 395–410.
An overview of research into dyslexia and the self-concept.
Buswell-Griffiths, C., Norwich, B. and Burden, R. (2004) 'Parental agency, identity and knowledge: mothers of children with dyslexia'. *Oxford Review of Education*, 30: 417–33.
This research revealed the contributions that parents can make to the assessment of any learners through a study of mothers of learners with dyslexia.

References

Bannister, D. and Fransella, F. (1986) *Inquiring Man: The Psychology of Personal Constructs*, 3rd edn. London: Routledge.
Bell, S.J. and Bell, R.C. (2008) 'An illustration of self-characterization in a child's drawing: the importance of process', *Personal Construct Theory & Practice*, 5: 1–9.
Burden, R. (2012) *Myself as Learner Scale (MALS)*, 2nd edn. Exeter: University of Exeter.
Burnham, S. (2008) *Let's Talk: Using Personal Construct Psychology to Support Children and Young People*. London: SAGE.
Buswell-Griffiths, C., Norwich, B. and Burden, R. (2004) 'Parental agency, identity and knowledge: mothers of children with dyslexia', *Oxford Review of Education*, 30: 417–33.
DfES (Department for Education and Skills) (2001) *Special Educational Needs: Code of Practice*. London: DfES.
Kelly, G. (1991) *The Psychology of Personal Constructs*, 2nd edn. London: Routledge.
Lamb, B. (2009) *The Lamb Enquiry: Special Educational Needs and Parental Confidence*. London: Department for Children, Schools and Families.

Norwich, B. and Kelly, N. (2004) 'Pupils' views on inclusion: moderate learning difficulties and bullying in mainstream and special schools', *British Educational Research Journal*, 30: 43–65.

Peer, L. and Reid, G. (ed.) (2012) *Special Educational Needs: A Guide for Inclusive Practice*. London: SAGE.

Ravenette, A.T. (1977) 'Personal construct theory: an approach to the psychological investigation of children and young people', in D. Bannister (ed.), *New Perspectives in Personal Construct Theory*. London: Academic Press. pp. 251–80.

Ravenette, A.T. (1999) *Personal Construct Theory in Educational Psychology: A Practitioner's View*. London: Whurr.

Ravenette, A.T. (2003) 'Constructivist intervention when children are presented as problems', in F. Fransella, . (ed.), *International Handbook of Personal Construct Psychology*. Chichester: Wiley. pp. 283–93.

Riddick, B. (2010) *The Social and Emotional Consequences of Specific Learning Difficulties/Disabilities*, 2nd edn. London: Routledge.

Rose, J. (2009) *Independent Review of the Primary Curriculum: Final Report*. London: Department for Children, Schools and Families.

CHAPTER 6

INFORMAL APPROACHES: ASSESSING DIFFICULTIES IN READING

Chapter Overview

This chapter enables the reader to:

- recognise which aspects of reading should be investigated when conducting an assessment of literacy difficulties;
- acquire knowledge and skills to devise and use informal methods to assess reading difficulties.

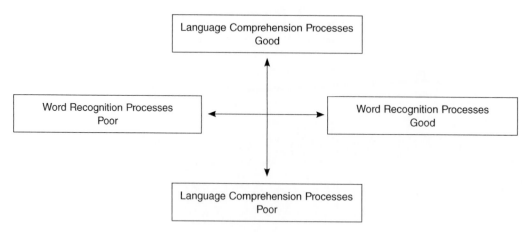

Figure 6.1   The Simple View of Reading (Rose, 2006)

Earlier chapters have suggested that the first indicators of literacy difficulties are observed in reading, whether these are of a specific nature (e.g. as a possible sign of dyslexia) or one aspect of more general learning difficulties. The Simple View of Reading (SVoR) model (Gough and Tunmer, 1986), which was adopted by the National Primary Strategy in England in 2007 (following the Rose Review of Early Reading in 2006), provides a useful basis for determining which reading skills should be assessed (see Figure 6.1).

The SVoR model suggests that reading (R) (which implies obtaining meaning from print) is a product both of decoding (D) and language comprehension (C), i.e. R = D × C. Gough and Tunmer (1986) used the terms:

- **decoding** to mean the ability to recognise/pronounce words out of context (i.e. have knowledge of grapheme–phoneme correspondence); and
- **comprehension** to mean linguistic or language comprehension (i.e. the ability to access meanings and combine words grammatically to form sentences/meaningful units).

These are considered to be two independent variables. Language comprehension is heavily influenced by the exposure to language and experiences a reader brings to a text. A wide vocabulary and good understanding of the grammatical structure of language helps a learner to predict words (what may come next) and previous experiences/knowledge helps a reader to check whether this makes sense (holds meaning) (see Figure 6.2.). Rose (2006) and others have substituted the term **word recognition** for decoding.

Fluent reading involves accuracy (in decoding) and an element of speed. It also builds on language comprehension because knowledge of how words are organised into phrases and sentences aids the ability to read quickly and with meaning. Learners

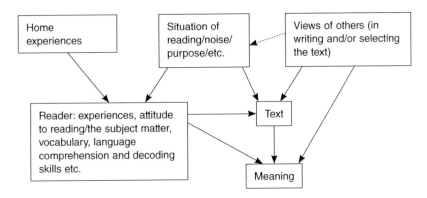

Figure 6.2   Model of how a reader extracts meaning from text

with dyslexia often have good language/listening comprehension but their reading comprehension may not reflect this because of their decoding difficulties. Word recognition is a major source of difficulty for many learners because it requires good knowledge of grapheme–phoneme correspondence (GPC). It also requires the ability to recognise some words 'on sight'. This is particularly the case for words that occur frequently but are not easily decoded using GPC (e.g. there). However, some 'high frequency' words may initially be read by decoding graphemes into phonemes, but, because of repetition, become stored in memory, and can therefore be responded to quickly and automatically (on sight).

Acquiring knowledge of GPC is particularly challenging for many learners with dyslexia (often because of an underlying phonological processing difficulty). They may also have a poor memory and slow speed of processing information, which means they do not retrieve information or respond quickly to print even when they have acquired some GPC skills. Assessing reading difficulties may therefore point to the need to probe underlying difficulties in cognitive processing, as discussed in Chapters 10 and 17. This chapter, however, is concerned only with the assessment of the reading difficulties themselves.

The starting point for assessment and devising appropriate methods and materials will depend on the age of the learner, the level of reading achieved so far and the methods of teaching reading used. The approaches suggested below are appropriate for learners who have failed to make expected progress in reading despite having been well taught. They draw on curriculum-based materials that can be easily used by teachers and incorporated within regular teaching/assessment procedures.

The SVoR, the Connectionist (Seidenberg, 2005) and Dual-Route models (Coltheart, 2005), as discussed in Kelly and Phillips (2011), lead to determining which aspects of reading should be assessed to build a profile of individual learners. These are summarised in Table 6.1.

Table 6.1   Reading difficulties: areas to be assessed

	Areas to be assessed	Purpose
1	Reading a passage aloud	To discover accuracy, fluency, comprehension including use of context
2	Single word reading	To discover ability to recognise words (particularly high frequency words) without the aid of context
3	Reading words using phonically regular words	To assess knowledge of grapheme–phoneme correspondence
4	Reading phonically regular non-words	To check knowledge of grapheme–phoneme correspondence
5	Reading comprehension (aloud and silently)	To establish levels of understanding a text
6	Reading speed/fluency	To establish rate of reading
7	Language comprehension of a text	To discover the knowledge of language brought to a text (when reading and when being read to)

The first step in assessing reading is to identify the strategies a learner uses. This involves asking the learner to read a passage aloud, to provide evidence of *how* they read and whether (and how) they decode words accurately.

'Miscue analysis' is a well-established method of obtaining this information. Although much of this chapter is allocated to an explanation of the approach, in practice the assessment procedure does not take long. It requires about five minutes with the learner and about 15–20 minutes to score and interpret (although frequent use of the technique can reduce this time).

Assessing a Passage of Reading Using Miscue Analysis

What is miscue analysis?

Miscue analysis is a means of observing, recording and analysing the strategies used by a learner when reading a passage aloud. Based on the work of Goodman (1973), who described it as providing a 'window on the reading process', it is a very useful assessment procedure for discovering what a learner understands about the reading process and to diagnose their 'strengths and weaknesses' (positive and negative strategies) in reading.

It is compatible with the Simple View of Reading model, as it considers strategies concerned both with decoding (word recognition) and the learner's knowledge of language (language/listening comprehension). The approach is similar to (but more detailed than) the 'Running Record' method of monitoring reading development (Clay, 2000). Although it is a method applied to reading aloud, Goodman emphasised that decoding from print to sound is ultimately not necessary, reminding us that the primary aim of reading is comprehension. However, accurate word recognition is initially essential to the process of learning to read.

The methods suggested below are based on Helen Arnold's version of miscue analysis (Arnold, 1982).

Miscues not errors

In miscue analysis, deviations from the printed text are viewed as 'miscues' not errors. This term is preferred because a mistake/incorrect response may reflect the fact that the reader has used certain psycholinguistic 'cues' but not integrated all available cues effectively. The term 'miscue' also avoids the negative connotation of 'errors', because a reader's miscues (mistakes) may indicate she/he is actually using a positive strategy, calling on useful knowledge, when responding to a text. In carrying out a miscue analysis the observer/teacher does not supply unknown words or 'correct' mistakes so that a reader has time to process the meaning/information read so far and to self-correct. (Many teachers find this non-interference difficult because they wish to support the learner, but it is important in this assessment method to see whether the learner is 'reading' to comprehend rather than simply decoding/'barking at print'. Self-correction may reveal this.)

There are three main cueing systems:

1 **Syntactic cues** The syntactic cueing system uses knowledge of the structure of the language (syntax: the rules that govern how words are combined into grammatical sentences). We draw on the spoken language we already know and our experience of book language to predict what is coming next in relation to the grammatical structure of a sentence.
2 **Semantic cues** The semantic cueing system uses links between the content of a text and a reader's experience in order to make it meaningful. In other words, as readers, we use our general expectations of meaning in life to try to predict what is coming. We use the immediate textual context (especially previous sentences/meanings) to help work out the meaning of the next words.
3 **Grapho-phonic cues** The grapho-phonic cueing system draws on knowledge of grapheme–phoneme correspondence, i.e. the way in which printed letters represent sounds within words. It is common to use the first two or three letters and the final letter to 'cue' into words. These miscues suggest that a learner is aware that there should be a letter–sound relationship, but has insecure knowledge of phonics.

All these cueing systems help learners to read. Fluent readers are competent in the use of all the systems and know when and how to use them effectively and efficiently. They can co-ordinate the strategies and use the most economical, leaving others redundant.

In the early stages of reading, learners often use both contextual cues and grapho-phonic responses but not integrated: finally, they use a combination of the two. Whilst we know the importance of using all cueing systems in learning to read, children need to understand grapheme–phoneme correspondence (phonics) and be able to decode words accurately in order to make maximum use of other cueing systems to comprehend a text.

Why use miscue analysis?

Miscue analysis can be used for:

- diagnosing strengths and weaknesses/areas for further development;
- planning next steps for teaching;
- evaluating text difficulty and the level of text a learner can read independently;
- monitoring progress;
- comparisons across groups of pupils.

Miscue analysis can contribute to the formative assessment of reading development of all children, providing evidence of their learning and monitoring progress. When a passage can be read with few miscues a learner can be presented successively with passages at higher readability levels in order to demonstrate progress. However, this book is concerned with its use as a means of identifying strengths and weaknesses to inform future teaching for learners experiencing difficulties in reading. There are three levels of interpreting the information gained:

- at a simple level it provides details about accuracy, fluency and general reading behaviour;
- it can be categorised to indicate general tendencies;
- each miscue can be analysed to indicate which strategies the learner is using – positively and negatively.

It is the latter which is particularly relevant in describing strengths and areas of difficulty in order to determine which areas require further investigation.

The Assessment Procedure

Selecting an appropriate text for reading

A miscue analysis is carried out using a passage of continuous prose. This can be:

- a learner's 'reading book' (i.e. one they are not reading independently). This would be the case for children who are using a reading scheme or 'graded' reading books;

- a previously unseen text at an appropriate level of difficulty level (see below);
- texts of three different levels of difficulty: easy, appropriate, challenging.

The second of these is the most commonly used and is described below.
  The teacher needs to ensure that:

- the content is interesting to the reader;
- the language is within the experience of the reader (this could be 'real life' or 'fictional' experience);
- there are no unfamiliar/irregular proper nouns, e.g. passages about Greek gods, historical figures, mountains, cities etc.

The level of text

A text that is challenging will provide the most useful information to reveal a reader's strategies. The readability level should normally be 12–18 months above the learner's *reading* age, as about 20–25 miscues are necessary to identify patterns of reading strategies used. Usually, a passage of 150–200 words will provide sufficient information to analyse. It can be useful to choose texts that are typical of reading materials used in the learner's curriculum as this shows how they respond to such materials. It is often a good idea to provide two or three passages (e.g. fiction and non-fiction) of equal difficulty and allow the learner to choose which to read.

  With regard to level of difficulty for reading, it is usually recognised that:

- when a learner can read a text with above 95% accuracy, the text is suitable for *independent* reading;
- when a learner can read a text with an accuracy level of between 90 and 95% the text is suitable for *instructional* reading. (i.e. with support/teacher input);
- when the learner is reading a text with below 90% accuracy, the text is unsuitable because it is at *frustration* level.

However, opinions vary, and a study by Burns and Parker (2010) working with learners 'struggling' to read suggested that instructional level is 93–97%, and over 97% accuracy (i.e. fewer than three mistakes/unknown words in 100) is necessary for independent reading. They suggest that text will be at frustration level if there is less than 93% accuracy. When assessing reading using miscue analysis, the passage chosen may well mean that some learners will be reading at frustration level and have to draw on *all* their resources to try to read. Teachers therefore have to explain carefully to learners why they are asking them to read a very 'hard' passage and how this information will be used to help them. (See note on discontinuing the assessment, p.83.)

  Readability may be assessed if thought necessary using Fog or Smog readability tests or by word-processing and using the Readability function in Microsoft® 'Word'.

Teacher requirements

The teacher needs:

- a copy of the text being read;
- a coding system with which they are familiar;
- a digital recorder – in order to analyse the reading later;
- a quiet room with no interruptions.

The **teacher's copy** of the text is used to record the learner's responses and allows comparison with the actual text thereby facilitating analysis and interpretation. The learner's name and the date of reading should be written on the teacher's copy.

There are several **coding systems** available, all of which are very similar. It is important that the teacher familiarises him/herself with the one they use. The system provided below is based on Arnold (1982) but offers suggestions for alternatives. Teachers may devise their own as long as they use it consistently.

Recording a learner's reading allows the teacher to analyse the responses at a later time, marking their copy to show a learner's actual responses. When they become familiar with the procedure some teachers code their copy while the learner is reading. However, recording the reading means that a teacher can 'replay' several times to ensure accuracy of coding the text and it is also makes it easier for a teacher to observe and write down a learner's behaviours during reading. (See the section below on 'Observing learners while they read'.)

Carrying out the miscue analysis

1   It is important that the learner feels comfortable about the reading. The teacher should prepare the learner by explaining the procedure, perhaps giving the learner an opportunity to read an introductory part of the text before recording the reading of the chosen passage. Every effort needs to be taken to reduce anxiety, especially as the text will be challenging for the learner. The teacher should also tell the learner that she/he will be asked about what has been read when they finish reading. The learner should be advised to carry on reading as far as possible without help from the teacher.

Note: Because the teacher doesn't 'correct' the child or substitute an unknown word, this assessment is not a reliable indication of comprehension but it may throw light on how reading accuracy is affecting their comprehension.

2   The learner will need a copy of the text to be read – either a book or photocopy (of good quality) of the passage. Usually this should be in a font familiar to the

learner and 12-point size (larger if the learner has a visual difficulty requiring enlargement). The learner can also use coloured overlays/lens or have the text presented on coloured paper if this is his/her normal practice (e.g. the learner has Meares-Irlen Syndrome).

3   The teacher records the learner's reading digitally, noting behaviours, but does *not* 'code' or 'mark' their copy so the learner can remain fairly relaxed. After reading, the teacher can ask questions about the text – again both the teacher and the learner are recorded. (If the learner becomes distressed or is clearly unable to read much of the text, the reading should be discontinued.)

4   The teacher later (not in the learner's presence) plays back the recording and marks/codes the miscues on his/her copy.

Which miscues will be noted?

Miscues (mistakes) can be analysed in many different ways. It is important to remember that the purpose is to find out whether there is a pattern in the learner's strategies: are the strategies being used in an integrated way or is there a reliance on only one strategy?

The miscue categories

The main categories that will be noted (based on the work of both Goodman and Arnold) are:

1   no response/teacher assistance sought;
2   substitutions (which will indicate the cueing strategy used);
3   omissions;
4   insertions;
5   self-corrections;
6   repetitions;
7   mispronunciations;
8   hesitations;
9   sounding out.

Note: We believe that hesitations and repetitions should be commented on as features of fluency rather than inaccuracies. Sometimes they may indicate uncertainty about what follows, and sometimes they may reflect that the reader is 'looking ahead' to what the next word or phrase says.

Substitutions are usually the most significant indicators of the reading strategies used and it is important always to write on the teacher's copy *exactly what the learner said*.

How to record/code the miscues

Table 6.2 suggests a useful system for coding miscues based on a generally accepted approach similar to those used in the work of (*inter alia*) Goodman (1973), Arnold (1982) and DfES (2003). It is important that teachers choose a system they understand and can use *easily and consistently* in order to ensure accurate recording, analysis and interpretation of a learner's reading strategies, strengths and difficulties. There is no *one* correct way of coding. The teacher replays the recording, coding their copy.

Identifying strengths and difficulties

Step 1. Analysing miscues

When the teacher is satisfied that the coded copy is an accurate record of the learner's reading, the first step is to list and analyse the miscues, using a grid such as that in Table 6.3.

The number of miscues in each category can be counted. The number of words read correctly should be noted, both as a number out of total words and also given as a percentage, because this indicates the 'level' at which the learner reads the text. Giving the total usually enables a positive statement to be made in any record/report e.g. 'Daniel read 117 words correctly in a passage of 139 words'.

Step 2. Analysing substitutions

Substitutions are usually the most significant indicators of a learner's strategies. A grid such as that in Table 6.4 is useful.

Firstly, the original word and the substitution are listed, and then the following questions are asked about each one:

- Have grapho-phonic cues been used? Is there some similarity to the original in terms of letters used and grapheme–phoneme correspondence?

Where 3/4 letters are the same, then the substitution suggests *some* knowledge of a relationship between graphemes and phonemes, and it is recorded as a grapheme–phoneme miscue. Some substitutions will resemble the original word more than others, which is one reason for recording the original *and* substitution, so that a qualitative judgement can be made, or a pattern noted, e.g. omission of a particular letter; regularly recognising specific letters rather than others. It is important to examine learners' grapho-phonic difficulties as these may well identify particular phonic skills that need further investigation.

Table 6.2   An example of a Miscue Analysis Coding System

Miscue Type	Coding Symbol / how to Code	Explanation
Non-response/no attempt	Ben is my <u>friend</u> Ben is my friend	Underline the word not attempted or use a box round the word
Substitution	house The white m̶o̶u̶s̶e̶	Cross out the word and write the substituted word (or non-word) above it
Self-correction	want ✓ I went to the park. want ⓢⒸ I went to the park. wandered w̶a̶n̶t̶ I went to the park.	Code first as substitution. If self-corrects, tick the new word or treat as substitution but then insert sc if self-corrects (Sometimes the 'correction' is incorrect, in which case write in the new word and code and score as another substitution)
Insertion	to She came ˄ home.	Use an insertion sign and write in the word(s) said
Omission	They went ⓣⓞ the shops.	Circle the omitted word(s)
Reversals (and transpositions)	She w̄as tired (learner said "saw") He took his bat and\ball (said "ball and bat") or s͡aw b͡at and b͡all	A form of substitution, but where there is evidence of some reversal, indicate positions by curved lines or use **arrows**
Repetition	They <u>felt</u> angry.	Solid underlining of repeated word(s)
Hesitation	They saw a/crash.	Put a stroke in front of the word following the pause / hesitation
Sounding out (not a miscue, but indicates a strategy)	s-h-e-d shed	Write word with hyphens between each grapheme sounded e.g. s-h-e-d suggests each sounded separately but sh-e-d indicates knowledge of the 'sh' digraph
Mispronunciation (may not be a miscue but indicates poor knowledge of the word/poor choice of alternatives)	présent presént present′	Use stress marks or breves / macrons to indicate inappropriate pronunciation

Table 6.3   Analysing miscues

Original Text	Actual Response	Miscue Type
silent	no response	no response
rose	nose	substitution
wish	hesitation	hesitation
was	saw	reversal
etc.		

Table. 6.4   Analysing substitutions

Text	Substitution	Grapho/phonic	Semantic	Syntactic
walked	winked	√	x	√
spend	decide	x	x	√
parent	present	√	x	x?
etc.				

• Does the substitution make sense within the sentence/text as a whole?

If so, then it is recorded as an indication of using the semantic system, i.e. the reader appreciates that reading material carries meaning. Again, some will be more effective than others – or may be meaningful within a sentence, but not the passage as a whole, e.g. 'The bird flew up into the *sky*' (substituted for 'tree') makes sense, but if the next part of the sentence says, 'to find its nest among the leaves', it does not.

• Is the substitution syntactically (grammatically) appropriate?

In the example quoted above, the substitution of 'sky' for 'tree' is acceptable grammatically, whereas if the substitution had been 'tired', it would not. 'Tired' may *look* more like the word 'tree' because it contains three of the same letters, but it suggests that the learner is decoding using (inaccurately) grapho-phonic cues rather than drawing on syntactic cues.

Learners with dyslexic-type difficulties in decoding often try to use their knowledge of language (both syntactic and semantic) to 'guess' words, usually with more success than learners with general learning difficulties or those with limited language comprehension.

Making a record of a miscue analysis

A record should be kept to summarise the assessment carried out. This could comprise a file of:

- the marked text (and a copy of the coding system used);
- the analysis of all miscues (as in Table 6.3);
- the analysis of substitutions (as in Table 6.4);
- a summary of the numbers of miscues under each category;
- a note of the learner's behaviour observed during the assessment (see below).

Alternatively, a record sheet, such as the example in Table 6.5, could be used to incorporate all information.

Is the learner using positive or negative strategies?

Arnold (1982) suggests miscues should be further analysed into 'positive' and 'negative' strategies, largely in relation as to whether these change the meaning of the text, thereby affecting comprehension. If wished, the following guidelines can be used. If the meaning of the passage is changed, they are seen as 'negative'. However, a report on the analysis will describe strategies but should *not* use the term 'negative'.

Guidelines for analysis

1 Omissions

    a Do the omissions change the meaning of the text?

    b Is there a pattern in the type of omissions (e.g. adjectives, adverbs, nouns, proper nouns, multisyllabic words, or parts of words)?

2 Insertions

    a Do the insertions change the meaning of the text?

    b Is there a pattern to the insertions (e.g. inserting adjectives or adverbs) possibly to aid comprehension?

    c Do insertions make sense when earlier miscues were taken into account?

3 Substitutions

    a Are the substitutions similar in shape to the text word?

    b Do the substituted words begin with the same letter or letters as the text word? Are grapho-phonic cues used?

    c Are the substitutions correct syntactically, that is, did the reader substitute the same part of speech for the text word?

    d Is the substitution semantically correct, such as 'leap' for 'jump'?

    e Are the substitutions real words or nonsense words?

4   Mispronunciations

    a   Do the mispronunciations suggest an attempt to decode using grapho-phonic cues?

    b   Are the mispronunciations of a particular type (e.g. proper names, multisyllabic words, or irregular words)?

    c   Are some parts of a word pronounced correctly? Is there a pattern in the mispronunciation (e.g. initial, middle, or ends of words)?

Addressing these questions enables a teacher to report *qualitatively* on the reading and with some detail.

Effects on comprehension/making sense of a text

1   Do any of the miscues change the meaning of the text?
2   Is there a pattern to the meaning change, such as tense, action, context, sequence, etc?
3   Do the miscues interfere with answering questions?
4   Are the miscues a result of earlier miscues? For example if the learner read 'Tom and Ann ate the cake' (instead of 'cakes'). 'They really liked it' (word in the text was 'them'), the second sentence agrees with the miscue that occurred in the preceding sentence, and could be seen as 'positive'.
5   Are any of the miscues the result of dialect differences? If so, they are not miscues, but their effect on comprehension should be evaluated.

Answering these questions enables you to understand and describe a learner's reading strengths and weaknesses, and also appreciate how their miscues affect comprehension.

What Information does Miscue Analysis Give Us?

The importance of using miscue analysis is its ability to indicate areas for planning teaching. The following information may be helpful in writing reports and setting targets.

Non-responses

Non-responses suggest the learner:

- has little or no knowledge of grapheme–phoneme correspondence;
- may be reluctant to 'guess', perhaps because she/he is not making sense of what has been read so far and is not using contextual clues, or perhaps feels very insecure as a reader lacking confidence;
- may be relying on whole-word recognition – has a visual approach to reading.

Table 6.5   Example of a Miscue Analysis Record Form based on the DfES (2003)
guidance booklet

	MISCUE ANALYSIS RECORD FORM						
Name:			**Date of birth:**				
Passage read (attached):			**Readability level:**				
Date of assessment:			**Chronological age:**				
Text	**Substitutions 'sc' denotes later correction**	**G–p**	**Sem.**	**Syn.**	**Mis.**	**Non-r**

No. of self-corrections: Insertions: Omissions:

Repetitions: Hesitations: Reversals:

Reading behaviours
e.g. use of intonation, word-by-word reading, finger-pointing, losing place/missing a line, use of
punctuation

Summary of strengths and areas for developing/improving

Further assessment required?

 Photocopiable
Assessment of Learners with Dyslexic-Type Difficulties © Sylvia Phillips, Kathleen Kelly and Liz Symes,
2013 (SAGE).

A pattern of non-responses can be followed up by asking a learner what they do when they see an unfamiliar/unknown word, e.g. do they look for particular sounds in response to letters; find little words in multisyllabic words?

Substitutions

Substitutions suggest the learner:

- may have limited grapho-phonic skills – this implies a need for assessment of phonic skills;
- may be impulsive and needs to slow down (if the first part of the word is correct, e.g. 'tries' for 'tractor', or there is 'first-letter-guessing').

Omissions

Omissions can be ignored if they are small words that do not affect meaning. Sometimes omissions suggest the learner:

- may be reading too quickly;
- has a visual difficulty, e.g. tracking letters in words, words in sentences and even missing a line.

Insertions

If they do not affect the meaning, insertions can be ignored, although if a learner is reading too quickly, s/he may need slowing down. However, additions to words can sometimes affect their meaning (and syntax).

Some insertions suggest the learner:

- may be adding words to make it more meaningful to him/herself.

Sometimes this is positive, but it *can* sometimes change the meaning. In such cases, the learner needs to be more accurate and look more carefully at words. Using phonic skills accurately and then using a morphological approach, particularly looking at prefixes and suffixes will be important.

Reversals

Some reversals of words or phrases may have little effect on meaning, e.g. reading 'shoes and socks' when the original text was 'socks and shoes'. (In fact, this may show the learner was reading ahead and putting the phrase into his/her own words.) Some reversals *can* change meaning, e.g. reading 'no' instead of 'on'.

Reversals may suggest a learner:

- may need to slow down and 'look more carefully', particularly at small words usually learned as 'sight' vocabulary;
- has limited grapheme–phoneme knowledge.

Repetitions

Repetitions suggest the learner:

- may be re-thinking the word and then confirming it;
- may be repeating a word to gain time to consider how to read the next word/or is reading ahead.

Sometimes, however, repetitions affect understanding of the text because they impede fluency.

Hesitations

It is important to note *when* hesitations occur. If, for example, they occur before polysyllabic or 'tricky' words, the learner may lack confidence in his/her reading ability or may have poor phonic skills. In many cases, however, the learner may read the following words correctly, suggesting that she/he needed time to 'process' the word. Whilst indicating that decoding is not yet an *automatic* skill, this could imply evidence of either a 'sight' vocabulary or some knowledge of decoding skills (using GPC). The latter interpretation would be reinforced if the learner starts to 'sound-out' the word, either the simple sound of each single letter or by grapheme–phoneme. Where there is a hesitation either at the end or start of a new line, it may indicate a difficulty in tracking.

Repetitions and hesitations whilst adversely affecting fluency should not necessarily be seen as negative. However, frequent use of either or both can affect comprehension because they disrupt the flow.

Self-corrections

Self-corrections can take two forms:

- those that change a substitution for the correct word either immediately or shortly after, e.g. 'the boy's house was brown' where the learner then realised that 'horse' made better sense;

- those where they 'correct' a substitution by another incorrect word or even several incorrect words, e.g. reading 'book' for 'look' then saying, 'I mean "like", no, "took", no, "liked"'.

'Good' corrections usually suggest the learner is reading for meaning. In some cases, where there are frequent substitutions followed by corrections, it may be that the learner is trying to read too quickly and needs to be slowed down. This is particularly true where a grapho-phonic substitution is made (as in book/look/took) whether or not the correction is 'good' or 'incorrect'. It suggests attention to shape or one or two letters in the word. (Sometimes a reader 'corrects' a word that has been read correctly. This is recorded as a substitution but it is noted that it had already been decoded correctly.)

As is the case with reversals and hesitations, over-use of corrections can affect comprehension.

An example of a passage 'coded' for miscues can be found at the end of this chapter and on the website so that readers can practise analysing and interpreting miscues using the record sheets provided in this chapter.

Checking the understanding of the text

Asking questions about a text read aloud by a learner who has difficulty in decoding is not an accurate assessment of that learner's reading comprehension. However, it can be useful to indicate how poor decoding skills affect comprehension of texts at that readability level. This, in turn, will have implications for how achievement in literacy-based lessons is affected if the learner is required to undertake reading at a level higher than his/her reading age.

Without allowing the learner to look back at the text, the teacher can ask simple questions such as:

- Can you tell me what the passage was about?
- Which bit did you enjoy best?
- Was there a bit you found hard?
- What character did you like best? Why?

The reader's answers will give an idea of the amount of the text she/he has understood. More specific questions about parts of the text can be used, e.g.:

- Why do you think 'such a thing' happened?
- What do you think was meant when it said ... (as a direct quotation)?

If wished, the teacher can then repeat the questions, first telling the learner she/he can look back at the passage/book before replying. This often reveals a higher level of understanding, not requiring the process of accurate decoding and pronunciation.

A more valid assessment of reading comprehension is discussed later in this chapter.

Observing learners while they read

During both informal and formal assessment of reading (see Chapter 14 on using stand-ardised tests of reading) it is important to observe and record the learner's behaviours.
   Aspects to note include:

- how the learner approaches the situation (whether they seem interested/well-motivated/at ease);
- use of volume/pitch/intonation in reading (whether they lower their voice when meeting a 'difficult' word, whether articulation is clear – this may affect the development of phonic skills);
- recognition of punctuation (e.g. through use of pitch/intonation);
- any requests for help (when/why?) – this may include verbal and non-verbal requests (e.g. looking at teacher for reassurance);
- losing place (e.g. omitting a line), which may suggest a tracking difficulty;
- use of finger pointing;
- looking away from text/fidgeting etc.;
- whether the 'test' situation has provoked anxiety, which could adversely affect the outcomes.

At the end of reading, responses to questions about what the passage was about should be noted, including whether the learner had any interest in the passage, or could make comments/parallels with their experience.

Fluency in reading aloud

Fluency is a combination of accuracy and speed. It is important to comment on the *appropriateness* of the rate of reading as this may well affect comprehension. Too many hesitations and repetitions in addition to non-responses and lack of appreciation of punctuation can all affect fluency. One suggestion may be that when a learner is read-ing accurately, but not 'fluently' (e.g. too fast/too slow or at an uneven or disjointed rate) the teacher could model 'fluent, expressive' reading (including timing it). Another approach would be to time the learner reading a passage and then ask them to read again to 'beat' their time (or equal that of the teacher). Speed of naming has been found to be related to reading comprehension (Johnston and Kirby, 2006).

Single Word Reading

Word recognition: sight vocabulary

Analysing the strategies a learner uses in reading is important to identify areas teachers can build on and those that need further development. However, use of context may sometimes compensate for difficulties in decoding/word recognition. An informal assessment of ability to read single words free from context may show the extent to which a learner has built a 'bank' of sight vocabulary.

Teachers of children in the primary phase can assess 'sight' vocabulary by devising a simple criterion-referenced test based on high-frequency words. We suggest that those listed in Letters and Sounds (DfES, 2007) could be used as they are part of the normal teaching/assessment cycle although this document may no longer be part of the Primary Strategy. The lists include both 'decodable' (phonically regular) words such as 'see' and more 'tricky' words which require learning as a 'sight vocabulary'. Single word testing for a sight vocabulary should include both, but with particular emphasis on irregular words. Criteria for reading tricky words by phase are given in an Appendix to Letters and Sounds – which was available on-line at the time of writing/publication.

Words can be presented on a card, with five to a line, well-spaced. Teachers should select the words, font and size which are appropriate for the age and teaching the child has received, in order to see whether they are attaining an expected level compared with their peers. Particular difficulties should be noted in relation to 'sight' words and those that are phonically regular. The items should be graded for difficulty. Between 30 and 60 words can be used at a time. Older learners with difficulties could be tested on a selection from the 300 words listed, although, on the whole, we would suggest that testing single-word reading for them is more appropriately carried out using a standardised test as suggested in Chapter 14. This is because 'selecting' words to use beyond those in 'Letters and Sounds' becomes very arbitrary. Some teachers in secondary schools, however, may wish to collate a number of words suggested by subject teachers as 'essential' to their teaching, to see whether or not these are recognised instantly out-of-context.

Examples of a teacher-made single word reading test can be found in Appendix 1(a).

Single word reading: assessing phonic skills

Performance in a single word 'sight' reading test does not yield much information about a learner's phonic skills (i.e. knowledge of grapheme–phoneme correspondence).

There are two main ways of assessing these:

1   reading phonically-regular real words;
2   reading non-words that can be decoded using phonic skills.

The general methods for assessing both are as follows.

Words can be printed on small cards or in rows across a page. Choice of words/word length should be appropriate to the age of the learner and should be graded from simple to challenging in both length and phonic complexity. A familiar font and appropriate size of print should be used.

Reading phonically-regular real words

Assessment should require a learner to read a set of **real words** graded according to phonic structure. These will start with CVC (consonant–vowel–consonant) words (or even, in the case of very young children, may start with two-letter words such as 'at, in, up'). The CVC words should include at least one example of each short vowel. A suggested structure for compiling an informal test would be:

- CVC words;
- initial consonant blends/adjacent consonants, e.g. sp-, st-, gl-, fr-;
- final consonant blends/adjacent consonants, e.g. -nt, -nd, -lk;
- consonant digraphs, e.g. th, ch, sh, ll;
- vowel digraphs, e.g. oa, ee, ai, oo;
- words using common prefixes (e.g. in-, dis-) and suffixes (e.g. -ed, -ing, -ness).

For older learners, also use polysyllabic words including those that assess morphological knowledge, e.g. stationary, antecedent, predecessor etc.

In this way, criteria are established for determining the skills which a learner appears to have attained and the point at which teaching may be required. An example of a teacher-made test can be found in Appendix 1(b).

One criticism of this sort of test is that it is possible that some of the words are familiar and have been stored in memory so that they are recognised as a whole word. A more reliable form of assessing a learner's decoding skills (and therefore their phonic skills) is to administer a non-word test (see *inter alia* Coltheart, 2005).

Reading non-words

A **non-word** reading test comprises sets of non-words that nevertheless follow regular grapho-phonic rules. A reader, therefore, has to decode using knowledge of GPC in order to pronounce them. Teachers should follow the phonic skills structure presented above in devising such a test. Thus, non-words such as 'nid' and 'plin' may be used. Learners need to be reassured that they are not being asked to read 'real' words – that they are 'nonsense' words. About 30–35 words can be used. See Appendix 1(c).

We consider that both these types of phonic-skills assessments should be carried out. For a teacher planning intervention they are more useful than a single-word reading test based on sight vocabulary.

Phonic skills can be 'checked' by comparing the learner's results on a non-word reading test with their reading of phonically regular words. Their phonics skills for reading should be compared with their application to spelling.

Assessing Comprehension

The Simple View of Reading (SVoR) model is useful for distinguishing between reading comprehension and listening/language comprehension. Accurate word decoding is important to reading comprehension, particularly in the early stages of learning to read. However, as word recognition skills develop, learners increasingly draw on their language comprehension, which includes both vocabulary (the meanings given to words in context) and their knowledge of language (syntactic knowledge of how words are formed and ordered in the grammatical structure of the language). Fluent reading aids comprehension because it draws on both dimensions (word recognition and language comprehension) to aid assimilation of meaning and help to predict the text. There is a mutual relationship, in that the greater the understanding (knowledge and experiences) a reader brings to a text, the more fluently she/he is likely to read. Comprehension requires the integration of decoding skills, syntactic knowledge, vocabulary and general knowledge, memory and automaticity of response and information processing. (A fuller account of reading comprehension can be found in Cain, 2010.)

Each sentence read has to be integrated into what has preceded it in order to make coherent sense and make inferences from the text. This draws substantially on background experiences, familiarity with written (literary) language and short-term memory. Some learners will have both poor decoding skills and also have poor language/listening comprehension (described by Snowling et al. (2009) as 'poor comprehenders' generally) whereas the reading comprehension of others (particularly those with dyslexic-type difficulties) is largely a result of decoding difficulties. A model of how different meanings may be brought to a text was suggested in Figure 6.2.

In order to ensure that learners can access an appropriate curriculum, it is important to assess the extent to which decoding difficulties (which should have been assessed by this point) affect their understanding of texts. Both reading comprehension (when reading aloud and silently) and listening comprehension (what they understand from a passage read to them) should be assessed.

Assessing reading comprehension

Reading aloud

Although questions can be asked at the end of conducting a miscue analysis, this is likely to be an underestimation of comprehension because of decoding difficulties. It can, however, vividly illustrate the impact of these, and is useful if the passage read is at the readability level of texts the learner is expected to read independently (e.g. for homework). (In such cases, the need for scaffolding and teacher support/instructional help in order to access the text will be apparent.) It may be more appropriate to assess comprehension by asking a learner to read aloud a text that is at their independent level – i.e. at least 95% accuracy. It is important in this case to note the readability level of the text where this is below chronological age. At first, the learner should not refer back to the text but afterwards, if there have been some incorrect responses (or no response), the learner can be told they can look at the text to 'find' the answer. Differences between the two scores should be noted.

Silent reading

The learner should be presented with a written text that is age-appropriate but may be at a readability level above their reading age, and asked to read it silently and then answer a set of questions orally. In the case of secondary school learners the passage may be taken from a text book used in a literacy-based lesson, e.g. history. Questions asked are unseen by the student although a teacher can choose to provide a written set of questions if they wish, which may, of course, offer 'clues' to the learner to identify certain aspects of the passage. Written answers should *not* be required, as this would involve other skills.

In both reading aloud and silent reading, memory/recall will be involved (as well as involvement of memory in the reading process). Looking back at the text can help here. Silent reading comprehension resembles the activities in which learners are increasingly involved as they progress through school and is particularly relevant for assessment in Key Stage 2 and above. (However, because the focus of the assessment of literacy difficulties is on their decoding skills, comprehension of reading aloud should also be assessed.)

What questions should be asked in order to assess understanding? Oral questioning can follow the same pattern whether assessing comprehension after reading aloud or silent reading or listening comprehension. It is important to ask questions that can be answered from information which is clearly stated in the text (literal level) and those that require an inference to be made, i.e. the reader has to make sense of the passage by contributing their own knowledge and experiences. Learners with good language comprehension and experience of literal language and vocabulary and of the structure of both narrative and expositional texts will be more skilled in answering inferential questions than learners who do not have these assets. At secondary level, appreciation of the nature of non-fiction texts will also aid comprehension, e.g. some texts describe structures (as in a science/biology text), others may describe processes (e.g. science/geography), others are narrative/descriptive (e.g. history, some maths problems). Knowledge of genre and style helps learners to interpret texts.

Comprehension questions may, therefore, at a **literal level** ask a reader to:

- recall facts or information;
- analyse, summarise, classify ideas presented in the passage.

Short-term memory is clearly involved in this, and speed of processing. Where a learner is unable to recall an answer, she/he should be allowed to refer to the text to see if this leads to a correct answer.

At an **inferential level**, a reader is asked to:

- infer/conjecture something, which may be implicit in the passage, drawing on their own ideas. Questions may ask learners to:

  - make comparisons (with experiences/ideas not in the passage)
  - explain cause–effect relationships (that are not stated)
  - suggest character traits – and justify what they say
  - predict outcomes;

- evaluate/consider the passage critically, making judgements, e.g. about:
  - reality versus fictionality of content
  - whether the story/argument is logical/well argued and justified;

- provide an affective/emotional response to the passage. This may be a very personal response and the reader should be asked to justify it. It can include comments on actions and characters. There should also be a response, particularly in older learners, to the appropriateness of the writer's language, use of imagery and a critical approach shown.

Examples of the sorts of questions that may be asked may be found in Appendix 1(d).

The relationship between listening comprehension and reading comprehension grows stronger with age and word recognition becomes less significant (Gough and Tunmer, 1986). However, this applies only when a reader has already acquired good word recognition/decoding skills. Learners who have good language/listening comprehension skills show good reading comprehension and an ability to 'read to learn' when they have acquired good decoding skills whereas those with poor language comprehension may become equally proficient in use of phonic skills but remain 'poor comprehenders' (see Cain, 2010). Teaching comprehension skills (rather than merely 'testing' it), can, however, lead to improvement in both literal and inferential skills (see *inter alia* Cain, 2010; Snowling et al., 2009).

Issues of Cultural and Linguistic Diversity

In Chapter 4 we drew attention to the fact that some of the characteristics of the literacy behaviours of learners with EAL are strongly affected by linguistic and cultural features which may resemble difficulties associated with dyslexia. These could lead to misidentifying a learner who presents such characteristics as having dyslexia or dyslexic-type difficulties when in fact they are evidence of 'emerging literacy in English'. When assessing the reading of learners with EAL, several factors should be taken into account.

One example of this may be that if a learner has been using a script that goes from right to left, there may be difficulty in scanning quickly and accurately from left to right, leading to omission of words, losing place or even missing a line. This tends to apply only to a few learners with EAL, as many of them may speak a language written right to left but are not able to read it. Nevertheless, it is a factor to bear in mind. A problem presented by larger numbers of children with EAL is a tendency to focus on decoding (because it is a 'new' skill) rather than reading for meaning. Their reading comprehension is not helped by this attention to word recognition, particularly if their proficiency in English (both language comprehension and vocabulary) is limited. This is not, of course, an issue only for learners with EAL: many other learners where English is a first language present similar behaviours. This points to the need to teach comprehension skills and emphasise that the purpose of reading is to obtain meaning from print, from the early stages of teaching reading.

Decoding skills may be affected by difference between the phonology of L1 and English, as discussed in Chapter 4. This may mean that these learners apply even more effort to decoding grapheme-phoneme correspondence, emphasising pronunciation and reading 'mechanically'. Developing listening comprehension, reading *to* learners and asking questions orally is therefore important. Where there appears to be a real problem in comprehension, it may be important to discover if there are any difficulties in L1. A problem in learning GPC, however, should be monitored closely as it *may* relate to dyslexia.

The materials used in assessment for all children should be culture- and age-appropriate and should take account of a learner's experiences both in and out of school. Non-words will assess any learner's ability to use phonic skills. It should be remembered, however, that 'high frequency words' and 'non-words' may be 'equally' familiar to some learners. It is important in the case of learners with EAL to remember that proficiency in both a first language and English (i.e. where a learner is bilingual or even multilingual) usually aids conceptualisation and therefore comprehension can be helped.

The informal methods of assessing reading suggested in this chapter, bearing in mind the points above, can all be used to assess strengths and weaknesses in reading, leading to intervention. They do *not* imply a learner is dyslexic, but they do point to implications for teaching.

Summary

This chapter proposed that the assessment of reading should include reading a passage of continuous prose to discover the strategies a learner uses when reading, particularly their use of context, their decoding skills and knowledge of language. Assessment must also include single-word reading and a detailed analysis of phonic skills reading both real words and non-words. The assessment of comprehension was considered in order to show the impact of poor word recognition on understanding but also to discover the extent to which some learners may use their knowledge and experience to understand texts, thereby compensating, to some extent, for poor decoding skills and dysfluency.

Note: Assessment should lead directly to devising teaching approaches. Table 6.6 provides a general overview of strategies that relate to methods of assessment described in this chapter. However, the main concern of this book is a focus on *decoding* difficulties and therefore the emphasis is on following up difficulties in accurate, fluent reading in order to establish more precisely the nature of those difficulties. This will include assessing underlying processes that might suggest a learner has dyslexia or dyslexic-type difficulties which require more systematic intervention to improve decoding skills.

Table 6.6   Some suggestions for interventions that could be used after analysing reading difficulties

Recommendations for intervention related to broad areas of difficulties	
Area	**Recommendation**
Accuracy in decoding: Poor knowledge of grapheme–phoneme correspondence	• further assessment of letter–sound knowledge • assessment of phonological processing/awareness • systematic teaching of synthetic phonics using structured multisensory programme: onset-rime etc. • if phonological difficulties: teaching phonemic awareness, e.g. segmentation, blending, manipulation
Losing place, omissions, insertions	• may need assessment of working memory and speed of processing • teach strategies of using a reading ruler/slowing pace/finger pointing
Reversals/inversions/ transpositions	• assess visual discrimination • compare with handwriting
Difficulty with polysyllabic words	• teach syllabification and morphological units (e.g. common affixes)
Makes no use of syntax in reading (NB most learners with dyslexic-type difficulties have **good** language comprehension)	• check learner's spoken language use: foster expressive language development • assess auditory and visual working memory (as learner may not be able to store the words long enough to make sense) • use cloze procedure/sentence completion exercises
Difficulties in understanding/ comprehension	• foster fluent reading • read aloud to learner/develop listening comprehension • develop vocabulary through first-hand experiential learning and reading • teach vocabulary and meanings: subject-specific dictionaries/ glossaries (also helps spelling). Use of picture clues for younger learners • talk about a book/passage before reading, i.e. 'pre-teach' and 'set the scene' using some of the vocabulary in the text • use comprehension-teaching strategies such as cloze procedure, sequencing, prediction, summarising, a questioning approach, (interrogating the text), writing reviews/critiques

Follow-up Activities

1 Practise analysing miscues, using the passage below, which has been 'coded' using the scheme provided in this chapter. The text was written by a teacher and

(Continued)

Tim and Anna were very excited. Today had been their last day at school before a week's holiday. Tomorrow they were going to the seaside with their parents for a week's holiday. Dad had borrowed a large tent from his brother, their uncle Ben, and last weekend Dad had taken Tim and Anna to their uncle's to practise putting up the tent. Now their Dad was outside packing the tent and some other equipment into the car. Their mother had finished putting all the clothes into a special kind of suitcase that fitted on to the roof of the car.

"Oh, no" said Tim, looking out of the window, "I think it's started raining!"

"Oh, no!" wailed Anna. "I want to play on the beach and go in the sea". *

Just then, Dad came back in. "Don't worry," he said, "I saw a weather forecast on TV and it said that it will be warm and sunny in Devon for the next three or five days, and that is where we're going."

"It's a long way," said Mum. "Come on, you two, time for bed. We need to set off early in the morning."

Activity 6.1   Example of marked passage for miscue analysis

(Continued)

has a readability of about 9 years. Although the reader is 10 she struggles to read like a 7–8-year-old child.

   a Identify the types of miscues made, using the record sheet provided, and write a summary of the reader's strategies.

   b Which areas would you target for intervention?

2 Assess a learner using a non-word reading test you devise (or develop the example provided in Appendix 1(c).

3 Choose a fiction passage of about 300 words and devise a set of comprehension questions using the taxonomy provided in Appendix 1(d).

Further Reading

Cain, K. (2010) *Reading Development and Difficulties*. Chichester: British Psychological Society and Blackwell.
An excellent comprehensive account of reading.
Jennings, J.H., Schudt Caudwell, J. and Lerner, J.W. (2009) *Reading Problems: Assessment and Teaching Strategies*, 6th edn. Upper Saddle River, NJ: Pearson.
An American text that considers a range of approaches to assessing reading difficulties.

References

Arnold, H. (1982) *Listening to Children Read*. London: Hodder.
Burns, M.K. and Parker, D.C. (2010) *Using the Instructional Level as a Criterion to Target Reading Instructions*. Minnesota Center for Reading Research: University of Minnesota. www.cehd.umn.edu/reading (accessed 12 July 2012).
Cain, K. (2010) *Reading Development and Difficulties*. Oxford: BPS Blackwell.
Clay, M. (2000) *Running Records for Classroom Teachers*. London: Heinemann.
Coltheart, M. (2005) 'Modeling Reading: the dual-route approach', in M.J. Snowling and C. Hulme (eds), *The Science of Reading: A Handbook*. Oxford: Blackwell. pp. 6–23.
DfES (Department for Education and Skills) (2003) *Miscue Analysis*. London: DfES.
DfES (Department for Education and Skills) (2007) *Letters and Sounds*. London: DfES.
Goodman, K. (1973) 'Miscues: Windows on the reading process', in K. Goodman (ed.), *Miscue Analysis: Applications to Reading Instruction*. Urbana, IL: NCTE. pp. 3–14.
Gough, P.B. and Tunmer, W.E. (1986) 'Decoding, reading and reading disability', *Remedial and Special Education*, 7: 6–10.
Johnston, T.C. and Kirby, J.R. (2006) 'The contribution of naming speed to the Simple View of Reading', *Reading and Writing*, 19: 339–61.
Kelly, K. and Phillips, S. (2011) *Teaching Literacy to Learners with Dyslexia: A Multi-sensory Approach*. London: SAGE.
Rose, J. (2006) *An Independent Review of the Teaching of Early Reading*. London: Department for Education and Skills.
Seidenberg, M.S. (2005) 'Connectionist models of word reading', *Current Directions in Psychological Science*, 14: 238–42.
Snowling, M., Cain, K., Nation, K. and Oakhill, J. (2009) *Reading Comprehension: Nature, Assessment and Teaching*. ESRC booklet: Lancaster University.

CHAPTER 7

INFORMAL APPROACHES: ASSESSING SPELLING DIFFICULTIES

Chapter Overview

This chapter enables readers to:

- consider how models of spelling development and the nature of the spelling process may provide frameworks for assessing learners' spelling difficulties;
- devise and/or adapt materials to assess spelling difficulties in ways that identify targets for intervention.

Learners with dyslexia often experience greater difficulties in spelling than in reading – and these difficulties often persist into adulthood. Spelling difficulties can affect written expression and performance in literacy-based subjects throughout school life (and in higher education). The draft National Curriculum for English at Key Stage 1/2 (DfE, 2012: 3) summarises both the significance and nature of good spelling:

> Writing down ideas fluently depends on effective transcription, that is, on spelling quickly and accurately through knowing the relationship between sounds and letters (phonics) and understanding the morphological (word structure) and orthographic (spelling structure) patterns of words.

Spelling, like reading, involves the integration of phonological awareness, phoneme–grapheme correspondence involving auditory and visual perception, and memory as well as morphological knowledge. It also includes orthographic knowledge (spelling structures and rules). Snowling (1994) commented that children with dyslexia present more errors that appear to try to represent the sounds of words (but do not show knowledge of grapheme–phoneme correspondence) than poor spellers who are not dyslexic. She suggests that poor phonological representations and knowledge of the alphabetic principle are largely responsible for their spelling difficulties. Although Treiman and Kessler (2005) accept that phonological processing is significant, they consider that visual processing plays a part. Earlier research (e.g. Peters, 1985) proposed that spelling is largely a visual activity, involving visual sequencing and memory. Her research also suggested that speed of handwriting is an important factor (as letters have to be held in working memory while writing a word).

Three models of spelling development are useful for identifying whether a learner's spelling is age-appropriate: those of Frith (1985), Ehri (2000) describing her model proposed in the 1980s, and Gentry (1987).

Both Frith and Ehri draw attention to an inter-relationship between reading and spelling, suggesting that children are first introduced to printed words for reading, but as they start to learn to write, they become more aware of the need to represent sounds by letters. In turn, this helps them to decode. Ehri's model describes four phases: pre-, partial-, full- and consolidated-alphabetic. (Later a fifth phase was added, 'automatic'.) Her model is not described here as it is less frequently used in England than Frith's model, which provides a simple but useful framework for assessment. Frith identifies three stages:

1 **Logographic** – a child recognises words as whole units. This is largely a visual approach and not based on 'decoding' in reading. 'Spelling' may be diagrammatic (e.g. a long stroke and short stroke may represent 'Daddy and me') or random letters may be used to represent sounds.
2 **Alphabetic** – as the child learns to read and write, alphabetic skills (letter–sound correspondence) develops. Storing this knowledge in memory means there can be both encoding and decoding. Writing/spelling at this stage helps reading development as decoding is developed. Development at the alphabetic stage requires good

phonological awareness. At this stage children often 'invent' spellings because they want to try to represent the sounds they hear in words using the letters they know. As they proceed through this stage, there is clearer representation of each phoneme, e.g. sed (said), myoozeum (museum), bekos (because). Accent may affect this, e.g. hospikl (hospital), uvver (other). Just as learning to spell and write at this stage helps reading, so, as children begin to decode unfamiliar words, their reading reinforces and enhances their ability to spell (and extend their vocabulary). In England, this stage normally occurs between ages 5 and 7.

3 **Orthographic** – the learner reaches this stage when their knowledge of letter–sound relationships becomes integrated with morphological knowledge (e.g. how morphemes are put together such as walk/ed; walk/ing) and common spelling patterns and rules (e.g. the differing rules for hop/hopping and hope/hoping). This normally occurs from the age of 7 onwards.

Frith suggests that a major hurdle for learners with dyslexia lies in the alphabetic stage because English has an 'opaque' or 'deep' orthography, i.e. the relationship between a phoneme and its written representation is not consistent compared with more 'transparent' orthographies where there is more regular phoneme—grapheme correspondence, such as Spanish and Italian.

This model provides a useful means of assessing a learner's spelling in relation to 'normal' development (assuming that they have been taught to read and write in English), as does that of Gentry (1987).

Gentry's model comprises five stages:

1 **Pre-communicative** – scribble-writing/drawing.
2 **Semi-phonetic** – a single letter or groups of letters are used to represent a word (or group of words). This can include 'invented' spellings (which Gentry would encourage to facilitate writing development and 'motivate' children to enjoy writing). Spellings often include only the main sounds in a word, and vowels are often omitted, e.g. ct (cat), skl (school), although, on the whole, sounds are represented in the correct order and blends/adjacent consonants often have one sound not represented, e.g. sip (snip) and mik (milk).
3 **Phonetic** – the 'surface sounds' are all represented (e.g. sed/said).
4 **Transitional** – spellings are influenced by some spelling rules (e.g. shine/shinning/shining). Visual memory may be used or generalisation of phoneme–grapheme correspondence (e.g. to/too).
5 **Correct** – conventional spelling used, including irregular words.

Kelly and Phillips (2011) point out that these models are compatible, but are open to the criticism that they follow traditional methods of teaching literacy, i.e. teaching a sight-vocabulary before teaching phonics. The models described above are based on identifying phases or stages, suggesting that children move through them as they grow older. It is important, therefore, not to use these stage-descriptors as 'categories' for determining a learner's spelling 'level'. Although the models suggest a progression, there will be 'transitional' spellings at any stage, where new knowledge is acquired and applied to some words, or on some occasions, but not consistently. To some extent, the Gentry model appears to have addressed this by proposing 'semi-phonetic' and 'transitional' stages, although this *could* be regarded as concealing the range of differences occurring at any stage.

Nevertheless, both provide a useful general framework to indicate whether a learner's spelling appears to be following a 'normal' pattern. Both models suggest that when **dysphonetic** spelling occurs (i.e. sequence of letters does not reflect the correct sequence of sounds in a word), a teacher should investigate further (particularly the areas of phonological processing, auditory/visual processing and memory as discussed in Chapter 10). Frith's model also points to the need to relate spelling and reading activities in early teaching. (Her model could also explain why some children can spell some words they cannot read, and vice versa.)

Although useful as a first step in assessing spelling, developmental models do not provide sufficient information to identify spelling difficulties in ways that can inform intervention. A model of the spelling process, such as that discussed in Kelly and Phillips (2011), suggests a framework for analysis of errors. Moreover, the model (reproduced here as Figure 7.1) implies that other related skills such as handwriting, (see Chapter 8) and underlying cognitive processes (see Chapter 10) should be considered.

The model suggests the need to examine spelling errors in more detail relating to phonemic and phoneme–grapheme knowledge, grapheme/orthographic representation and ability to give 'meanings' to words (not only vocabulary, but meaningful units of words – morphemes). What is important is to see spelling as an integration of these. This will involve analysing a learner's spelling to discover:

- their skills/knowledge of grapheme–phoneme correspondence;
- their knowledge of the rules that govern spelling, where they exist, e.g. the rule involved in forming 'hoping' from 'hope', but 'hopping' from 'hop' (how many times have we seen, 'the sun was shinning down'?);
- any evidence that sounds are not being distinguished correctly and therefore not represented correctly (or at all), e.g. a sound omitted, such as 'ct' for 'cat' or 'tact' for 'tract';
- if there is incorrect sequencing of letters, e.g. 'saet' for 'seat'; letter omission, e.g. kiten, set (seat), nife;
- evidence of their morphological knowledge, e.g. '-ed', '-tion', etc. not recognised as a meaningful unit or conventional spelling.

The inter-related nature of these can be seen from the 'overlaps' when trying to categorise the above!

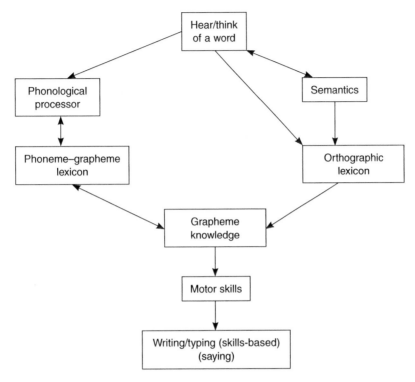

Figure 7.1   Application of a dual-route model to spelling

Most teachers, particularly at primary school level, assess children's spelling informally as part of 'marking/evaluating' written work. Some give 'spelling tests' based on
'testing' how well a learner can spell a given set of words. These may be families of
words, e.g. based on phonic rules and onset–rime (e.g. shore, fore, tore, snore) or
subject-specific terms (e.g. glacier, valley, moraine). Learners are asked to 'learn' them
and then correctly spell the words when dictated. There can be many problems with
this approach. Although the latter, subject-related words may be associated with a
particular topic and may be considered essential to a learner (thereby motivating them
to 'learn' them) they are not phonically/visually related. In the case of the former list, which
presents words following a clear grapheme–phoneme/rule system as an 'aid' to memory
and visual/auditory channels, some of the words may have no or little relevance/
meaning for a learner.

However, Peters' (1985) research showed that spelling improved where schools did
conduct regular testing of spelling, e.g. 'weekly spelling tests', even when there was
no direct instruction in spelling. We are not suggesting, therefore, that teachers should

discontinue to use this approach, although it is worth adding that spelling improved even more when it was taught as well as tested.

Methods for Assessing the Nature of Spelling Difficulties

Three approaches are recommended to collect information on which to base diagnostic assessment using error analysis:

1   Analysis of spelling based on free writing
2   Single word spelling test
3   Spelling of phonetically-regular words

Note: Some teachers may additionally include a passage of dictation given to an individual or whole class. A major issue is establishing the criteria for selecting a passage.

Analysis of spelling based on free writing

Copies of a learner's unaided writing (handwritten) are obtained. (These may also be used to assess handwriting as described in the next chapter.) They may be stories, reports, or assignments, but should be written in school and without the use of dictionaries/spellcheckers. Some learners may, of course, limit their choice of vocabulary to words they believe they can spell, although in our experience this occurs less frequently than many suggest and therefore this method is highly recommended. Sufficient writing must be obtained to generate enough errors to establish a pattern (as was suggested when carrying out a miscue analysis of reading, see Chapter 6). Normally, 25–30 errors are sufficient, although many teachers suggest a higher number. In some cases, this may involve more than one piece of writing, as many learners with literacy difficulties produce little written work in one session.

Analysing the errors in free writing/dictation
Several methods may be used and teachers should select one which they find easy to use, and which will form the basis for setting targets for direct teaching. Readers might like to try one of the alternatives outlined below. In all cases, it is useful to record the 'target' or intended word, and the actual word as written.

Method 1: 'POM'
The 'POM' method is based on analysing errors broadly as Phonological, Orthographic or Morphological:

- **Phonological** – two aspects:
  - ○ not all sounds represented/wrong order, e.g. had/hand; mael/meal;
  - ○ additional or omitted letters.
- **Orthographic** – two aspects:
  - ○ all sounds represented but poor grapheme–phoneme correspondence (e.g. sed/said, stashun/station);
  - ○ poor knowledge of spelling rules (e.g. doubling, -ck or –k).
- **Morphological** – three aspects:
  - ○ incorrect letters in affixes (or root word);
  - ○ misuse of homophone;
  - ○ apostrophe wrongly used (e.g. as in contractions such as you're – your).

A grid, similar to that described below as Method 2, can be drawn up but with the above headings.

Method 2: Diagnostic Spelling Assessment Record (DSAR)

This method is based on that suggested by Peters and Smith (1993) but distinguishes apparent visual and auditory difficulties and considers omissions and insertions separately from knowledge of spelling rules. It acknowledges that sometimes it is difficult to analyse a learner's spelling strategies/weaknesses but does not use the Peters and Smith category of 'bizarre', which some teachers consider to be a very negative description. Table 7.1 provides a copy of a record form which can be used to analyse the errors.

An alternative form of recording these errors is to list and number the type of error (as in the columns on the grid) and then to 'tick' the type of error made, as in Table 7.2.

Method 3: Analysing spelling errors

This approach is an amalgamation of both of the above and also acknowledges the importance of the pre-alphabetic stages (suggested by Frith and Ehri) and the semi-phonetic stage suggested by Gentry. It also draws on our experience of assessing spelling. This suggests analysis into the categories indicated in Table 7.3. A similar, but more detailed analysis is suggested in WIAT-II[UK]-T, a standardised test which is described in Chapters 14 and 15. Teachers can use this guidance to analyse errors by writing the target word, the actual spelling and putting the corresponding 'number' of the category in a third column.

When using *any* system of analysis, it becomes clear that many misspellings can be described by more than one category. This reflects the fact that spelling involves the integration of phonological, morphological and orthographic knowledge. An example is 'had' for 'hand', which could be described as an auditory/phonological difficulty or

Table 7.1   Diagnostic spelling assessment record

DIAGNOSTIC SPELLING ASSESSMENT

Name: ....   Date of birth: ....   Year group: ....

Date of assessment: ....   Chron. age at assessment date: ....

Analysis based on free writing/dictation   Work/copy attached Yes / No   Number correct .... Out of ....

Phonic alternative with G–P correspondence correct		Phonic attempt but incorrect use of phonics (GPC)		Visual sequencing problems/transpositions/ visual shape etc.		Possible auditory/ phonological difficulties		Omissions/ insertions		Poor knowledge of spelling rules, e.g. doubling rule		No evidence of strategies	
Target word	Attempt	Target word	Attempt	Target word	Attempt	Target word	Attempt	Target word	Attempt	Target word	Attempt	Target word	Attempt

Table 7.2 Example of alternative record form (Method 2)

Diagnostic Spelling Assessment Record

Name: **Date:**

Error Type

1. Phonic alternatives using good grapho-phonic knowledge
2. Phonic alternatives not following grapho-phonic correctly
3. Visual errors (e.g. sequencing/shape/discrimination)
4. Auditory errors (e.g. incorrect vowel/consonant blend)
5. Omissions/additions (of letters/syllables)
6. Poor knowledge of spelling rules (e.g. doubling)

Number of words correct   ....
Number of words attempted   ....

| Word | | Error Type | | | | | |
Target	Attempt	1	2	3	4	5	6
bark	barck		√			√	√
stone	stoan	√					

Table 7.3   Categories for analysis of errors (Method 3)

	Category	Example	Target
1	Pre-alphabetic stage: random letters not representing sounds	Mt	(began)
2	Semi-phonetic: a. some phonemes represented b. phonemes omitted/inserted	sin bgin	(spring) (begin)
3	Phonograms/letters transposed	was, tap	(saw/pat)
4	Phoneme substitution (in CVC words look particularly for the vowel)	cot went	(cat) (want)
5	Some GPC knowledge shown but incorrect choice	liet	(light)
6	Omission of silent letter(s)	thum, no	(thumb, know)
7	Poor morphological knowledge, particularly prefixes and suffixes	eggsepshun	(exception)
8	Spelling rule errors	easyer carefull	(exception) (careful)
9	Incorrect homophone	herd there	(heard) (their)
10	Inaccurate representation or use of contraction	your, your'e you'r	(you're) (your)

as an omission; the spelling of 'herd' for 'heard' could be incorrect choice of homophone, or omission, or phonetic – because the phonemes are represented. Teachers can therefore use more than one category by ticking each one that is applicable or can make a choice based on which they believe is most appropriate. As long as there is consistency in how this decision is reached, a teacher will be able to 'make sense' of the results.

Using the analysis

The record of errors should be scrutinised to see if there are any patterns in the errors, indicating major difficulties. These may then become targets for teaching.

Some recommendations can be found in Table 7.4. However, because some learners may restrict their choice of words in free writing, possibly because they use words they think they can spell and also because their subject matter may put constraints on vocabulary, assessment of free writing should be followed by two approaches that assess single word spelling.

Testing spelling of single words

Single word spelling is usually best assessed by a standardised test, partly because of a need to compare a learner's spelling with that of their peers, and also because, as in the testing of single word reading (Chapter 6), there is difficulty in determining which words to include. When an informal assessment is used, it should be based on high-frequency words, including 'irregular' words, and particularly at secondary level, can include subject-specific vocabulary. A list of about 20–30 words is sufficient and should be graded for difficulty and length. In selecting words, teachers should try to include a range of morphological aspects and spelling rules. Testing should stop when it is clear that the learner is experiencing difficulty. It is important to say the word, then say a short sentence containing that word, and then repeat the word. The purpose of stating the sentence is not only to help the learner identify the word (particularly when a homophone is used) but also because some people process spelling through their semantic lexicon. Answers should be made in writing unless this is an area of particular difficulty for a learner, in which case it can be oral.

Responses can be analysed using the method suggested above.

Single word spelling of phonetically regular words
Where a learner's spelling (and reading) suggests they have an insecure knowledge of grapheme–phoneme correspondence, it is useful to test their spelling of phonetically regular words. We suggest that the words on a single word reading test of phonetically regular words can be given (although on a different day from the one used as a reading test). In this case, only the word itself is spoken, but it can be said twice. (An example of this type of test is provided in Appendix 1c.)

This test will provide information about any weaknesses in GPC and establish a baseline for phonics teaching. Results can be compared with the knowledge shown for reading.

Next Steps

Evidence suggesting phonological difficulties and poor knowledge of GPC should be followed up by an assessment of processing skills (Chapter 10) and knowledge of letter–sound correspondence, as described in Chapter 9. This is particularly the case where, for example, there is vowel confusion in CVC words, and omission of the penultimate letter in final blends. Further assessments may indicate severe difficulties suggesting a need for one-to-one intervention based on a structured literacy programme.

Where a learner's spelling mistakes appear to lie in very specific areas and not be associated with other literacy difficulties, then a specific rule (or set of rules) or convention can be targeted. A useful resource for teaching spelling, offering a choice of strategies, can be found in Brooks and Weeks (1999).

Table 7.4   Some recommendations for teaching spelling related to analysis of errors

Area of difficulty	Recommendations for teaching
Phonological awareness/ basic phoneme-grapheme correspondence	Phonemic awareness training: systematic teaching of synthetic phonics: letter-sound correspondence. Onset-rime. Practice in reading and writing. Practice in blending/segmentation.
Insecure morphological knowledge	Direct teaching concepts of base/root word plus affixes. Teaching of common pre-fixes/suffixes with meanings (e.g. origin and meaning of prefixes).
Orthographic/spelling rule errors	Target specific rule where a difficulty. Use **discovery learning** methods so learner 'discovers' rule e.g. soft/hard 'c' as /s/ or /k/.
Contractions	Teach concept of use of an apostrophe for contractions e.g. it's, you're. Explicitly teach correct use of words where confusion occurs. On a different occasion teach concept of possession in relation to possessive pronouns (their, its) and use of apostrophe to denote possession e.g. child's, children's.
Incorrect choice of homophone	Teach words/spelling in context and teach how to use context to determine spelling choice.

Note: Teaching spelling should always include teaching good letter formation and developing fluent, speedy handwriting.

Issues of Cultural and Linguistic Diversity

As has been made clear from earlier chapters, all aspects of literacy in English will be affected by the level of proficiency in the language. When assessing spelling it is important to bear in mind the vocabulary used in free writing is likely also to be restricted by a learner's experiences and knowledge. This implies that it is even more important to carry out single word spelling but to ensure that the words used mainly lie within the learner's spoken or reading and listening vocabulary. The 'phonics' reading test provided in Appendix 1(c) can be used to discover which phonic skills a learner can use in spelling.

Different forms of pronunciation between first language and English, as noted in earlier chapters, should be taken into consideration. Analysis of the 'errors' can still be used, however, to target appropriate intervention, which may be phonological/linguistic because of first language rather than indicating an assumed learning difficulty. The concept of 'response to intervention' (see Reynolds et al., 2010) is important here, i.e. an area should be targeted for direct teaching and progress monitored. If there is no improvement *then* further assessment should be undertaken (see Chapter 2, Figure 2.1).

Summary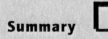

This chapter provided an overview of some approaches to assessing learners' difficulties in spelling. It proposed that using models of literacy development and of the complex nature of the spelling process together provide a framework that teachers can use in the informal assessment of spelling to set targets for teaching.

Follow-up Activity and Discussion

1 Analyse a piece of unaided free writing using one of the methods suggested in this chapter. Identify an area either for further assessment or as a target for teaching.
2 How might spelling assessment outcomes influence the kind of feedback you give to learners when you mark their work?

Further Reading

Bourassa, D. and Trieman, R. (2008) 'Morphological constancy in spelling: A comparison of children with dyslexia and typically developing children', *Dyslexia: An International Journal of Research and Practice*, 14: 155–69.

A useful discussion of the use of a morphological approach in spelling for all learners.

Brooks, P. and Weeks, S. (1999) *Individual Styles in Learning to Spell: Improving Spelling in Children with Literacy Difficulties and All Children in Mainstream Schools*. London: (DfEE) Department for Education and Employment.

Provides an account of different methods of teaching spelling and considers children's individual preferences.

References

Brooks, P. and Weeks, S. (1999) *Individual Styles in Learning to Spell: Improving Spelling in Children with Literacy Difficulties and All Children in Mainstream Schools*. London: (DfEE) Department for Education and Employment.

DfE (Department for Education) (2012) *Draft Curriculum for English at Key Stage 1/2*. London: DfE.

Ehri, L. (2000) 'Learning to read and learning to spell: Two sides of a coin', *Topics in Language Disorders*, 20: 19–49.

Frith, U. (1985) 'Beneath the surface of developmental dyslexia', in J.C. Marshall, K.F. Patterson and M. Coltheart (ed.), *Surface Dyslexia in Adults and Children*. London: Routledge and Kegan Paul. pp. 301–30.

Gentry, J.R. (1987) *Spel is a Four Letter Word*. Leamington Spa: Scholastic.

Kelly, K. and Phillips, S. (2011) *Teaching Literacy to Learners with Dyslexia: A Multi-sensory Approach*. London: SAGE.

Peters, M.L. (1985) *Spelling: Caught or Taught?* London: Routledge and Kegan Paul.

Peters, M. and Smith, B. (1993) *Spelling in Context: Strategies for Teachers and Learners*. Windsor: NFER–Nelson.

Reynolds, C.R., Livingston, R.B. and Willson, V. (2010) *Measurement and Assessment in Education*, 2nd edn. Upper Saddle River, NJ: Pearson.

Snowling, M.J. (1994) 'Towards a model of spelling acquisition: the development of some component skills', in G.D.A. Brown and N.C. Ellis (eds), *Handbook of Spelling: Theory, Process and Intervention*. London: Wiley. pp. 111–28.

Treiman, R. and Kessler, B. (2005) 'Writing systems and spelling development', in M.J. Snowling and C. Hulme (eds), *The Science of Reading: A Handbook*. Oxford: Blackwell. pp. 120–34.

CHAPTER 8

INFORMAL APPROACHES: ASSESSING DIFFICULTIES IN HANDWRITING

Chapter Overview

This chapter will enable the reader to:

- consider the impact of dyslexia on compositional skills;
- have a framework for assessing handwriting skills.

Writing involves three major aspects: composition, legibility and speed. Aspects of compositional skills such as genre, style, content and the use of grammar are described in the National Strategies for Literacy (2006, 2007, 2012) and other literature on teaching and assessing English. Although this chapter considers the possible impact of dyslexia on composition, the main focus is on the assessment of handwriting in terms of legibility and speed. All three areas can be assessed informally although assessment of the speed of handwriting for access arrangements is usually undertaken using a norm-referenced test such as Detailed Assessment of Speed of Handwriting (Barnett et al., 2007, as described in Chapter 15). Where there is any concern about presentation, legibility or speed, handwriting should be assessed in order to determine whether there is a need to develop a specific handwriting programme or whether it will be addressed as part of a multi-sensory literacy programme.

Impact of Dyslexia on Composition

> Effective composition involves articulating and communicating ideas, and then organising them coherently for a reader. This requires clarity, awareness of the audience, purpose and context, and an increasingly wide knowledge of vocabulary and grammar. (DfE, 2012: 3)

In assessing compositional skills, it is useful to collect three samples of unaided writing to include both fictional and non-fictional pieces. After evaluating these in relation to content, style and genre, they should be analysed in relation to possible indicators of dyslexia. The main effects of dyslexia on composition are listed below:

- limited use of vocabulary compared with oral use (may be inhibited by spelling ability);
- poor organisation (paragraphs and ideas may appear to be disjointed and lack flow);
- poor sequencing of events and ideas (lack of order in paragraphs and in sentences) affecting narrative and reporting skills as well as assignment writing;
- lack or inconsistent application of punctuation (concentration on content and spelling may lead to ignoring punctuation rules);
- words or phrases omitted (possibly due to ideas running ahead of speed of handwriting or due to poor working memory and ability to hold ideas in memory long enough to write them down).

Any of these characteristics should be noted and recorded when assessing a piece of written work. It is important to recognise that composition can also be affected by legibility and speed (see Kelly and Phillips, 2011).

Legibility of Handwriting

As handwriting can change according to the situation or demands (e.g. topic chosen, pressure of time, free writing or copying) it is useful to collect three or four different samples, e.g.:

- unaided writing in class (untimed);
- copying from a board as much as possible in 5–10 minutes according to age;
- copying from a book or worksheet on the desk as much as possible in 5–10 minutes;
- copying something they have written in their 'best' handwriting (untimed).

Observing a Learner

Observation should be conducted during at least *one* copying task and if possible during free writing, and comment made using a checklist such as that in Table 8.1.

Seating position should be noted, together with any factors that may contribute to illegible handwriting. Sometimes it is worth checking eyesight, especially if a learner's head is placed close to or sideways on to the paper. The paper should be rotated slightly anti-clockwise for a right-handed person, or clockwise for a left-handed person so that the bottom of the page is where the mid-bodyline is to avoid writing across the body line (see Alston and Taylor, 1993).

Distance of hand to tip of pen should be checked, as it might affect size of letters. If writing is too large, the learner could be asked to move their fingers closer to the tip and vice versa. Pen grip and pressure should also be observed as they affect pencil control: a tight grip can lead to very small handwriting (and vice versa), too much pressure also leads to indentations or even holes in the paper and can cause muscle cramp and general tiredness. Particular note should be made in the case of left-handed learners to ensure correct pen/pencil hold, not with the hand hooked, which causes muscular pain in hand and shoulders. Observations made should always be checked against the evidence of the piece of writing produced.

Analysing Handwriting: Legibility and Presentation

Table 8.2 provides a list of the characteristics of handwriting that the teacher should consider when assessing a piece of writing. Age-appropriateness should be taken into account in commenting on the writing performance. Comparisons should be made between pieces of writing conducted under the different conditions described above to note particular effects in work making different demands on a learner, e.g. generation of ideas, spelling etc. (as in free writing); pressure of time; distance copying and 'near' copying. Indicators of working memory difficulties include frequent referring back to the text when copying (which will have been observed), and losing their place and missing out words or phrases, will be noted in their writing. Particular attention should be paid to their 'best writing', as it is an indicator of what they are capable of producing without time constraints and the effort required when composing an assignment or story.

Detailed comments should be made in each case so that, for example, letters that are formed correctly are specified and the nature of any problems described. Choice

Table 8.1   Observation of handwriting: record sheet

Observation	Comment
Seating position e.g. • Position on chair • Distance of eyes from paper • Relative height of seat and desk • Position of non-writing hand	
Position of paper in relation to handedness	
Pen/pencil hold • Handedness • Position of fingers • Distance from tip • Hook position?	
Grip and pressure	
How each letter of the alphabet is formed	
In the case of cursive writing, are letters joined appropriately?	
Frequency of looking at original during copying task	

Photocopiable

Assessment of Learners with Dyslexic-Type Difficulties © Sylvia Phillips, Kathleen Kelly and Liz Symes, 2013 (SAGE).

Table 8.2   Assessment of handwriting: record sheet

Characteristic	Comment
Print or cursive	
Consistency of form/shape	
Consistency of size	
Appropriateness of size	
Orientation of letters (reversals, inversions)	
Correct use of upper and lower case	
Mixes upper and lower case	
Ability to write on the line or write in a straight line	
Appropriate height of ascenders and descenders	
Appropriate size and use of punctuation	
Spacing between words	
Appropriateness of layout on page	
Frequent crossing out	
Pressure on page (inconsistency, too much or insufficient)	
Letter joins (where appropriate)	
Handwriting affected by the nature of implement used	

of implement can in some cases make a large difference to the legibility of the writing and so further assessment should include an opportunity to explore a range of different implements, e.g. pens of different thicknesses, weight and length; different casing, e.g. smooth, rough, straight edges, curved or angled; different types of nib/tip, e.g. felt tip, roller ball, pencil. An over-use of crossing out, which often severely affects presentation, may indicate the learner's insecurity about writing or spelling, or that they cannot think of the next idea or that their handwriting cannot keep pace with their ideas. Presentation of work and legibility have been shown to affect marks in examinations and course work (Briggs, 1980). If we are overly concerned with presentation, the quality of writing may go unrecognised.

There are many instances where teachers have found a learner's writing so difficult to decipher that they 'give up'. Asking a learner to read it back (which they sometimes can on the day it was written, although they may not always be able to do so later), while a teacher word-processes it, can reveal creativity and ideas that would otherwise be unrecognised. The following poem by a 10-year-old boy is an example. It was almost illegible, with inconsistent form of letters and crossings out. The teacher 'gave up' after line 3 as it took so long to 'decode'.

Night

Slivry lihgt shinning throw the curtns.

Eerie, dark and kwivring shdoes.

Fear! Friht!

A screaching owl

And wining wind rattling roud the chimmeny.

A shadoe dances on the cealing

Downstars

A door bangs.

I cannot move, palarised

Fear! Friht!

Suddenly –

Footstepps on the sters.

I pull the doovay over my hed.

The dor creecks open.

"Goodnight", sais Mum.

Too scerd to anser, but

I new it was her all the time.

(Jonathan, aged 10)

Although he had great spelling difficulties they did not affect his confidence in using words. He clearly had the concept of a poem and also demonstrated the use of strategies for inserting additional words as he used asterisks and arrows to insert words such as 'wining' and 'palarised'. This added to the difficulty in reading it! Most teachers who read the poem when typed and with the spelling corrected agree that it is a good poem for a 10 year old.

Speed of Writing

Speed of handwriting is important because of its relationship to spelling attainment. Writing speed depends not only on motor skills but also on the ability to select, name and write letters quickly. Labelling difficulties may affect the speed of retrieval of letter shapes and spellings. Poor working memory may also affect writing speed if the learner loses track of where they are up to during the activity. Speed of handwriting can affect the ability to compose, because automaticity in this area allows a learner to concentrate on style, content, organisation and spelling. Grahame et al. (2000) found this true even in young children. There are great variations in the handwriting speed of learners of secondary school age. Montgomery (2007) found that nearly 20% of secondary school students she studied were writing at 40% below the mean speed for their age. Slow handwriting speed can become a reason for requesting extra time in examinations (see Chapter 20). It is important to distinguish between copying speed and speed of free writing because the latter can be affected by difficulties in organising ideas, memory and spelling, and therefore it is necessary to collect samples of both.

Speed in free writing

The learner could be offered a choice of age-appropriate topics on which to write. In the case of young writers, they could be told that they are going to have five minutes to write as much as they can about that topic, whereas older learners could be given half an hour to write but should be asked to put a mark on their paper every five minutes (when signalled to do so). In this way it is also possible to see if writing deteriorates over time. The number of words is calculated for each five-minute interval and divided by five in order to establish the number of words written per minute. A learner who is unable to keep up sustained, legible writing may be eligible for a scribe in examinations, whereas one who writes extremely slowly may be eligible to have extra time. The expectation in Year 6 SATs is that a child must be able to write at a speed of at least 10 words per minute in a free writing task. At age 16 the learner needs to write at least 19 words per minute in order to access formal examinations according to the DASH manual (Barnett et al., 2007).

Copying

The learner could be asked to copy from a class text (even if they have difficulty reading at this level). The length of the passage given will vary according to age of learner. For example, a young child could be asked to copy 20–50 words depending on age whereas a student in Year 10 might be asked to copy 150–200 words. The total number of words copied (deduct any omitted from the total given) should be divided by the number of minutes taken.

What to Do Next

In analysing the writing samples, patterns of strengths and difficulties will emerge. Questions to consider include asking whether reversals are found in both free writing and copying and/or words omitted in both. The next step is to compare the conclusions reached from the assessment of handwriting to the findings from assessment of reading and spelling, to look for consistencies and discrepancies, such as whether, if there are reversals in writing, these are also evident in reading. Consideration should be given to the implications for intervention. If the learner prints and their speed is very slow, then the teacher might consider teaching cursive writing to improve writing speed. In some cases there may be indications that further assessment is needed by another professional, such as an occupational therapist. A teacher may question the possibility of dyspraxia (Developmental Co-ordination Disorder) where difficulties in spatial awareness have been observed, (e.g. 'rivers' of white space; inconsistent word spacing; writing increasingly moving away from the margin; inability to stay on the lines); the learner has an awkward pencil hold; too much tension in the pencil grip; evidence of muscle cramps such as frequent rubbing of wrist.

Issues of Cultural and Linguistic Diversity

Not all scripts are written from left to right and this may affect presentation, particularly for learners who have acquired some literacy in their first language. Writing requires rapid retrieval of letter shapes and names and so learners who do not have an alphabetic language may have difficulty in learning how to write in English and writing quickly. Some languages do not leave spaces between words or use joined writing (e.g. Thai), so in the early stages learners may not understand the need for spaces. Older learners of such languages may have particular difficulty in learning cursive writing if they have had substantial experience of using print and may find that cursive writing does not necessarily improve their speed. Some cultures may put greater emphasis on accuracy than speed and this is particularly true where even a minor inaccuracy in writing changes meaning.

Summary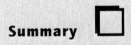

Handwriting is normally assessed informally even when part of a more formal diagnostic assessment of dyslexia is carried out (although speed of handwriting would usually be assessed using a norm-referenced test for formal assessments). It is important, therefore, that teachers can develop and use a framework for analysing handwriting which will be useful in deciding whether a learner should be given a specific handwriting programme or whether, if other assessments indicate a need for a multi-sensory literacy programme, handwriting can be taught within its structure. This chapter has suggested criteria that may be used to develop procedures to assess three aspects of writing – compositional skills, legibility and speed of handwriting – using informal, curriculum-based methods.

Follow-up Activities

1 Observe a learner doing a piece of free writing, particularly noting seating position, position of paper and pen hold. Is there any relationship between this and handwriting that would lead you to make recommendations for intervention?
2 Analyse the handwriting produced using the checklist from this chapter.
3 Ask the learner to copy the sentence 'The quick brown fox jumped over the lazy dog' three times and consider any inconsistencies in letter formation.

Further Reading

Montgomery, D. (2007) *Spelling, Handwriting and Dyslexia: Overcoming Barriers to Learning.* London: Routledge.
Covers both spelling and handwriting and the relationship between them.
Sassoon, R. (2006) *Handwriting Problems in the Secondary School.* London: SAGE.
A practical text that is appropriate for both primary and secondary school teachers.

References

Alston, J. and Taylor, J. (1993) *The Handwriting File.* Wisbech: Learning Development Aids.
Barnett, A., Henderson, S.E., Shelb, B. and Schutz, J. (2007) *Detailed Assessment of Handwriting Speed Manual.* London: Pearson Educational.

Briggs, D. (1980) 'A study of the influence of handwriting on grades in examination scripts', *Educational Review*, 32: 185–93.

DfE (2012) Draft National Curriculum for English KS1–2. www.education.gov.uk/schools/teaching andlearning

Grahame, S., Harris, K.R. and Fink, J. (2000) 'Is handwriting causally related to learning to write? Treatment of handwriting problems in beginning readers', *Journal of Educational Psychology*, 92: 620–33.

Kelly, K. and Phillips, S. (2011) *Teaching Literacy to Learners with Dyslexia: A Multi-sensory Approach*. London: SAGE.

Montgomery, D. (2007) *Spelling, Handwriting and Dyslexia: Overcoming Barriers to Learning*. London: Taylor and Francis.

National Strategies for Literacy (2006, 2007, 2012) www.education.gov.uk/schools/toolsand initiatives/nationalstrategies accessed 17 December 2012. Current documents are available at www.education.gov.uk/schools

CHAPTER 9

ASSESSING ALPHABETIC KNOWLEDGE

Chapter Overview

This chapter will enable the reader to:

- appreciate the significance of assessing two aspects of alphabet knowledge;
- develop informal approaches for assessing alphabet knowledge.

The first area for assessment is to assess knowledge and understanding of the alphabetic principle, i.e. a letter or letters represent sounds. This involves assessing knowledge of grapheme–phoneme correspondence in relation to the letters of the alphabet, which is crucial for both reading and spelling, as indicated in Frith's model of literacy development outlined in Chapter 7 (see Frith, 1985). She emphasised the interaction between reading and spelling at all stages and proposed that the greatest difficulty for learners with dyslexia is in the alphabetic stage. Muter (1996) found that for children to make progress in reading they need to make links between sounds and knowledge of letters (both letter names and graphic representation). However, a study by Blomert and Willems (2010) found no link between poor letter knowledge of young children and later reading difficulties and proposed that learning letter names and the ability to learn grapheme–phoneme correspondence are two separate processes. Their finding has yet to be replicated. It is important to note that they were concerned only with reading. We maintain that letter knowledge is particularly important for spelling. Treiman and Kessler (2005) emphasise the significance of phonological skills and the alphabetic principle in spelling but also consider the contribution of visual processing. This implies a need to assess not only knowledge of grapheme–phoneme correspondence when assessing spelling but also to discover whether a learner can identify individual letters, the phoneme each separate letter represents and the name of that letter. A further reason why learners need knowledge of letter names is so that they can be secure in identifying and labelling letters because a letter has only one name although it may make several sounds.

The second aspect of alphabet knowledge is the ability to sequence the letters of the alphabet accurately and quickly, as this is an important study skill for accessing information, e.g. dictionaries and indexes.

Assessing Letter Names and Sounds

Before assessing letter sounds and names, we need to be sure that a learner can visually distinguish letters (particularly in the case of young children). This can be done by a matching exercise in two main ways:

- two sets of alphabet letters which children are asked to pair;
- give letters on a printed sheet with a target letter in the left-hand column and a row of letters next to it. The child has to circle or highlight the one that is the same:

| G | M | J | G | K | P |

The same approach can be used with lower case letters:

| b | u | p | z | d | b |

Devising a test sheet of 10–15 items is sufficient to see if the child understands the principle of matching.

Elements of the assessment

Responding to visual presentation

a   Knowledge of letter sounds: The learner is presented with either wooden or plastic letters or cards with printed letters. Letters must be presented randomly and the learner is asked to say the sound for each. This should be done for both upper case and lower case letters.

b   Knowledge of letter names: A similar approach is used to elicit letter names. See Figure 9.1 for an example of a test card. Print size and spacing can be adjusted to a size considered appropriate by the teacher. (See also Appendix 2.)

F	D	V	P	J
C	Q	Z	I	X
O	G	B	M	E
K	R	H	A	L
T	W	Y	S	U
N				

Figure 9.1   Knowledge of letter names

Responding to auditory presentation

a   Knowledge of letter sounds: A set of letters (or letters on cards) is presented to the learner. This could be either the full alphabet or a section, depending on age. The teacher says the sound and the learner has to select the correct letter (sounds have to be presented randomly and not in alphabetical order). This is then repeated with lower case letters.

b   Knowledge of letter names: The same procedure is used for assessing letter names.

Writing letters

a   Knowledge of letter sounds: The teacher says (with small pause for the learner to respond in each case) all the single sounds of the alphabet (in random order) and the learner writes each down in upper case in print. On a separate occasion, the activity is repeated and the learner writes them in lower case using print or cursive writing.

b   Knowledge of letter names:

The teacher says the name of all 26 letters of the alphabet (in random order) and the learner writes them down in upper case in print. On a separate occasion, the activity is repeated and the learner writes them in lower case using print or cursive.

The above activities have emphasised that although letters can be written in a number of different forms, e.g. upper case, lower case, print and cursive, they retain the same letter name and simple sound representation. (At this stage /s/ is looked for in response to 's' and /z/ is 'z'.) Learners also need to recognise that these letters can be represented in a number of different fonts and sizes. The following activities could be used to assess their ability to do so.

Representing letters in different fonts and sizes

a   Given a set of upper case and lower case letters, the learner is asked to pair them and say the letter name.

b   The teacher asks the learner to track a particular letter, e.g. 'a', when it is written in different formats (see Figure 9.2).

Figure 9.2   Tracking activity

Recording information

In all the above activities the teacher should note the errors made by the learner, e.g.:

*   confusion of the terms 'name' and 'sound';
*   specific sounds that cause confusion or are not known;
    reversal or inversion of letters;
*   slowness of response suggesting there is difficulty in rapid retrieval;
*   any inconsistencies across the activities, suggesting insecure knowledge.

More than two or three errors suggest that there is need for some direct input at this level.

Assessing Knowledge of Alphabetical Order

Elements of the assessment

Reciting the alphabet aloud

The learner is asked to say the alphabet starting at 'a'.

Setting out the alphabet

Given a set of 26 letters, the learner is asked to sequence them from A to Z in a line or arc.

Writing the alphabet

The learner is asked to write the alphabet in correct order in either upper case or lower case (not mixing them).

Sequencing activities

a   For this activity the alphabet can be set out for the learner. The learner is asked to turn away while the teacher removes one or two letters, closing the space. The learner has then to identify the missing letters.
b   The teacher gives the name of a letter and the learner has to say (or lay out) the alphabet from that letter.
c   The teacher gives the name of a letter and the learner states the letters before and after the named letter, e.g. the teacher says 'h' and the learner responds 'g' and 'i'.

Recording information

The following aspects should be noted:

- the time taken to set out the alphabet in correct sequence, as this tends to reflect how secure the learner's knowledge is or could be an indication of slow speed of processing (as a rough guide, learners over the age of 9 should be able to set out the alphabet in under two minutes if knowledge is secure);
- whether or not they rely on singing the alphabet;
- if when asked to set out the alphabet from a particular letter, they start to say the alphabet from the beginning until they come to the letter, as this suggests that they are relying on rote learning;
- any letters that are left over and only inserted later;

- any letters that are out of sequence or reversed;
- incorrect orientation of letters – while this is not a characteristic of poor knowledge of alphabetical order it should still be recorded because it may be found in other aspects of their work, e.g. handwriting.

These informal assessments of the learner's current knowledge of the alphabetic principle and alphabet sequencing can be used to set targets for teaching. Ideas for activities for alphabet work are described in Chapter 10 of Kelly and Phillips (2011).

Issues of Cultural and Linguistic Diversity

Not all languages are based on the alphabetic principle: some may be logographic (whole word representation) or pictographic. There may be difficulty, therefore, in grasping the concept that letters of the alphabet represent sounds and in appreciating grapheme–phoneme correspondence. The very act of setting out the alphabet in sequence from left to right may be problematic for children who have learned to read from right to left (as in Urdu) or where a script is presented vertically (as in Japanese). Many alphabetic languages do not contain 26 letters, e.g. Spanish, Polish and Italian, which all have a different number of letters although they are based on the Latin script.

The sounds that occur in some languages are not found in English and therefore not represented alphabetically. This may be puzzling to some learners seeking to represent those sounds. Some letters in English do not have a corresponding letter in other languages. For example, the Polish alphabet has 32 letters including nine vowels and 23 consonants, but no 'v', 'q' or 'x'. Some languages spell sounds differently from English e.g. the sound |j| is represented 'gi' in Italian (which has no letters j, k, w, x, y). Some letters in English do not have a corresponding sound or have a different sound in other languages, e.g. 'j' in Spanish.

Summary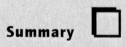

This chapter describes two aspects of alphabetical knowledge which should be assessed for learners presenting literacy difficulties. These are knowledge of letter names and letter–sound correspondence, that is, the alphabetic principle, and knowledge of alphabetical order. It suggests some informal methods that teachers may use in conducting diagnostic assessment. These are also applicable when carrying out formal literacy assessments to gain more specific detail of difficulties than a standardised test of reading or spelling can provide.

Follow-up Activity

Carry out two of the assessment tasks described above on a learner who is known to have weak phonic skills in both reading and spelling to see how long they take and what additional information they provide.

Further Reading

Kelly, K. and Phillips, S. (2011) *Teaching Literacy to Learners with Dyslexia*. London: SAGE. Contains a chapter on teaching alphabet skills.

References

Blomert, L. and Willems, G. (2010) 'Is there a causal link from a phonological awareness deficit to reading failure in children at familial risk of dyslexia?', *Dyslexia, Special Issue: Part 2: Investigating the Links between Neurocognitive Functions and Dyslexia*, 16 (4): 300–17.

Frith, U. (1985) 'Beneath the surface of developmental dyslexia', in J.C. Marshall, K.E. Patterson and M. Coltheart (eds), *Surface Dyslexia in Adults and Children*. London: Routledge and Kegan Paul. pp. 301–30.

Kelly, K. and Phillips, S. (2011) *Teaching Literacy to Learners with Dyslexia: A Multi-sensory Approach*. London: SAGE.

Muter, V. (1996) 'Predicting children's reading and spelling difficulties', in M. Snowling and J. Stackhouse (eds), *Dyslexia, Speech and Language: A Practitioner's Handbook*. London: Whurr. pp. 31–44.

Treiman, R. and Kessler, B. (2005) 'Writing systems and spelling development', in M.J. Snowling and C. Hulme, *The Science of Reading: A Handbook*. Oxford: Blackwell. pp. 120–34.

CHAPTER 10

ASSESSING COGNITIVE PROCESSING SKILLS

Chapter Overview

This chapter will enable the reader to:

- appreciate which processing skills may hold difficulties for learners presenting dyslexic-type difficulties;
- develop informal approaches for assessing these cognitive processing skills.

Causation theories point to a number of processing skills which are often impaired in learners with dyslexia. Hatcher and Snowling (2002) point to a core deficit in phonological processing which encompasses a range of aspects such as phonological awareness, verbal memory and rapid naming. This includes what is often referred to as 'auditory discrimination' and other behaviours such as verbal repetition. Stein (2008) and Stein et al. (2001) propose that impairments in the magnocellular system affect visual and auditory perception, and consequently visual and auditory memory, as well as scotopic sensitivity (a problem in visual perception characterised by print appearing to move on the page). The third main theory of causation is the cerebellar/automaticity deficit theory (Nicolson and Fawcett, 2008) which offers explanations for problems in rapid retrieval, speed of processing, sequencing (particularly in motor skill activities such as handwriting) and organisation. These three main theories based on extensive research offer different explanations for the same characteristics (see Kelly and Phillips, 2011, for further discussion) and point directly to areas for assessment, intervention and curriculum support. These are:

- phonological awareness;
- auditory/visual processing (discrimination);
- sequencing;
- short-term and working memory;
- speed of information processing.

Most cognitive processing skills can be assessed using teacher-made materials such as those provided in Appendix 2. These can either be used as they stand or teachers can devise their own following the same principles. In all cases, the strategies a learner uses should be observed and their actual response recorded for later analysis. The record sheet should include: learner's name, age, date of birth, the date of assessment, and name and role of the assessor.

Phonological Awareness

Adams (1990) identified five different levels of phonological awareness. These are: knowledge of nursery rhymes, knowledge of rhyme and alliteration, blending and syllable-splitting, phoneme segmentation and phoneme manipulation. An example of teacher-made assessment is given as Appendix 2(a). When devising tests teachers should use age-appropriate vocabulary/pictures. (For an example of a published informal test see Hatcher, 2000.)

Auditory/Visual Processing (Discrimination)

This section is concerned with auditory and visual discrimination whereas auditory and visual sequential memory is considered below.

The magnocellular deficit hypothesis suggests that phonological deficits could be a result of poor temporal processing in the magnocellular system. Stein, Talcott and Witton (2001) point out that phonemic awareness seems to depend on the ability to track changes in both sound frequency and amplitude. Difficulty in processing rapidly changing stimuli in the auditory pathways of the magnocellular system can compromise phonological awareness and suggests why many phonemes (speech sounds) (e.g. /p/, /b/; /t/, /d/; /k/, /g/) may not be distinguished. Similarly, poor visual perceptual processing may cause letters to be mis-sequenced, transposed or blurred. Examples of auditory and visual discrimination tasks are given as Appendices 2(b) and 2(c).

Sequencing

The three main causation theories point to difficulties in retrieval of information from long-term memory and in organising it in working memory, particularly being able to retrieve sequences of information. Informal assessment of sequencing can be carried out using resources available in the classroom or easily made, e.g. sets of pictures for picture stories in the case of young children, alphabetical order, number sequencing, sentences on cards for sequencing a story, writing instructions in the correct order and knowledge of common sequences such as days of the week and months of the year (check knowledge of 'what comes before and after' a given day or month). In the case of older learners the teacher should look for a sequential structure in assignments (e.g. reports, accounts of science experiments).

Short-Term and Working Memory

Memory can be divided into short-term (recent memory) and long-term. Short-term memory refers to the immediate recall of information presented verbally or visually. If a learner needs to work on information (e.g. following an instruction or performing a mental calculation), then it must be kept in working memory long enough to act on it. Working memory also has a vital role in retrieval from long-term memory. If information cannot be held on to long enough to be organised and communicated, it may be lost or mis-sequenced (e.g. in spelling or recalling times tables). Learners with dyslexia usually show signs of poor working memory as they tend to have very few strategies for retaining information in working memory long enough to process it effectively (see Gathercole and Packiam-Alloway, 2008). Teachers should assess both auditory and visual short-term and working memory.

Auditory memory

The most common form of assessing auditory short-term memory is through a 'digit span' test which asks the learner to listen to and recall a list of between three and seven numbers in the order in which they were dictated. Working memory is normally tested by dictating a series of digits and asking the learner to recall them in reverse order, thereby requiring information to be held on to whilst the sequence is reversed. This form of assessment is included in most dyslexia screening tests but teachers can devise their own, as in Appendix 2(d). In teacher-made tests this could be extended to include verbal sequences of colours, items in a shopping bag, or any vocabulary that is age-appropriate. Teachers should note any discrepancy between short-term and working memory. The length of the sequence that can be recalled will vary according to age and so the learner should be compared to children of the same age with no literacy difficulties. Where a learner can recall a sequence of five or more items it is useful to ask them how they remembered it, to find out if they have used any strategies such as rehearsal or chunking.

Visual memory

Visual short-term memory can be assessed using a sequence of letters, pictures or shapes. Two identical sets of materials (up to seven cards) are needed, one for the teacher to make a sequence with and the other for the learner to recreate the sequence. Starting with a sequence of two pictures, shapes or letters the learner is asked to look at them for five seconds and then the sequence is covered up and they recreate it with their set of cards. The teacher shows the correct sequence so the learner can self check. There should be two sequences for each level. The ceiling is reached when the learner fails both attempts at the same level (e.g. fails both trials in recalling a sequence of five).

Working memory can be assessed by putting in a time delay or by asking the learner to recreate the sequence in the reverse order. If a time delay is used the learner is asked to wait for five seconds before setting their cards out, which means that they must hold on to the information in working memory.

Learners need to be able to do this as activities such as copying require the ability to hold visual information long enough to write it down. The ability to name letters or use language to label what is being copied will facilitate it. Speed of copying will be affected by the amount of information that can be held in working memory. Observation of a copying task could be carried out when assessing handwriting (see Chapter 8) and the teacher should note how many letters they copy at a time, frequency of looking back at the text, words or lines missed out, inaccuracies, and length of time taken.

Speed of Information Processing

Rapid naming is the most common form of assessment of speed of processing. The learner is asked to name rapidly a series of objects, letters, colours or numbers presented randomly. This type of assessment is included in most dyslexia screeners (see Chapter 13) and also tests of cognitive processing (see Chapter 17). The need for norms in order to interpret the information means that it is not appropriate for teachers to develop their own test. However, observation can indicate possible slow processing speed: e.g. speed of reading and writing, laying out and naming the alphabet, delay in response to following instruction, length of time taken to perform mental calculations or answer questions (although they answer correctly). Such observations may indicate the need to follow up using standardised tests of rapid naming, rate of reading and handwriting speed.

Issues of Cultural and Linguistic Diversity

It is clear that the level of proficiency in English and knowledge of concepts and vocabulary will affect performance in these areas of assessment. In our experience many of the children with EAL who have acquired Basic Interpersonal Communication Skills (BICS) perform well on phonological tests and indeed these skills may have been facilitated because they have had to listen intently and imitate sounds and parts of words. Speed of processing may sometimes appear slow, particularly where they have not yet acquired Cognitive Academic Language Proficiency (CALP), as they may be translating from first to second language or vice versa. Care needs to be taken in selecting the materials to use to make sure they are culturally appropriate as far as possible, e.g. pictures and story sequences.

Summary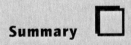

This chapter has suggested some informal approaches which may indicate underlying processing difficulties in literacy and numeracy. However, because there is no means of comparing this information with a normal population, more valid and reliable data may be obtained from standardised tests described in Part III.

Follow-up Activity

Use the approaches described above to assess the processing skills of a learner presenting difficulties and identify areas requiring further development.

Further Reading

Gathercole, S.E. and Packiam-Alloway, T. (2008) *Working Memory and Learning*. London: SAGE.
A comprehensive account of working memory drawing attention to behaviours that may be observed in the classroom.

Goswami, U. (2010) 'Phonological development across different languages', in D. Wyse, R. Andrews and J. Hoffman (eds), *The Routledge International Handbook of English Language and Literacy Teaching*. London: Routledge. pp. 98–109.
Provides a general introduction to phonological development, making some cross-cultural comparisons.

References

Adams, M.J. (1990) *Beginning to Read: Thinking and Learning about Print*. Cambridge, MA: MIT Press.

Gathercole, S.E. and Packiam-Alloway, T. (2008) *Working Memory and Learning*. London: SAGE.

Hatcher, P.J. (2000) *Sound Linkage: An Integrated Programme for Overcoming Reading Difficulties*, 2nd edn. London: Whurr.

Hatcher, J. and Snowling, M.J. (2002) 'The phonological representation of dyslexia: from theory to practice', in G. Reid and J. Wearmouth (eds), *Dyslexia and Literacy: Theory and Practice*. London: Wiley. pp. 69–83.

Kelly, K. and Phillips, S. (2011) *Teaching Literacy to Learners with Dyslexia*. London: SAGE.

Nicolson, R.J. and Fawcett, A.J. (2008) 'Learning, cognition and dyslexia', in G. Reid, A. Fawcett, F. Manis and L. Siegel (eds), *The SAGE Dyslexia Handbook*. London: SAGE. pp. 192–211.

Stein, J., Talcott, J. and Witton, C. (2001) 'The sensorimotor basis of developmental dyslexia,' in A. Fawcett (ed.), *Dyslexia, Theory and Good Practice*. London: Whurr. pp. 65–88.

Stein, J. (2008) 'The neurobiological basis of dyslexia,' in G. Reid, A.J. Fawcett, F. Manis and L. Siegal (eds), *The SAGE Handbook of Dyslexia*. London: SAGE. pp. 53–76.

CHAPTER 11

ASSESSING DIFFICULTIES IN MATHEMATICS

Chapter Overview

This chapter will enable the reader to:

- understand the effect of specific learning difficulties on mathematical development;
- consider the different profiles of learners with dyslexia, dyspraxia or dyscalculia and the implications for assessment.

Research into specific learning difficulties in mathematics is a relatively new area compared to the long history of research into dyslexia. In fact, definitions of dyslexia only began to acknowledge possible problems in arithmetic and mathematical symbols from the 1980s onwards. In the UK, mathematical difficulties were acknowledged by the government in the first Code of Practice (DfE, 1994), when it included 'difficulty in manipulating number' in its definition of dyslexia. Such difficulties were further acknowledged by the DfES (2001) in the National Numeracy Strategy, which made clear the difference between the difficulties in number experienced by children with dyslexia and those with dyscalculia.

This chapter considers the differences and similarities between learners with different forms of specific learning difficulties in mathematics and those with difficulties of a more general nature. The implications for assessment are discussed as a basis for planning appropriate intervention.

Dyslexia and Mathematics

Most learners with dyslexia experience some difficulty with certain aspects of mathematics. Many have difficulty with memorisation and recall of facts, problems in holding information in working memory, difficulty in sequencing and with the language aspects of maths (Kay and Yeo, 2005). These difficulties are usually seen as a consequence of the impact of dyslexia on mathematics rather than with the mathematics itself.

The phonological difficulties experienced by learners with dyslexia often lead to labelling difficulties in mathematics (word for symbol and vice versa), uncertainty in deciding which procedure is required in word problems, difficulty in learning and remembering number fact knowledge (such as number bonds, multiplication facts and number sequences) and slower retrieval of learned facts, requiring more thinking time to be given. In addition, working memory difficulties often mean that the learner can hold less information and fewer steps in their working memory which may result in the learner struggling to follow calculation procedures, forgetting where they are up to in a calculation (not sure what the next step is or forgetting the question being asked) and being slower at oral calculations. Slower processing speed results in fewer examples being worked, making automatic recall of number facts harder to establish. Auditory processing difficulties may lead to confusion between similar sounding numbers (e.g. fifty, fifteen) and poor auditory memory may fail to alert the learner to any mistaken steps that may occur in number sequences as they have 'poor ability to know that the incorrect step sounds wrong' (Kay and Yeo, 2005, p. 19), leading to sequencing difficulties. The degree to which these difficulties can be overcome varies from learner to learner and depends to some extent on their individual cognitive learning style. Some have good visualisation skills and spatial ability which helps them to see questions in their head, understand relationships and recognise patterns (Clayton, 2005). They are more likely to have what Chinn (2011) refers to as a 'grasshopper' learning style (see section on learning styles), which can help them to overcome weak number fact knowledge by looking at the problem as a whole and using their knowledge of number relationships to take 'short-cuts' in carrying out a calculation. These learners may be performing at chronological age or above in mathematics despite having dyslexia, but difficulties with the language aspects of mathematics may still become evident through appropriate questioning.

Dyspraxia and Mathematics

Yeo (2003) noted that there are many constraints in processing number that learners with dyslexia and those with dyspraxia have in common, including difficulty recalling number facts, poor working memory and sequencing skills. Learners with dyspraxia also have difficulty with visual–spatial processing, tactile perception and psychomotor skills (Dixon and Addy, 2004), which often leads to problems in understanding spatial concepts including telling the time, fractions, weights and measurements, estimation and recognising mathematical symbols and numbers when presented in different formats. Motor planning difficulties can result in difficulty writing numbers and symbols, forming shapes correctly in geometry, copying from the board, setting work out on a page and manipulating mathematical materials. Kay and Yeo (2005) suggest that poor visualisation skills means that learners with dyspraxia tend to have an 'inchworm' learning style, processing numbers in ordered steps following a set procedure and lacking flexibility of thought in solving numerical problems. They also suggest that poor ability to visualise maths questions is strongly correlated with severe maths difficulty. Yet learners with dyspraxia can achieve in some aspects of mathematics: often they can learn the procedural aspects of maths (due to their relative strength in verbal skills) and can perform well in familiar situations, and many can reason well in certain areas of maths while having inordinate difficulty understanding aspects requiring good visual spatial skills such as fractions, ratios, decimals and percentages. They may, therefore, present a 'spiky' profile in mathematics with possibly several levels difference on National Curriculum across different areas.

Dyscalculia

Sharma (2003) referred to dyscalculia as a dysfunction in the reception, comprehension, or production of quantitative and spatial information that affects the most basic aspect of arithmetical skills. Learners with dyscalculia have a specific difficulty with mathematics and often do not acquire the basic concepts that underpin the skills necessary for performing mathematical procedures (Hannel, 2005). This can affect very simple activities such as counting and comparing numbers (e.g. which is bigger, 4 or 6?). Butterworth and Yeo (2004) note that learners with dyscalculia often use immature strategies such as counting on fingers to solve problems and may be unable to recognise even small numerosities without counting. They have no intuitive number sense and find it difficult to visualise numbers and therefore see patterns and number relationships, e.g. that six ones are the same as 3 + 3 or 2 +2 +2. Like learners with dyspraxia, they usually have an 'inchworm' learning style. Bird (2009) suggests that an informal way of identifying those who need further assessment is to check if they have any difficulty counting backwards, if they can remember times tables reliably and if they have no calculation strategies other than counting in ones. Further information may be gained using a diagnostic assessment (see Emmerson and Babtie, 2010) or the computer-based Dyscalculia Screener (Butterworth, 2003), which provides standardised scores.

Specific Learning Difficulties in Mathematics

There is considerable overlap between the characteristics displayed by learners with dyslexia, dyspraxia and dyscalculia. However, learners with dyslexia are seen to have a difficulty due to the impact of their dyslexia, rather than a difficulty with the mathematics itself, and they usually have a good conceptual understanding despite weaknesses in computational skills. Their difficulties may appear mild compared to learners with dyspraxia who have problems with psychomotor skills and visual-spatial processing, affecting ability to form numbers, visual questions and see relationships, which can lead to severe difficulty with certain aspects of mathematics. Learners with dyscalculia also have problems with visual–spatial processing but are characterised by their lack of intuitive grasp of number, leading to severe impairment in developing an understanding of basic mathematical concepts. Specific learning difficulties in mathematics might be seen as a continuum, then, with dyslexia at one end of the continuum and dyscalculia at the other. We have provided a checklist for the main areas affected by specific learning difficulties (Table 11.1) which might be used by teachers as part of an informal assessment of mathematics to consider where on the continuum a learner's difficulties might lie. The left-hand column lists areas that learners with specific learning difficulties often find difficult in mathematics. The teacher should highlight any difficulties observed that may be a potential barrier to learning. The right-hand column notes which specific learning difficulties are most commonly affected: dyslexia (DL), dyspraxia (DP) or dyscalculia (DC).

General Learning Difficulties and Mathematics

The National Council for Curriculum and Assessment in Ireland (NCCA, 2012) notes similar areas of difficulty to dyscalculia, e.g. maths language, estimation, fractions, recall of facts, concentration, understanding mathematical concepts, spatial awareness, applying previously learned knowledge, visual sequencing, confusion with signs and symbols, following instructions, being overwhelmed with the learning process, but notes also difficulties in *reading* (a strength for learners with dyscalculia) in those with general learning difficulties. Butterworth and Yeo (2004) suggest that another difference lies in working memory. They argue that learners with dyscalculia only seem to have working memory difficulties in relation to numerical information rather than a reduced working

Table 11.1   Checklist for specific learning difficulties in mathematics

Area of Difficulty	SpLDs commonly affected
• Mental calculations	DL, DP, DC
• Slow to respond to questions	DL, DP, DC
• Little written output	DL, DP, DC
• Keeping place in calculation	DL, DP, DC
• Retrieving learned facts e.g. number bonds, multiplication tables	DL, DP, DC
• Linking vocabulary to maths symbols and vice versa	DL, DP, DC
• Reading word problems	DL, DP
• Recognising which operation is implied by a particular word in word problems	DL, DP, DC
• Telling the time from an analogue clock	DL, DP, DC
• Poor working memory – cannot stay 'on track' in calculations	DL, DP, DC*
• Coding and sequential thinking, e.g. algebra	DL, DP, DC
• Cannot remember next step in a process	DL, DP, DC
• Poor setting out on page	DP, DC
• Seeing patterns in strings or sequences of numbers	DP, DC
• Poor spatial skills, e.g. writes numbers or symbols incorrectly	DP, DC
• Understanding place value	DP, DC
• Understanding fractions, decimals, ratios and percentages	DP, DC
• Profound difficulty in estimating	DP, DC
• Visualisation, e.g. seeing questions in head, seeing how numbers are written and how they relate to each other	DP, DC
• Weak perception, e.g. interpreting diagrams, discriminating similar symbols	DP, DC
• Logical thinking	DC, DP **
• Understanding simple number concepts	DC
• Lack of intuitive grasp of numbers	DC
• Generalising from one type of calculation to another, e.g. 5p–2p to 5–2	DC
• Poor understanding of money	DC
• Uses fingers in simple calculations	DC
• Does not ask questions even when she/he clearly does not understand	DC
• Finds it difficult to remember basic number facts	DC
• Forgets previously mastered procedures very quickly	DC
• Problems in understanding difference in size between numbers	DC
• Finds rounding numbers difficult	DC
• Does 'sums' mechanically – cannot explain procedure	DC
• Reliance on rote learning rather than understanding	DC
• Anxiety (e.g. playing games that involve calculations)	DC
• Moving from concrete to abstract level at secondary school	DC

*Only for numeric information (according to Butterworth and Yeo, 2004)
**Erratic.

memory capacity in general. One explanation they offer is that if a learner is not good at representing numbers then this could reduce working memory capacity rather than the other way round. This may account for literacy skills normally being unaffected in learners with dyscalculia. Bird (2013) suggests that a teacher might suspect that a learner has dyscalculia if they have a surprising level of difficulty with simple numeric operations despite being competent in other areas of the curriculum, and they rely on strategies such as finger counting well beyond the age that others have progressed to more efficient strategies.

In practice, distinguishing between a general learning difficulty and dyscalculia may not be that clear cut. Specific learning difficulties are often co-morbid and a learner with dyscalculia may also have dyslexia or dyspraxia leading to literacy difficulties as well as problems in mathematics. Bird (2013) questions if the label is important as long as appropriate teaching methods are used. However, different resources may be needed for learners with poor motor skills and those who are unable to subsitise (see without counting), whilst the teaching approach may be influenced by the learner's thinking/learning style (see Chinn, 2011; Clausen-May, 2013). Consideration of both the nature of the learning difficulty and the student's preferred cognitive learning style is necessary to inform teaching intervention.

Cognitive Learning Style

Chinn (2011) describes two styles of thinking in mathematics as 'inchworm' and 'grasshopper'. He points out that ideally learners should be able to use both learning styles flexibly depending on the kind of problem to be solved. If a learner has a preferred thinking style this will influence how they use numbers and the choice of operation.

'Inchworms' tend to:

- look at the details;
- follow a set procedure in sequential steps;
- use one method of working out;
- use the numbers in the order presented;
- apply rules mechanically (may not understand the reasoning behind the procedure);
- use pen and paper;
- not check the answer (or check using the same procedure).

'Grasshoppers' tend to:

- overview the problem (look for 'short cuts');
- estimate the answer before calculating;
- use a range of methods;
- adjust numbers, for example by rounding up or down, to make calculations easier;
- see the question in their head rather than write it down;

- use their estimate to evaluate their answer;
- check their answer using a different procedure.

A learner's preferred thinking style can be identified through observation and careful questioning (see example 1 below). The teacher should start by asking the learner to read the question and note any confusion over symbols. Observe if the learner writes down the question or tries to work it out mentally. Ask the learner to explain their method of working out. Skilful questioning can help to discover how the answer was reached and the reasoning behind the procedure used.

Example 1: Ask the learner to perform a simple calculation and note the method used, e.g.

$$14 + 9 + 6 + 11 =$$

Those who favour an 'inchworm' learning style will start the question at the beginning and perform each step in order.

'Grasshoppers' look for patterns that involve easier calculations, and so would calculate $14 + 6 = 20$, $9 + 11 = 20$ and then $20 + 20 = 40$.

The introduction of the Numeracy Strategy in the UK encouraged learners to use more flexible approaches in mathematics. This was reinforced through the Primary Strategy (DfES, 2006). Learners are expected to use mathematical language and develop a good memory for sequential information (which favours inchworms) but are also expected to be able to estimate answers to simple calculations, carry out mental calculations, visualise shapes, work out a problem using more than one method and check solutions (an approach that favours grasshopper thinking style). For learners with a specific learning difficulty in mathematics a grasshopper thinking style can help to compensate for weak number fact knowledge (see Example 2 below) as they have a range of alternative methods available to make the calculation easier.

Example 2: Ask the learner how they can calculate an unknown multiplication fact such as:

$$8 \times 6 =$$

Those with an 'inchworm' thinking style tend to use repeated addition (e.g. $6 + 6 + 6 + 6 + 6 + 6 + 6$) and may rely on counting strategies to calculate the answer.

'Grasshoppers' may use a simpler multiplication fact and solve it by doubling (e.g. I know $8 \times 3 = 24$ so 8×6 is $24 \times 2 = 48$); round up to $10 \times 6 = 60$ then subtract 2×6 (12) $= 48$, or use a method derived from their knowledge of money, e.g. 8×5 (40) $+ 8 \times 1$ (8) $= 48$.

Questioning should be extended to find out not only the strategy a learner has used to solve the problem but also if they can check their answer using an alternative method. This can be done in a supportive manner by asking the learner if they can think of 'another way' to solve the problem. Further, through the use of appropriate questioning the teacher may identify any misconceptions that have arisen and help to develop the learner's understanding.

Choice of support materials can also inform the teacher about the learner's thinking style. Given the choice of a range of materials 'grasshoppers' are more likely to choose coins, Cuisenaire, Geoboards, multiplication squares or Numicon while 'inchworms' are more likely to choose linear materials such as a number line, Unifix or counters. Those with an 'inchworm' thinking style may also find Numicon shapes useful for calculations because, for example, the 5 shape has five holes which they can count but they are unlikely to see patterns such as '5 is made up of two 2s and a 1' or visualise that the '3 and the '7 shape can fit together to make the '10' shape, in the way that 'grasshoppers' do.

Anxiety in Mathematics

The emphasis in the Primary Strategy on grasshopper approaches will suit learners with dyslexia who have good visualisation skills. However, those with an inchworm thinking style may resist being taught different methods as they can find it confusing. Too many methods introduced too quickly may cause anxiety in learners with specific learning difficulties (particularly if they have an extreme inchworm thinking style). Butterworth and Yeo (2004) note that most learners with dyscalculia do not enjoy number work, feel discouraged in maths lessons, suffer from maths anxiety and often use avoidance strategies. Chinn (2011: 99) considers several factors that may contribute to maths anxiety, including poor understanding of maths, teaching that does not differentiate sufficiently, badly designed tasks, a curriculum that does not take into account the range of learners (including differences in thinking style), constant underachievement, teacher and parental attitudes, the pressure of having to do maths too quickly, the abstract nature of maths and the way that maths is usually marked as 'right' or 'wrong'. He suggests that teachers need to create a classroom ethos where learners feel able to take risks, one that encourages flexibility in thinking without scaring those for whom flexibility will never be an option (he maintains that a small number of learners have such an extreme thinking style that flexibility is not possible). The Maths Inventory (Table 11.2) can be used to find out more about the learner's attitude to maths and to elicit possible causes of anxiety that may have been observed. The teacher should use sensitive questioning/probing to follow up responses where necessary to get to the root of the anxiety.

Table 11.2   Attitudes to mathematics

I like doing maths	**Y**	**N**
I find maths easy	**Y**	**N**
I enjoy maths lessons	**Y**	**N**
I wish we had more maths lessons at school	**Y**	**N**
I would like to do a job that involves maths when I leave school	**Y**	**N**
I like playing with numbers and exploring patterns	**Y**	**N**
I can do maths homework without any help	**Y**	**N**
I prefer to have an adult working with me in maths lessons	**Y**	**N**
I like maths when we carry out investigations	**Y**	**N**
Sometimes I find maths hard	**Y**	**N**
I do maths at home with my parents	**Y**	**N**
If I get a sum wrong I want to know why	**Y**	**N**
I always try my best at maths even when it is difficult	**Y**	**N**
I am worried about getting the answer wrong	**Y**	**N**
I feel sick when it is time for a maths lesson	**Y**	**N**
I often ask my friends for help in maths lessons	**Y**	**N**
My friends think I am good at maths	**Y**	**N**
I usually get the answers right	**Y**	**N**
I often put my hand up in class to answer questions	**Y**	**N**
I like explaining my answers to others	**Y**	**N**
I get embarrassed if I answer a question wrong in class	**Y**	**N**
I think maths lessons are fun	**Y**	**N**
Maths is my least favourite lesson	**Y**	**N**
I often find it hard to understand the teacher's explanation	**Y**	**N**
Being shown different ways of solving a problem is confusing	**Y**	**N**
Having counting materials available in maths lessons is really helpful	**Y**	**N**
I sometimes try to find ways of avoiding doing maths	**Y**	**N**

Issues of Cultural and Linguistic Diversity

Some of the difficulties presented by learners with dyslexia in understanding and using mathematical language may also be observed in children with EAL, particularly in the early stages of learning English. A small research study by Issa and Eve (2009) found that children struggling with a particular mathematical concept such as 'estimate' were better able to understand that concept and apply it in English when supported by staff who spoke their first language (Turkish) and who could relate it directly to their cultural experiences. While many schools will not be able to adopt this approach, they should still try to determine if the learner's difficulty is due to limited English proficiency or phonological and other cognitive processing skills. Some of the confusion between similar sounding words which may be the result of problems in auditory processing in learners with dyslexia may also be noted in learners with EAL, but attributable to level of proficiency in English.

Some languages have different scripts and use of symbols, which may cause confusion either for young children who have been introduced to these scripts in their home or for learners who have recently arrived in the country having experienced some maths teaching in their first language.

Examples of these are as follows:

- In Chinese the symbol for the number one looks like a minus sign (–) and the symbol for the number ten looks like a plus sign (+). When counting above the number ten, the tens digit is stated first so that the number eleven is written as ten one (+ –).
- In Gujarati the symbol for the number seven resembles the English 9 (nine) as it does in Bengali, although the Gujarati and Bengali symbols are not identical.
- In Hindi the symbol for the number seven resembles an English 6 (six).
- In Arabic the symbol for the number six looks like an English 7 (seven).
- In Bengali the symbol for the number four looks like an English 8 (eight). The symbol for the number two is very similar to the English 2 so that the number twenty-two looks the same in both scripts, but the number twenty-four looks like 28 and the number twenty-seven looks like 29.

These may cause some initial difficulties in carrying out calculations, but where teaching number concepts is reinforced it is usually easily resolved. Some knowledge of first language and script can be helpful in assessing the nature of the difficulty and helps the teacher to understand possible reasons for errors rather than assuming underlying processing or mathematical difficulties. However, learners with EAL normally learn the English number system quickly and basic numeracy is often a strength.

Summary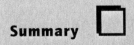

Informal assessment of maths difficulties may start with classroom observation and the use of a checklist or diagnostic screener. This should be followed by appropriate questioning, not only when the learner gets a question wrong (to ascertain if any misconception has arisen) but also when the answer is correct, to discover how the answer was reached and the reasoning behind the procedure, providing valuable information about the learner's cognitive learning style. Many children and adults with specific learning difficulties have maths anxiety and this can be explored using the inventory provided. Further questioning or probing of some responses may be necessary to discover the root cause of the anxiety and this should be handled sensitively.

Points for Discussion

- To what extent is it useful to provide a label such as 'dyslexia' or 'dyscalculia' to explain the difficulties being experienced?
- Is the range of mathematical materials provided in your setting appropriate for both cognitive learning styles?
- How can the use of observation and questioning in assessment inform mathematics teaching?

Follow-Up Activity

Use the Maths Inventory with a group of learners in your setting. Follow this up by in-class observation of any learner whose answers cause concern.

Further Reading

Chinn, S. and Ashcroft, R. (2007) *Mathematics for Dyslexics: Including Dyscalculia*, 3rd edn. Chichester: Wiley.
A comprehensive coverage of how to address difficulties often experienced by learners with dyslexia and/or dyscalculia.
Dixon, G. and Addy, L.M. (2004) *Making Inclusion Work for Children with Dyspraxia*. London: RoutledgeFalmer.
Contains a useful chapter on mathematics and dyspraxia.

References

Bird, R. (2009) *Overcoming Difficulties with Number*. London: SAGE.
Bird, R. (2013) *Dyscalculia Toolkit*, 2nd edn. London: SAGE.
Butterworth, B. (2003) *Dyscalculia Screener*. London: NFER–Nelson.
Butterworth, B. and Yeo, D. (2004) *Dyscalculia Guidance*. London: NFER–Nelson.
Chinn, S. (2011) *The Trouble with Maths*, 2nd edn. London: RoutledgeFalmer.
Clausen-May, T. (2013) *Teaching Maths to Pupils with Different Learning Styles*, 2nd edn. London: Paul Chapman Publishing.
Clayton, P. (2005) *How to Develop Numeracy in Children with Dyslexia*. Cambridge: LDA.
DfE (Department for Education) (1994) *The Code of Practice on the Identification and Assessment of Special Educational Needs*. London: HMSO.
DfES (Department for Education and Skills) (2001) *The National Numeracy Strategy: Guidance to Support Pupils with Dyslexia and Dyscalculia*. London: DfES.
DfES (Department for Education and Skills) (2006) *Primary Framework for Literacy and Mathematics*. London: DfES. Available at www.educationengland.org.uk/documents (accessed February 2013).
Dixon, G. and Addy, M. (2004) *Making Inclusion Work for Children with Dyspraxia*. London: RoutledgeFalmer.
Emmerson, J. and Babtie, P. (2010) *The Dyscalculia Assessment*. London: Continuum Publishing.
Hannell, G. (2005) *Dyscalculia*. London: David Fulton.
Issa, T, and Eve, P. (2009) *Making Maths Curriculum More Accessible: Strategies for Children Learning EAL*. NALDIC (National Association for Language Development in the Curriculum). Available at www.naldic.org.uk/eal-teaching-and-learning/eal-resources/maths-eal (accessed February 2013).
Kay, J. & Yeo, D. (2005) *Dyslexia and Maths*. London: David Fulton.
NCCA (National Council for Curriculum and Assessment) (2012) *Guidelines Mild General Learning Difficulties: Mathematics*. Dublin: NCCA. Available at www.ncca.ie/uploadedfiles/P_Mild_Maths.pdf (accessed February 2013).
Sharma, M. (2003) *Dyscalculia*. www.bbc.co.uk/skillswise/ (not available since 2012)
Yeo, D. (2003) *Dyslexia, Dyspraxia and Mathematics*. London: Whurr.

PART III

FORMAL ASSESSMENT

This section is concerned particularly with developing teachers' skills in selecting and using standardised tests. In order to carry these out in ways that adequately describe a learner's strengths and difficulties, there must be knowledge and understanding of the principles and concepts of psychometrics, as summarised in Chapter 12. The remaining sections provide overviews and comments on the main areas of standardised testing used to assess dyslexic-type difficulties. Each chapter includes summaries, in tabular form, of some of the tests in current use, so that readers can evaluate the information in relation to their needs. However, as these are *only* summaries, teachers wishing to purchase copies for use are advised to send for inspection copies and read details from the test manuals which provide more comprehensive information. Sufficient comment on these, references to other useful tests and information on how to choose standardised tests provide guidance for teachers in evaluating any new tests that may be developed.

This section of the book is designed for use by SENCOs, teachers in learning support services and specialist teachers, although as many classroom teachers use some form of standardised testing of reading and spelling, they should find Chapters 12, 15 and 16 useful. This part of the book is, however, particularly useful for teachers training to be specialist teachers of learners with dyslexia and can be used to support both academic study and practice.

CHAPTER 12

PRINCIPLES AND CONCEPTS OF PSYCHOMETRICS

Chapter Overview

This chapter enables readers to:

- understand some of the basic concepts of psychometrics;
- select and use standardised tests appropriately;
- know how to score tests accurately, report and interpret results.

Previous chapters have described the sort of informal procedures which teachers use to assess the nature of a learner's difficulties in ways that can inform teaching. Such approaches can yield detailed information leading directly to intervention. There are many occasions, however, when a more formal approach is required and teachers, therefore, need to know how to select and use appropriate standardised tests. These may be necessary when:

- there is a request to explore a learner's difficulties to see whether these indicate that she/he has dyslexia or dyslexic-type difficulties and if so, their severity;
- there is a need to compare attainments and difficulties with others of that age;
- there is an administrative requirement, e.g. in order to request specialist provision (teaching/technical aids/support etc.) which carries resource/funding implications – such provision has to be transparent in its fairness to all learners and the use of standardised tests makes comparisons fairer;
- applying for 'Access Arrangements' in external examinations (as described in Chapter 20);
- conducting an assessment for someone applying for a Disabled Student Allowance (DSA). As this provision is only available post-school it is not discussed in this book.

As most schools use some form of standardised tests (e.g. Cognitive Ability Tests, group reading tests) it is often surprising to find that many teachers do not have a proper understanding of the basic psychometric concepts underpinning their use. Indeed, some admit to 'flicking through' the pages of test manuals which contain details of the psychometric properties of the test – particularly where test standardisation statistics are reported. This chapter provides an overview of the basic concepts teachers need to understand in order to select, use and interpret the results of standardised tests.

Standardised Tests

A standardised test allows us to compare the performance of an individual with that of the group used during the process of test development and standardisation (sometimes referred to as the 'norm group' or 'standardisation sample or population'). This group should be as representative of the general population as possible if we are to find out what is 'average' (or above/below) for the population. Test constructors must decide which aspects of a population they wish to represent in their standardisation sample, e.g. social class, gender, geographical distribution, age, ethnicity, language. Each time a factor is added it increases the number needed in the sample. Groups should be selected in proportion to their size in the general population. It is always important, therefore, to check that the standardisation sample of any test used has included learners similar to those you wish to assess. There is a particular problem where a test has been 'standardised' on a specific population if we wish to compare performance with the average for a total age group. Similarly, if a test has been standardised on, say, learners in only one local authority or region the norms may not be appropriate for use elsewhere. An example of this was the first edition of the Salford Reading Test which was standardised only on children in Salford. Schools in some other authorities found that when used with their children they obtained higher scores than on other tests of reading which had a 'national' standardisation sample.

It is always important to note the *size* of any standardisation sample. The number of sub-groups used will be related to the population characteristics included, as noted above. On the whole, the larger the standardisation sample, the better the test, as it is more likely to represent the general population.

The age range of the standardisation sample is a further factor to consider. Tests that cover a wide age range and present scores in yearly or even three-monthly divisions may have very small numbers at each of those age levels. This may mean that the sample is not large enough to reflect performances 'typical' of that age. Standardisation samples are usually larger for the years of formal schooling than for adults, but these should always be checked for each age group in addition to the demographic composition.

A further consideration is that pace of development of knowledge, skills and understanding is more rapid in childhood than in later years. Tests that cover a wide age range (such as the Wide Range Intelligence Test [WRIT] and the Comprehensive Test of Phonological Processing [CTOPP]) often provide norm tables at six-monthly intervals for young children (primary ages), but then only for year groups in adolescence and often five year (or more) intervals in adulthood, when there is usually less change in the factor being measured.

Sampling and test statistics mean that tests are most reliable for those in the middle of the claimed age range, so where possible a learner should be assessed using a test where she/he is well within the extreme boundaries (the basal/'floor' age and the top/'ceiling' limit). In Chapter 20 it will be noted that the Joint Council for Qualifications (JCQ – the regulating body for GCSE/A-level examinations) – currently requires assessors to state the 'test ceiling' to ensure an appropriate test is being used when applying for access arrangements.

The date of test standardisation is also highly significant, as populations, educational experiences, language and other factors change over time. Norms established several years ago might be less representative of the current general population. Test materials, pictorial images and vocabulary may also be less appropriate. Checking the date of the test norms is always necessary. A 'new' edition of a test does not necessarily imply new norms

When a test is standardised, the test instructions, materials and scoring are all stipulated and used in a consistent, standardised manner. It is under these conditions that the scores were standardised for that population. When giving a standardised test, therefore, the instructions for test administration and scoring must be followed exactly for the resulting scores to be valid. A good manual will provide clear instructions and wording for the assessor to use. This will usually include whether or not a learner can be encouraged to 'guess' if they do not think they 'know' an answer, and how many times an instruction or question may be repeated. There may be some unscored 'practice' items to make sure a learner knows what to do. The criteria for deciding whether an item has been answered correctly/incorrectly or given a certain number of points will be stated. Following the set procedures, using the materials as stated 'replicates' the conditions under which the norms were established. It is important to practise giving and scoring a test until confident that it will be properly conducted. Giving the test will mean you need to read the words from a manual (or have them *exactly* copied on a 'cue' card). Deviation from the correct procedures renders scores meaningless. The standardisation procedures should mean *all* those being assessed on that test have experienced the same process and this should also minimise 'tester-bias'.

Standardised Scores

An assumption of a standardised test is that the underlying attribute (or psychological construct) it is attempting to measure is normally distributed within the general population. Most people would score in the middle (average) range with decreasing numbers scoring at the extremes. This produces a bell-shaped curve (often known as 'the curve of normal distribution') as shown in Figure 12.1.

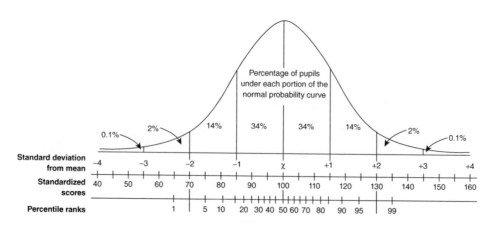

Figure 12.1 Normal curve of distribution

In order to appreciate standardised scores and the normal curve of distribution it is necessary to understand the concept of central tendency. When reporting on the scores of a group of testees, e.g. a class, year group or standardisation sample, it is useful to consider what score is the most **representative** of the group as a whole. This is known as the 'central tendency' of the group. There are three commonly used measures. The **mean** is the arithmetical average score obtained by adding together all the scores and dividing by the number of them. The other two you may find referred to are the **median** – the middle score when the scores are arranged in order – and the **mode** – the score obtained by most people. If the scores are normally distributed all three will be the same and be where the distribution peaks. In an informal spelling test, for example, a group of 11 learners may score as follows: 5, 6, 6, 7, 7, 8, 10, 11, 13, 17, 18. The **median** is the middle score dividing the distribution in half, five above and five below 8. The **mode** is the most frequently occurring score – in this case there are two – 6 and 7 – so the distribution is **bimodal**. The **mean**, however, is 9.82, a score no one actually achieved. Knowing about these three measures of central tendency is useful also because they can reveal if the scores of a group are **skewed**, i.e. the 'peak' of the distribution is not in the centre, as in Figure 12.1, but to the left or right. Understanding how 'extreme' scores or a group of scores obtained by specific sub-groups of the population can affect the way a mean is established further points to the need to ensure that a standardisation sample adequately (or proportionately) represents the general population.

The scores that people in the standardisation sample actually achieved (raw scores) are converted into **derived scores**, following the normal curve of distribution. This shows a person's position in relation to peers. When we score a test, we use the tables in the test manual to convert a raw score into a standardised score so that we can compare the learner's score with those gained by similar testees in the standardisation sample. There are three main forms of derived scores:

- standard score (or standardised score);
- percentile score;
- age equivalent score (American tests often also, or alternatively, quote 'Grade Equivalent').

Before discussing these, it is important to understand two essential criteria for a good standardised test:

- reliability – results must be consistent;
- validity – the test must measure what it claims to.

Reliability

When we use a test we need to be sure that it measures the named skill area/construct consistently, i.e. any score will be reliable. There are various ways in which the reliability of a test can be assessed and test manuals will always state the form(s) used to establish reliability. The main approaches are as follows:

Test–retest reliability

This measures the degree to which the same group of testees, when given the same test on two separate occasions, obtain the same scores. This method is often used, but it should be noted that usually there is a gap of only 2–4 weeks between testings, as intervening learning experiences could be expected to bring about changes. Even with this short gap, there is often a 'drop-out' in the sample so that there is a smaller sample involved in the second test situation. Questions to ask include:

- Is the drop-out random?
- Is the sample population still representative?
- What period of time elapsed between the two administrations? (There is an implication here in relation to the length of time any score obtained by a learner can be relied on.)
- Were the two situations the same? (Place of testing, assessors?)

In test–retest reliability, the possibility of a higher score due to 'practice' effect is taken into account.

Note: It is *not* good assessment practice for teachers to carry out the same test within a short period of time because of the 'learning' that results from the experience of undertaking the test (sometimes called the 'practice effect' or 'test familiarity').

'Split-half' or Internal Reliability

The internal reliability of a test indicates the extent to which a testee's scores/achievements in a test are due to his/her ability or skills in that area rather than a sampling error. The most common form of doing this is by correlating the scores on two halves of the test where items have been arranged into equal order of difficulty from easy to most difficult (usually by dividing them into 'odd' and 'even' numbered items). The correlation coefficient (see below for an explanation) reflects the confidence we can have that the test measures individual differences in that area. Learners with 'high ability/skill' in that area should gain higher scores and get the harder items correct whereas low scores will suggest poor skills.

The formulae used to estimate reliability need not concern users, but the three most common ones are Cronbach's Alpha, Spearman–Brown and Kuder–Richardson. Teachers should not be deterred by references to these – and those who wish to pursue the statistics underpinning them may do so. The first two are known as 'parametric' in that they assume the scores approximate to a numerical scale (i.e. a score of four means twice the amount of whatever is being measured as a score of two) and therefore can be added and divided. The latter is non-parametric and therefore does not make these assumptions about the scores. It merely says that two is more than one and therefore the scores can be put in order. It is usually used when the items in the test are answered either 'yes/no', or 'right/wrong' rather than being scored a number of points. However, simply noting the use of any of these with a high correlation should reassure an assessor that the test has high reliability for measuring that attribute in an individual.

Inter-scorer Reliability

Clear administration and scoring instructions should lead to the same results being obtained, regardless of who is conducting and scoring it. It is very common to find reference to evidence of this form of reliability, which shows that different scorers obtain the same results.

Parallel Forms

Some tests provide two forms of assessing an attribute, each of which contains similar but different items, and each being a valid and reliable test. To ensure that both produce equally reliable results, the scores on these have been correlated. It is important to look for high reliability (e.g. 0.9) of parallel forms (sometimes called 'alternate forms'). Having parallel forms is useful where a teacher wishes to look for signs of progress, particularly at the end of an intervention. Reading/maths tests often include parallel forms (e.g. Wide Range Achievement Test 4 – WRAT-4 – has 'Blue' and 'Green' forms).

Other considerations

The reliability of a test is also affected by test length (the number of items/questions rather than the length of time allocated). Some single word reading tests (of non-words or real words) may take very little time (and, in fact, may also be tests of reading speed) but contain sufficient number of words to be a reliable test, e.g. Test of Word Reading Efficiency (TOWRE-II). On the whole, the longer the test the less likely the effect of any random factor on the performance of the testee (such as stress, a 'one-off' error, guessing etc.). The greater the number of possible scores, the higher the reliability, because there is more likelihood that the testee demonstrated understanding or knowledge. This suggests that the results of any very short tests (i.e. few items) should never, in themselves, be relied on. (There is a similar implication for informal assessment – e.g. word-reading tests to assess phonic skills must contain a considerable number of items in order to assess the skills. However, as informal testing is not used as the main basis for formal assessment, but will become part of ongoing assessment, this is not as serious a problem as it is in the case of standardised tests.)

Validity

Validity describes the degree to which an assessment procedure measures what it claims to measure. It is important, therefore, when choosing a test, to find one that claims to be testing the attribute(s) you wish to assess. The next step is then to see whether it is a valid test of that attribute.

Reynolds et al. (2010) point out that although many test manuals have classified the forms of determining validity as 'types of validity', it is more appropriate to conceptualise validity 'as a unitary concept' (Reynolds et al., 2010: 127) and therefore see the categorisation as representing different ways of collecting evidence of validity.

The main ways are:

- content validity;
- criterion validity (concurrent and predictive);
- construct validity.

Content Validity

This refers to how adequately the test covers all relevant aspects of the area it claims to assess. Sometimes this is based on 'face' validity e.g. a panel of experts in the field scrutinise test items to determine whether they tap into/test the targeted area/skills. It can involve deeper analysis of items and consideration of the rationale and research basis for selecting items.

Construct Validity

This is a consideration as to whether the assessment reflects the attributes (psychological constructs that help us to make sense of what people do/are like) or skills considered to be involved in or underpinning test performance. Many tests provide little evidence of this, but judgements are usually based on discussing the results of extensive research. Good examples of the rationales justifying the construct validity of tests of 'intelligence' and underlying ability can be found in the manuals for WRIT and Raven's Progressive Matrices.

Criterion Validity

This approach considers the relationship between performances on this test and other variables which are considered to measure the same attribute. There are two forms:

- **Concurrent validity** compares performance on this test with the performance on an established valid test of the same aspect taken shortly later. Pierangelo and Giuliani (2009) suggest this needs to be within two weeks of taking the 'new' test. It can also be used to compare performance with 'known' groups, e.g. learners who are known to have decoding difficulties would be expected to have low scores on a new non-word reading test.
- **Predictive validity** seeks to establish whether the results can predict a future outcome, e.g. whether a test of expressive vocabulary will predict a result in written English examinations.

Note: If a test does not have high reliability, it is unlikely to be valid.

These terms are still those most commonly found in test manuals. In the USA, the 'Standards for Educational and Psychological Testing' (AERA et al., 1999) identified five categories of evidence relating to the validity of tests. These are:

- based on test content (analysing questions/tasks);
- based on relationships between test performance and external criteria;
- based on internal structure (relationship between test items and the construct);
- derived from analysis of processes engaged in making responses;
- based on the consequences of testing (both intended and unintended outcomes).

These correspond to the more commonly found terms, with the latter three all relating to content validity evidence. As many of the standardised tests used to assess dyslexic-type difficulties are American and as future tests are developed, test-users need to be aware of possible differences in terminology they may find in test manuals.

Correlation Coefficients

Relationships between variables are often expressed as correlation coefficients. Reliability of tests is often presented as a reliability coefficient.

Coefficients (usually referred to as 'r') are expressed as between −1.0 and +1.0. A coefficient of −1.0 is a perfect negative correlation (e.g. the relationship between the money spent from an account and money left in the bank) whereas +1.0 is a perfect positive correlation – a perfect relationship (e.g. average speed of a car over a journey and the time taken to travel). A coefficient of *less* than 1.0 means that one measure/ factor is influenced by some factor not found in the other or found to a lesser extent. Coefficients are normally reported for all forms of reliability to show agreement, e.g. if a test–retest coefficient of 0.8 is reported this means that there is a high level of agreement between the two scores achieved by individuals taking the test on two separate occasions. An internal reliability coefficient of 0.89 suggests that about 79% of the variance (differences in scores) is due to individual differences and 21% due to test errors/sampling errors. (See note below on how to calculate variance.) In the case of validity, coefficients are only reported for concurrent validity evidence, where test scores may be compared with those on another valid test or predictive validity where they may be compared with future (or earlier) performances.

In most cases it is important to look for coefficients of at least 0.8 and, preferably, 0.9 and over. In some cases (e.g. where an apparently unitary construct 'comprehension' is being assessed, but where readers bring very different experiences and knowledge to texts and requiring decoding, inferential understanding etc.) there may be many factors involved in performance resulting in lower correlations, e.g. 0.6 (see the manual for the York Assessment of Reading Comprehension – YARC – for further discussion of this).

Understanding how correlations can be used is not only useful to evaluating a test. When interpreting the extent to which a relationship between scores on two different tests suggests a common factor, it is useful to consider the coefficient. An example might be to look at a correlation between non-verbal ability on one test and a receptive vocabulary score on another test. If this were given as 0.49, it is possible to estimate the proportion of these two tests that is due to a common factor. This is the **variance** (accounting for the variation in scores). This is done by multiplying the coefficient by 10 and then squaring the result. (4.9×4.9 = approximately 24%). This means that 76% of the variation of each score is accounted for by **other factors**, including random variation. Whether you consider 24% a high or low or useful predictor depends on how many other variables may affect the scores. If the 76% implies your teaching can affect the results then what appears to be a low correlation between these two measures is useful. (Other variables might be: the background experiences of the learner, the actual items used, motivation, health, test relies on memory, speed of processing etc.)

Reporting and Interpreting Test Scores

Raw scores

Raw scores are the actual scores obtained by a testee. The manual (and often the Record Form/Booklet itself as in WRIT: see the record form for the Diamond subtest) contains the criteria for scoring and these must be strictly applied. In some cases there are various 'levels' or 'weighted' scores (as in WRIT Vocabulary sub-tests). Raw scores are converted into **derived scores** which are reported in tables (usually in the manual but sometimes in a separate document). These tables are arranged in sets of age bands. The manual gives instructions as to how to calculate a chronological age for the purpose of referring to the appropriate band. Whilst this may sound unnecessary, standardised tests vary in their methods of calculating this – some requiring 'rounding up/down' and others not.

Accuracy in scoring, reading the conversion tables carefully and then interpreting them is essential.

Standard Scores

In standardised tests, raw scores are arithmetically converted to a **mean** in relation to the **normal distribution.** A Standard Score (SS) indicates a testee's score in relation to the mean for his/her age group. The mean is the calculated average for the age group in the standardisation sample adjusted to fit the normal curve of distribution (Figure 12.1 above) where the mean is 100. The 'average' range will contain approximately 68% of the population (34% either side of the mean/average). A **Standard Deviation** (SD) is the average deviation of the scores from the mean. The diagram of the curve of normal distribution shows that almost the whole of the population measured on an attribute assumed to be normally distributed would fall within 3 SDs of the mean with very small numbers at the extremes (very high or low scores). A good example would be the scores/times of Olympic athletes. This concept of 'normal distribution' led to the term 'norms', i.e. giving the normal range of performance for any age group (or a specific group of people).

SDs are very important when carrying out diagnostic testing. As the scores of the majority of learners (68%) are average and therefore fall within 1 SD of the mean, when assessing a learner it is important to note where there may be scores that lie outside the average range (either above or below). This helps to draw up a profile, as suggested in Chapter 19, and make a comparison with the learner's peer group.

A Standard Score is considered the most appropriate score to use when evaluating a learner's results and if only *one* type of score is to be recorded in a report, it should be the Standard Score.

Reporting and explaining Standard Scores

In addition to providing a score in an assessment report, it is important also to describe it in words both to demonstrate position in relation to others and to ease discussion of the range of scores across different tests in any summary, where explicit links should be made to explain consistencies/discrepancies in performance. Most test manuals suggest a terminology that can be quoted directly if wished. However, we suggest an assessment report should use terms consistently. At the time of writing, the most commonly used terms are:

Score	Description	Score	Description
Score	**Description**	**90–110**	**Average**
130+	Well above average	85–89	Low average
116–119	Above average	70–84	Below average
111–115	High average	69–	Well below average

It may be that an assessor may prefer to use 85–115 as 'Average', which is correct, and then state, 'at the lower (or higher) end of the range'.

Please note that some test manuals may use different descriptors.

These descriptions are useful when explaining scores which may *appear* to a non-specialist to be different, but are actually in the same range. This is particularly so when **Confidence Bands** (see below) are taken into consideration. An example might be that Standard Scores of 85 and 89 appear 'different' but, in fact, both indicate 'low average' and the difference between them may be assumed to be 'by chance'.

Percentile Scores

Percentile scores offer a form of 'ranking' which is easy to understand. They show the percentage of a group whose scores fall *below* that of a learner. Thus, a percentile (sometimes called a 'centile') score of 80 means that 80% of learners of that age would not be expected to score as well and only 20% would score better than the testee. It is *not* the same as a percentage score and this often needs to be explained to parents/others reading a report; this is one reason for always giving explanations of the meaning of scores within, or at the end of, an assessment report (see Chapter 20, Figure 20.1). The distribution of percentile scores in relation to Standard Scores can be seen in Figure 12.1 above, showing the normal curve. This indicates that percentile ranks 16–84 are within the 'average' range and there is very little real difference between scores near the mean (note the very small spaces!). Thus giving a percentile score near the mean (say at the 54th centile) may imply a more significant difference in scores than is the case. The difference in performance between a percentile rank of four and 12 is far greater than between 44 and 52, although the **ranking** does not show this. A Standard Score, on the other hand, reflects performance more accurately because an interval scale is used. Similarly 'moving' from the 95th to the 99th percentile is a bigger jump than from the 50th to the 55th. However, because percentiles give a direct comparison with percentages of others, local authorities or schools often use them in allocating (and justifying) resources. Sometimes percentiles are reported in 'bands' such as quartiles, e.g. 1–25, 26–50, 51–75, 76–99, or even more rarely 1–10, 11–20, et. seq., but we do not recommend this for writing reports to inform teaching.

Age Equivalent Scores

An Age Equivalent Score gives the estimated age level *in that attribute* based on the average raw scores for learners of that age. It is usually reported in years and months. Sometimes a 'band' or 'range' is given, e.g. 9.3 to 9.6 years, suggesting performance lies in this area (better than children aged 9.3 but not as good as those aged 9.7 in the standardisation sample). Caution must be exercised. Just as when a learner has a particular Standard Score and percentile rank on a test of single word reading (e.g. WRAT-4) it does not mean that the learner's **general reading attainment**, including comprehension, is at that level. Having a 'Reading Age' (RA) of, say, 7.6 on single word reading does not mean that they read *overall* like a 7½-year-old child. (This is one reason why, when someone says a child, 'Has a reading age of 8' we need to know *which test* was used, what aspect of reading was tested and the date of assessment.) Age equivalent scores become less useful as a learner becomes older, because their *rate* of development becomes slower. Examples of this can be found in WRAT-4 reading tests and TOWRE-II, where raw scores for young adults when converted into standard scores may show they are within the average/low average range, but their Age Equivalent Score suggests they have *regressed* and now read *less* efficiently than when they were 15 years old. Whilst age equivalent scores may be considered useful by teachers in primary schools to indicate a 'readability' level of books for independent reading, they are less useful at secondary school and beyond. (A Reading Age based on silent reading comprehension may, however, be useful at secondary school when considering appropriateness of reading material presented to students in different subject areas. A group reading test may be a first step used as a screener to provide this information.)

In some American tests 'age scores' are presented as *Grade* Equivalents, although usually they also provide Age Equivalents. It is *not* appropriate to use Grade Equivalents in reports in the UK even if a 'rough conversion' (add five years to give Age Equivalent) is offered.

Using and Interpreting Scores

It might be useful to emphasise that a *high* score is rarely wrong! It shows what the learner *can* achieve. It may be exceptional for the learner – and if achieved only once may be as a result of responses to specific questions/items on a particular occasion. Therefore, it may not be 'typical'. However, we advise against using the term 'over-achievement'. On the other hand, a multitude of factors may lead to *under-performance* on a test. It is always worth considering what reasons may underpin a 'judgement' that a learner's performance is not what a teacher/assessor 'expected'.

Having obtained a score, or set of scores, what confidence can an assessor have in the scores representing the 'true' score?

Significance

One indication of this will have been given in the accounts of reliability and validity coefficients and information about the significance of test results. This is often reported as probability (p) or significance, indicating the likelihood that the score/result could occur by chance. If the reported value is 0.05, that result *would* have occurred by chance five times in 100. The smaller 'p' is, the less the likelihood that this result could occur by chance – i.e. the more **significant** the result. If the reported value is 0.001, then it would only occur by chance once in a thousand times – therefore it is *very* significant.

Confidence Bands Intervals

All tests contain some 'errors' in that their reliability and validity is never perfect. Test manuals, therefore, usually include information about the **Standard Error of Measurement**

(SEM) which indicates the probable discrepancy between a 'true score' and the range of obtained scores within which it lies. The SEM, therefore, represents the confidence we can have in the score obtained. The smaller the SEM, the more 'accurate' an obtained score will be. Very reliable tests (e.g. r = 0.9 and above) will have small SEMs.

The range or band of scores within which we can have confidence a true score will lie is usually called the 'confidence band' (sometimes confidence 'interval') and this is based on the SEM of a test. They are usually reported as:

68% confidence (based on 1 SEM on either side of the Standard Score)
95% confidence (based on 2 SEMs on either side of the Standard Score)
99% confidence (based on 3 SEMs on either side of the Standard Score).

Many test manuals provide this information (and in some, have converted it also to give a range of Age Equivalent scores), so it is possible to obtain the range of scores in which we can have confidence, directly from the 'norm' tables in a manual. Care needs to be taken as to which confidence level is used particularly where it is *not* one of the above to make sure that the appropriate Confidence Band is quoted. (Some tests give 80% and/or 90%.)

What the Confidence Band shows is the level of confidence we can have, so that if we show a narrow range of scores, on the whole this shows we can have *less* confidence that it represents the 'true' score. This makes particular sense if you relate it to an everyday event such as getting to a workplace on time. You will know the shortest and longest time this can take and the 'average' (in the sense of the 'usual') time (unless road works etc. unexpectedly impede the journey). However, if you want to be 99% 'confident' you'll be there for a specific event, you are likely to leave home allowing a 'longer-than-usual' time.

It is important, therefore, to remember that an actual 'score' on a test only tells you about the 'range' into which the true score may fall. How wide that band is will depend on your evaluation of how the results are to be used. Confidence bands are particularly useful to interpret apparent differences/discrepancies between scores, e.g. Standard Scores of 85 and 89 in particular tests *may* imply at 95% confidence level a range of 80–90 and 85–93 respectively and these can then be compared with other scores before commenting on overlap/discrepancies/consistencies, rather than a rigid interpretation of a single score. Explaining the range of possible scores to colleagues and parents is often part of an assessor's role.

Other ways of reporting scores on standardised tests

Although most standardised tests used in the UK report standardised scores with a mean of 100 and an SD of 15, some tests or assessment reports refer to other forms of standard scores as below:

Stanines – based on nine intervals	Mean 5, SD 2
T-scores (as in BAS II)	Mean 50, SD 10
Subtest scores (e.g. CTOPP) (often called scaled scores)	Mean 10, SD 3

Scaled scores (standardised with a mean of 10) are often found in test 'batteries' where a number of short tests (sub-tests) of specific skills or attributes can be combined to give a composite measure. Examples are tests of proposed underlying ability (such as WISC-IV-R used by educational psychologists) and CTOPP (used particularly by specialist teachers) and described in Chapter 16. The reliability and validity of these batteries is high *overall* and they contain a large number of items. The variety of content in the sub-tests is based on research and/or theory in relation to proposed underlying attributes. It is always tempting, therefore (and sometimes encouraged) to 'profile' the sub-tests to try to indicate where teaching may be targeted at apparent areas of difficulty. It is important to exercise caution. Any one sub-test may have very low reliability because of its short length. Most tests involving these then show how results on some sub-tests should be considered together to look at a 'composite' score that will be more reliable. This is not to say that 'profiling' using sub-tests should not be used. Sometimes the results of more than one sub-test can be compared (a good example might be to give all four sub-tests of rapid-naming in CTOPP – or compare two of its sub-tests with results from rapid-naming in DEST or PhAB, described in Chapter 17). Another approach might be to see whether results on a sub-test correspond with observations/informal testing results (e.g. results of the 'elision' sub-test in CTOPP compared with informal assessment of phonological difficulties and phonic skills). Information obtained on sub-tests of 'Screening Tests', for example, are not in themselves reliable as *evidence* of a difficulty (their *purpose* is different), but they can be used as 'further' or 'first' information about a difficulty to be followed up. The issue then is to find which reliable test could be used to follow-up/confirm or inform this result.

How to Choose a Standardised Test

This account of the basic psychometric principles and concepts involved in using standardised tests provides important information not only about how to use the tests and interpret findings, but also points to the criteria for choosing a test. It is clear from the expertise, time and resources that are involved in standardising tests (leading to tests that are expensive) and from the ethical considerations of the way in which the results of an assessment can affect a learner's life at school and beyond, that teachers/assessors need to use robust procedures.

Table 12.1 suggests the general criteria that should be used in selecting and evaluating appropriate tests in order to assess performance of the designated attribute(s). It is based on an understanding of the principles and concepts in this chapter. The checklist can also be used to examine the information included in the summaries of tests provided in later chapters.

Table 12.1   Choosing a standardised test

CHECKLIST FOR CHOOSING A STANDARDISED TEST

Does the stated purpose of the test match what I wish to assess? (for what purposes can it be used?)

1   Can the test be used to assess individuals? (Needed for diagnostic assessment.)
2   What is the age range?
    A test is only appropriate for learners who are well *within* this level, i.e. not at the extreme limits – and certainly not above.
3   When was the test standardised? (How old are the norms? What has changed since then? e.g. population/education/language use)
4   Standardisation sample: appropriateness/size
    How representative is it of the general population? Does the sample include learners similar to the learners I wish to assess? Size of sample – and for different groups, e.g. age/language spoken etc.

5   Is the test reliable? What forms and correlations are quoted? (Look for 0.8 and above.)
6   Is the test valid? What evidence is quoted?
7   How are the scores reported? (e.g. standard scores, percentiles, age equivalents)
8   Are confidence bands quoted in tables? What levels?
    (If not, what is the SEM so the confidence bands can be worked out?)
9   Administration implications:

   • length of time to administer – implication for learner as well as assessor
   • format/materials
   • are there parallel forms?
   • how is a starting point (baseline) determined?
   • how is the 'ceiling'/point to discontinue testing determined?
   • clarity of instructions (information re: guessing, repetition of items etc.)

In addition you might consider whether the manual:

   • states how to report the scores
   • suggests how to interpret the scores
   • suggests other testing to verify/extend the information yielded
   • makes recommendations for intervention/support.

Issues of Cultural and Linguistic Diversity

It follows from what has been written here that a major consideration is the extent to which a learner's cultural and language background has been represented in the standardisation sample. In many cases American tests are used – the norms may therefore *not* be the same as would be established on a UK population. Geographical and social class representation are also important factors, even in tests standardised in the UK: are rural/urban populations proportionately represented? In a UK test, are there populations from Scotland, Wales, England and Ireland? Different backgrounds and educational systems may affect results.

Racial/ethnic minority group representations may have very different implications in different countries. The issue of EAL is also significant, because different languages, together with levels of proficiency in English, will have implications for interpreting scores. In some tests, where a standardisation sample included learners with EAL, they may *all* have spoken *one* home language, but it is likely they would have had different levels of EL2 proficiency, whereas in another sample a large number of different languages might be used. A major problem is the fact that often learners with EAL are treated as a homogeneous group (but see Kelly and Phillips, 2012).

All tests used, as noted earlier in this book, tend to be based on a white, western, English-speaking culture, even when they were standardised on a multiethnic, multilingual population. Test materials need to be scrutinised in relation to 'fairness' or 'access' for an individual pupil before deciding either to administer the test or, having given it, how to interpret the results. Other aspects, particularly regarding language issues, have been discussed in earlier chapters of this book.

Summary

This chapter considers the basic psychometric properties that teachers need to know in order to carry out assessments of learning difficulties using standardised tests. It included information about how to interpret a range of scores and proposes that Standard Scores provide the most useful form of reporting performance. These should be seen within a degree of the 'confidence' they reflect in a score.

Discrepancies between scores on different tests are seen as important in profiling a learner's strengths and difficulties and the use of Standard Deviations is important here. The area of profiling is discussed in Chapter 19. The chapter concluded by offering a checklist for choosing a 'good' standardised test based on its psychometric properties and the implications for conducting an assessment for both testee and assessor.

Follow-up Activities and Discussion

1 Obtain a copy of a standardised test for an area you wish to assess and use the checklist to decide whether you consider it a 'good' test to meet your requirements.
2 What alternatives are available for this purpose?
3 What advantages/disadvantages does the test have compared with others? You might like to take 'cost' into consideration, but this should not be the first priority.
4 Discuss (with colleagues) the use of Confidence Bands in interpreting test scores.

Further Reading

Reynolds, C.R., Livingston, R.B. and Willson, V. (2009) *Measurement and Assessment in Education*, 2nd edn. Upper Saddle River, NJ: Pearson.
A good overview of the principles of psychometrics for teachers.
Mather, N. and Wending, B.J. (2011) *Essentials of Dyslexia Assessment and Intervention*. Hoboken, NJ: John Wiley and Sons.
An American text which looks at identification, assessment and intervention for learners with dyslexia.
Further reading on the topic of the use of standardised assessment with learners from different ethnic groups may be found in, for example:
Everatt, J. (ed.) (2012) *Dyslexia, Languages and Multilingualism*. Bracknell: BDA.
Richardson, B. (ed.) (2007) *Tell It Like It Is: How Our Schools Fail Black Children*, 2nd edn. London: Bookmarks/Trentham Books.

References

AERA (American Educational Research Association), American Psychological Association and National Council on Measurement in Education (1999) *Standards for Educational and Psychological Testing*. Washington, DC: AERA.
Kelly, K. and Phillips, S. (2012) 'Identifying dyslexia of learners with English as an Additional Language'. in J. Everatt, (ed.), *Dyslexia, Languages and Multilingualism*. Bracknell: BDA. pp. 55–71.
Pierangelo, R. and Giuliani, G.A. (2009) *Assessment in Special Education: A Practical Approach*, 3rd edn. Upper Saddle River, NJ: Pearson.
Reynolds, C.R., Livingston, R.B. and Willson, V. (2010) *Measurement and Assessment in Education*, 2nd edn. Upper Saddle River, NJ: Pearson.

CHAPTER 13

SCREENING PROCEDURES FOR DYSLEXIC-TYPE DIFFICULTIES

Chapter Overview

This chapter will enable the reader to:

- understand the advantages and limitations of screening procedures;
- become familiar with a range of screening methods and procedures.

The early identification of learners with dyslexic-type difficulties can be facilitated if schools adopt a systematic process for screening, as proposed in Chapter 4. Informal approaches are neither sufficient nor practical to screen large numbers of learners. Published screening tests are available for use at all ages from pre-school to adult. Fawcett and Nicolson (2004a) point out that the availability of a range of standardised screening tests (including their pre-school test for 3–4-year-olds) places the UK at the forefront in terms of early identification. In addition to using screening as a basis for further internal assessment in a school, standardised screening tests can also provide evidence to justify the request for a formal assessment to be made by an educational psychologist or specialist teacher. Most screening tests are designed to be used by teachers, SENCOs or health professionals. To obtain information that is of diagnostic value they should be given and interpreted by those who are appropriately trained both in dyslexia and the use of standardised tests.

In the UK a number of standardised screening tests are available, including paper-based tests such as Dyslexia Portfolio (Turner, 2008), the Dyslexia Screening Test Junior (DST-J) and Dyslexia Screening Test Secondary (DST-S) (Fawcett and Nicolson, 2004a, 2004b) and the Bangor Dyslexia Test (Miles,1997) as well as computer-based tests such as the Dyslexia Screener (Turner and Smith, 2004) and the Lucid range of screeners for children and adults, e.g. Lucid Assessment System for Schools LASS 8–11 (Thomas et al., 2001), LASS 11–15 (Horne et al., 1999) and Lucid Adult Dyslexia Screening LADS (Singleton et al., 2002). In this chapter we give an overview of screeners commonly used in primary and secondary schools as a first step in the identification process. Tables are provided in this chapter summarising: details of the standardisation of the tests, administration time, age range and subtest descriptions to help teachers to decide which screener might be the most appropriate for their particular situation.

Dyslexia Portfolio

Dyslexia Portfolio is a paper-based assessment that draws together a number of literacy and literacy-based processing tasks into one test to provide a detailed individual assessment (see Table 13.1). Turner (2008) suggests that it is more suitable for specialist teachers or those on postgraduate specialist training courses than the computerised Dyslexia Screener (Turner and Smith, 2004), as only paper-based tests can enable the tester to record moment-by-moment observations that can provide useful additional information to the test results. The manual advocates that after the assessment session the teacher should produce a table of scores and examine the profile in the light of other information they may have (e.g. any specialist teaching she/he may have received) before entering data on line to produce a Dyslexia Index. The knowledge and skills of a specialist teacher or one with a good knowledge of dyslexia are therefore utilised in interpreting the results. It is sometimes seen as a useful follow-up to

Table 13.1   Dyslexia Portfolio

Name of Test: Dyslexia Portfolio			
Author: Turner, M.	**Publisher:** GL Assessment, 2008	**Age Range:** 6–16	**Date of Norms:** 2008

Standardisation Sample:

603 (Years 1, 2, 3, 5, 7, 9) across 25 primary and 10 secondary schools. Children with less than two years' exposure to English were excluded.

Purpose/Function:

To identify learners 'at risk' of dyslexia through a battery of tests

Test Description:

An individual assessment that can be used with children from age 6 to identify dyslexia and other literacy-learning difficulties. The test contains eight subtests.

Administration time:	Reliability:	Validity:	How scores are reported:	Confidence intervals:
40 minutes approx. Four timed subtests, the rest untimed	Split-half reliability 0.87–0.98	0.57 to 0.9 when subtests correlated with single word reading and single word spelling. Full table provided	Standard scores Dyslexia Index A–E provided on line	N/A

Subtest Information: (as stated in manual)

- Naming Speed – pupil identifies by name common objects over a two minute interval
- Reading Speed – pupil has three minutes to decide if each statement is true or false
- Phoneme Deletion – pupil must say the whole word then the new word with phoneme deletion
- Non-word Reading – probes the pupil's alphabetic coding skills
- Single Word Spelling – teacher says the word, then the sentence, then the word again for pupil to write
- Digits Forwards/Backwards – strings of digits presented at a rate of one digit per second which the pupil repeats (forwards) or says backwards
- Single Word Reading – pupil reads a list of words
- Rate of Writing – a measure of writing productivity. For pupils aged 5–6 a timed copying task (four minutes); for all other pupils, the task is free writing (five minutes)

Comments:

Standard scores are provided on the accompanying disc so that the teacher can construct their own pupil profile. A Dyslexia Index from A (no dyslexia signs) to E (severe dyslexia) is given if data are entered on-line but scores from an ability test are needed as a discrepancy definition is used in providing the Dyslexia Index. The ability test chosen may influence the grading of the Dyslexia Index.

the Dyslexia Screener Digital Test as it examines a learner's difficulties in more detail, so that intervention can be planned. However, there have been some inconsistencies noted in the Dyslexia Index allocated in relation to the cognitive ability test selected. Tests such as CATs, British Picture Vocabulary Scales and Raven's Matrices (all considered appropriate tests to use with Dyslexia Portfolio) do not measure the same things and are therefore likely to produce different scores. As a discrepancy between ability and attainment is used to determine the Dyslexia Index this may result in some variation in the index produced.

Although the test is advertised as being suitable for children between the ages of 6 and 16 years, the norms were developed on pupils up to the age of 14:06 and therefore may be less reliable with 15–16-year-olds. It should also be noted that not all year groups were included in the norms as there were no children from Years 4, 6 and 8 even though ages 7–8, 10–11 and 12–13 are included in the tables.

Dyslexia Screener Digital

Dyslexia Screener is a popular computerised screening tool that is designed to give impartial, objective screening without specialist knowledge and can be used by SENCOs and other teachers to obtain an 'estimation of the degree of dyslexia in the profile of any pupil of school age' (Turner, 2008). An on-line version is now available providing instant scoring and analysis although the original CD-Rom format can (at the time of writing) still be purchased. It is quick and easy to administer and can be used for screening whole year groups. A discrepancy-based definition of dyslexia is used in producing a profile of the pupil's strengths and weaknesses. It includes tests of verbal and non-verbal ability which are compared to results on attainment tests of reading and spelling and diagnostic tasks involving auditory and visual processing to produce a Dyslexia Index (see Table 13.2). This provides more consistency in the Dyslexia Index allocated than the Dyslexia Portfolio (where teachers can select the cognitive ability test to use). However, it gives less detail of the individual's strengths and difficulties and is not as useful in planning intervention.

Lucid Screeners

Lucid produces a range of computerised screeners that pre-date Dyslexia Screener Digital. The use of Lucid Rapid Dyslexia Screener (Singleton et al., 2003) is gaining popularity in schools in the UK as it takes only 15 minutes to administer. It claims to have relatively low numbers of false positives and negatives whilst using only three diagnostic assessments: phonological processing, auditory sequential memory and phonic skills (non-words) (8–16-year-olds) or visual-verbal integration memory

Table 13.2   Dyslexia Screener

Name of Test: Dyslexia Screener			
Author: Turner, M. and Smith, P.	**Publisher:** GL Assessment, 2004	**Age Range:** 5–16	**Date of Norms:** 2004

Standardisation Sample:

1,356 pupils (Years 1.2, 3.5.7.9) across 30 primary and secondary schools in England

Purpose/Function:

Computer based assessment to help to identify 5-16-year-olds with dyslexic tendencies

Test Description:

Dyslexia Screener is a diagnostic tool which distinguishes between those with general literacy difficulties and those whose difficulties are likely to be associated with dyslexia. Recommendations are given about the next steps to take. It has six subtests which are offered as a continuous test.

Administration time:	Reliability:	Validity:	How scores are reported:	Confidence intervals:
30 minutes	Split-half reliability: 0.9–0.95	Correlations of reading with spelling, vocabulary, word sounds and non-verbal reasoning are between 0.7 and 0.83. Correlation with visual search is between 0.34 and 0.39.	Standard Age Scores Stanines National Percentile Rank	N/A

Subtest Information: (as stated in manual)

Six tests covering three areas: two ability, two diagnostic and two attainment tests

- Non-verbal Reasoning – missing pieces, the pupil must pick which answer fits the empty square
- Verbal Ability – pupils must select the photo that matches the word given
- Word Sounds – the pupil must decide how many syllables are in a spoken word
- Visual Search – the pupil must match the symbol as quickly as possible
- Reading – audio instructions give a sentence with one word missing, pupils must select the missing word from the choices given
- Spelling – audio instructions give a word and the pupil must select it (or a section of it) from the choices given

Comments:

The assessment is easy to administer and many learners are motivated to work on the computer. Sample profiles and sample reports are provided. It can be used to screen whole year groups. A Dyslexia Index A–E is given.

Table 13.3   LASS 11–15 (Lucid Assessment System for Schools for 11- to 15-year-olds)

Name of Test: **LASS 11 to 15** (Lucid Assessment System for Schools for 11- to 15-year-olds)			
Author: Horne, J.K., Singleton, C.H. and Thomas, K.V.	**Publisher:** Lucid Research Ltd, 1999	**Age Range:** 11.0–15y 11m	**Date of Norms:** 1998

Standardisation Sample:

505 students in 14 schools across the UK

Purpose/Function:

Can be used for routine screening on entry to secondary, screening for literacy problems and identification of dyslexia

Test Description:

Presents eight assessment modules on disc. Tasks use cartoon style graphics and high quality sound.

Administration time: 45 minutes	Reliability: Test–retest: 0.51–0.93	Validity: Concurrent validity: 0.33–0.88 Predictive validity suggests it correctly identified 79% of dyslexic students as having dyslexia.	How scores are reported: Standard scores Centile scores Standard deviation Age equivalent	Confidence intervals: N/A

Subtest Information:

- Single Word Reading – identify from choice of five the printed word that corresponds to a spoken word
- Sentence Reading – cloze procedure using multiple choice
- Spelling – single word spelling dictated by the computer
- Reasoning – multiple choice for completion of a spatial matrix
- Auditory Memory – digit span presents 2–9 digits in correct (forwards) sequence
- Visual Memory – recall of objects in position (2–7 items)
- Phonic Skills – non-word reading from a choice of four alternatives.
- Phonological Processing – segmentation and deletion of syllables and phonemes from four spoken alternatives

Comments:

In most of the subtests the computer automatically adjusts the difficulty of the items to the pupil, thereby keeping them more engaged. Learners can be assessed without supervision. The manual suggests that the low correlations for validity may be because of comparing computer based test with conventional tests. The manual (available on-line) provides ideas for intervention including reference to published resources. A template of comments sheet is provided to record observations during testing.

(4–7-year-olds). However, the manual recommends that if a more detailed understanding of the learner's difficulties is required, initial screening should be followed up by using another screener, either Lucid COPs Cognitive Profiling System (Singleton et al., 1996) for 4–8-year-olds, LASS 8–11 (Thomas et al., 2001) or LASS 11–15 (Horne et al., 1999), in order to profile cognitive strengths and weaknesses that will help to plan an individualised teaching programme. These screeners include tests of attainment (reading and spelling) as well as non-verbal reasoning. LASS 8–11 and LASS 11–15 (Table 13.3) contain similar subtests, which according to the manual are based on a well-established view of dyslexia as weaknesses in literacy, phonological skills and auditory memory 'that are not due to low intelligence'. The inclusion of non-verbal reasoning allows a discrepancy definition to be used.

While it is considered desirable to follow up the Lucid Rapid Dyslexia Screener with a screener such as LASS to give a more detailed profile of the individual as a basis for planning intervention, in practice this often does not happen because of the cost of annual licence fees. Careful consideration should be given therefore to the use a screener will be put to before making a decision about which test/s to purchase for a particular establishment.

Dyslexia Screening Test Junior (DST-J)

The original Dyslexia Screening Test (Fawcett and Nicolson, 1996) was revised in 2004 and split into two tests: DST-J for primary and DST-S for secondary age pupils. Two new subtests were added to DST-J and two of the existing subtests were re-normed (see Table 13.4). The At Risk Quotient (ARQ) was lowered from 1.0 to 0.9 with a new category of 0.6–0.8 indicating mild to moderate risk of dyslexia. These revisions were made to reflect changes in theory and practice since the initial publication (Fawcett and Nicolson, 2004a and 2004b). According to the manual, the test has been modified in response to suggestions from teachers involved in the nation-wide testing of the original version in 1995. For example, computer software has been added to generate the 'At Risk Quotient' and produce a profile for each child tested. Like the screeners described earlier, it includes subtests to assess attainment (reading and spelling), phonological processing and cognitive ability (vocabulary and semantic fluency as opposed to non-verbal reasoning) but also includes subtests to assess hand–eye co-ordination, postural stability and writing speed and accuracy, taking into account cerebellar deficit theory which suggests that children with dyslexia 'show difficulties consistent with slight abnormalities in the cerebellum, a structure which is involved in motor skill, balance and control of eye-movements' (Fawcett and Nicolson, 2004a: 15).

Further changes have occurred in primary schools since the revised version was produced in 2004. There has been an even greater focus on the teaching of phonics with the introduction of the new Primary National Strategy in 2006. As a consequence some of the subtests may be in need of re-standardisation, such as 'non-word reading',

Table 13.4   The Dyslexia Screening Test-Junior (DST-J)

Name of Test: The Dyslexia Screening Test-Junior (DST-J)			
Author: Fawcett, A.J. and Nicolson, R.I.	**Publisher:** Harcourt Assessment, 2004	**Age Range:** 6y 6m – 11y 5m	**Date of Norms:** 2002

Standardisation Sample:

800 children in Sheffield and Middlesbrough for the 3/4 new or modified tests (rhyming skills, one minute reading, receptive vocabulary). Segmentation test re-normed on 774 pupils aged 6–11 years. Norms for the remaining subtests are derived from the original 1995 nation-wide norms.

Purpose/Function:

Designed to identify children 'at risk' of reading failure and can be used to request further formal assessment

Test Description:

A battery of subtests as listed below. New category of mild risk at 0.6 has been introduced and 'at risk' is 0.9.

Administration time: 30 minutes	Reliability: Test–retest: all above 0.7 Inter-rater: 0.98	Validity: Correlation between WORD and One Minute Reading: 0.673	How scores are reported: 'At Risk Quotient' Centile range	Confidence intervals: N/A

Subtest Information:

- Rapid Naming – learner has to name pictures of common objects quickly and accurately
- Bead Threading – assesses hand–eye co-ordination and manipulative skill (30 seconds)
- One Minute Reading – single word reading test
- Postural Stability – tests the child's ability to remain stable when pressure is applied to the back (this is based on clinic procedures for establishing cerebellar abnormalities)
- Phonemic Segmentation – tests ability to break down words into constituent sounds
- Rhyme – only given if a child is unable to cope with segmentation. Child is given two words orally and has to say if they rhyme or not
- Two Minute Spelling– a list of single words is dictated and the child has to write down as many as they can in two minutes
- Backward Digit Span – child listens to strings of numbers and repeats in reverse order
- Nonsense Passage Reading – child reads a short passage containing real and non-words but only the non-words are scored
- One Minute Writing – child has to copy a sentence or short passage (assessed for accuracy and legibility)
- Verbal Fluency – tests ability to generate words beginning with a stimulus letter (one minute)
- Semantic Fluency – tests ability to generate words in a given category
- Vocabulary – a test of receptive vocabulary – can be given as a group test

Comments:

The Two Minute Spelling test requires the child to write and the score will be affected by their writing speed as well as spelling ability. Materials include CD-Rom for digit span and one for a scoring guide.

as it could be expected there would be improvements in this skill as a result of teaching reading using synthetic phonics.

Dyslexia Early Screening Test (DEST-2)

The Dyslexia Early Screening Test was designed to identify children at risk of reading failure early enough for them to be given support at school. As education starts very early in the UK the test was developed for children between the ages of 4 years 6 months and 6 years 5 months. The aim was to address difficulties as early as possible in order to minimise long-term failure. The second edition of the test includes two additional subtests for spatial memory and receptive vocabulary, 12 subtests altogether (see Table 13.5). As might be expected of a screening test for very young children, a number of the subtests assess early phonological skills (some of which are pre-requisites for reading) and are therefore different from those in DST-J. In addition to the rapid naming test, DEST-2 contains digit naming (timed) and letter naming (timed) and more tests of phonological processing, e.g. a test of phonological discrimination, alliteration and sound order. The latter assesses the ability to determine which sound comes first of two sounds. The gap between the two sounds is shortened as the test proceeds. When they are presented close together, learners with slow processing speed may still be processing one sound when the next is introduced, resulting in confusion with sound order. A timed test of shape-copying is also included as 'dyslexic children usually have difficulty in writing fast and neatly. These later difficulties often show up in terms of difficulty in copying outline shapes' (Nicolson and Fawcett, 2003: 27).

Dyslexia Screening Test Secondary (DST-S)

Similar revisions were made in 2004 to DST-S as those described above for DST-J: the ARQ was lowered to 0.9, a new category of 'mild risk' at 0.6 was introduced and two new subtests were added, one for phonological processing (spoonerisms) and one for cognitive ability (non-verbal reasoning). The other subtests remained the same as in the first edition (see Table 13.6), with norms derived from the 1995 testing.

As a paper-based test, the DST-S has the same advantages as Dyslexia Portfolio in that it allows the assessor to make an on-going record of test behaviour, providing useful additional information. It gives detailed information for the specialist teacher to help in planning intervention. However, knowledge of dyslexia theory is required in order to fully understand which cognitive processes it taps into and why they are considered to be important in building a profile of a learner with dyslexia. For instance, it may not be clear to a non-specialist why

Table 13.5   The Dyslexia Early Screening Test – Second Edition (DEST-2)

Name of Test:			
The Dyslexia Early Screening Test – Second Edition (DEST-2)			

Author: Nicolson, R.I. and Fawcett, A.J.	**Publisher:** Pearson, 2003	**Age Range:** 4y 6m – 6y5m	**Date of Norms:** 2001

Standardisation Sample:

400 children for the two additional tests (spatial memory and receptive vocabulary). Norms for the remaining subtests are derived from the original 1995 UK norms involving over 1,000 children.

Purpose/Function:

Designed as a screening instrument for routine use within school as a first step in deciding whether to request further assessment by an educational psychologist. It provides a profile of strengths and weaknesses that can be used to guide the development of in-school support.

Test Description:

A battery of subtests as listed below. New category of mild risk at 0.6 has been introduced and 'at risk' is 0.9.

Administration time: 30 minutes	**Reliability:** Test–retest: all above 0.6 Inter-rater: 0.98	**Validity:** No similar test to use for comparison	**How scores are reported:** 'At Risk Quotient' Centile range	**Confidence intervals:** N/A

Subtest Information:

- Rapid Naming – child has to name pictures of common objects quickly and accurately
- Bead Threading – assesses hand–eye co-ordination and manipulative skill (30 seconds)
- Phonological Discrimination – ability to hear sounds in words, e.g. difference between 'hit' and 'hip'
- Postural Stability – tests the child's ability to remain stable when pressure is applied to the back (this is based on clinical procedures for establishing cerebellar abnormalities)
- Rhyme/First Letter – tests the ability to tell if two words rhyme or alliterate
- Forwards Digit Span – child listens to strings of numbers and repeats in same order
- Digit Naming – child has to name digits within 10 seconds per digit
- Letter Naming – child has to name letters within 10 seconds per letter
- Sound Order – child has to listen to two sounds and say which is presented first
- Shape Copying – child has to copy a series of shapes within a set time
- Backward Digit Span – child listens to strings of numbers and repeats in reverse order
- Corsi Frog – child has to jump a 'frog' on to numbered lily pads in the order demonstrated
- Vocabulary – a test of receptive vocabulary – can be given as a group test

Comments:

Materials include a CD for digit span and one for sound order and a scoring guide on CD-Rom. Case studies are included of how DEST-2 has been used in intervention.

Table 13.6   The Dyslexia Screening Test-Secondary (DST-S)

Name of Test:			
The Dyslexia Screening Test Secondary (DST-S)			

Author: Fawcett, A.J. and Nicolson, R.I.	**Publisher:** Harcourt Assessment, 2004	**Age Range:** 11y 6m – 16y 5m	**Date of Norms:** 2001/2002

Standardisation Sample:

700 students in Sheffield and Middlesbrough for the two new tests (spoonerisms and non-verbal reasoning). Norms for the remaining subtests are derived from the original 1995 nation-wide norms.

Purpose/function:

Designed to identify learners 'at risk' of reading failure and can be used to request further formal assessment

Test Description:

A battery of subtests as listed below. New category of mild risk at 0.6 has been introduced and 'at risk' is 0.9.

Administration time: 30 minutes	**Reliability:** Test–retest: all above 0.7 (except non-verbal reasoning: 0.631) Inter-rater: 0.98	**Validity:** Correlation between WORD and One Minute Reading: 0.673	**How scores are reported:** 'At Risk Quotient' Centile range	**Confidence intervals:** N/A

Subtest Information:

- Rapid Naming – learner has to name pictures of common objects quickly and accurately
- Bead Threading – assesses hand-eye co-ordination and manipulative skill (30 seconds)
- One Minute Reading – single word reading test
- Postural Stability – tests the learner's ability to remain stable when pressure is applied to the back (this is based on clinical procedures for establishing cerebellar abnormalities)
- Phonemic Segmentation – tests ability to break down words into constituent sounds
- Spoonerisms – involves memory as well as ability to break down words (learner has to swap over the sounds at the beginning of two words)
- Two Minute Spelling – a list of single words is dictated and the learner has to write down as many as they can in two minutes
- Backward Digit Span – learner listens to strings of numbers and repeats in reverse order
- Nonsense Passage Reading – learner reads a short passage containing real and non-words but only the non-words are scored
- One Minute Writing – learner has to copy a sentence or short passage (assessed for accuracy and legibility)
- Verbal Fluency – tests ability to generate words beginning with a stimulus letter (one minute)
- Semantic Fluency – tests ability to generate words in a given category
- Non-Verbal Reasoning – given three shapes the learner has to work out the next one in the sequence – can be given as an individual or group test (timed)

Comments:

As for DST-J, the Two Minute Spelling test requires the learner to write and so the score will be affected by their writing speed as well as spelling ability. Materials include CD-Rom for digit span and one for a scoring guide.

bead threading and a test of postural stability have been included in a dyslexia screener alongside tests of phonological processing, working memory, reading, spelling and writing.

The use of computer software makes it easier to produce individual profiles than in the first edition (where they had to be hand drawn). While standard scores are not provided, a centile range (decentile score) is given which allows comparisons to be made between individual subtests identifying strengths and weaknesses. However, many teachers find these more difficult to work with than standard scores.

Issues of Cultural and Linguistic Diversity

The assessor should consider how reliable any screener is for the population being assessed. None of the tests discussed above have bilingual norms and the number of ethnic minority children included in the standardisation sample may not be representative of the percentage in the general UK population. No detail is given of the ethnic or linguistic breakdown of the normed group, which is a serious consideration when interpreting the results and shows the importance of taking other information into account in interpreting scores. The presentation of material tends to represent Western culture and some of the tests require knowledge of English vocabulary and reading ability. Therefore the same caution should be exercised regarding level of language proficiency.

Summary

This chapter has described a number of standardised screening tests, including paper-based, computerised and on-line tests. The subtests within them in some cases can be used independently as part of diagnostic assessment. Tests vary in length of time taken and ease of administration, which is a consideration for schools.

Discussion Point

- If your school already uses a standardised screening test, discuss what appear to be its strengths and weaknesses. To what extent is the diagnosis useful for teaching?

Follow-up Activity

Try out the demo videos of:
Dyslexia Screener Digital – www.gl-assessment.co.uk/products/dyslexia-screener-digital
Lucid Screeners – www.lucid-research.com/freedemo.htm

Further Reading

Further information on the development and use of screening tests is provided in the test manuals and general texts cited earlier.

References

Fawcett, A.J and Nicolson, R.I. (1996) *The Dyslexia Screening Test 7–15.* London: Harcourt Assessment.

Fawcett, A.J. and Nicolson, R.I. (2004a) *The Dyslexia Screening Test-Junior (DST-J).* London: Harcourt Assessment.

Fawcett, A.J. and Nicolson, R.I. (2004b) *The Dyslexia Screening Test-Secondary (DST-S).* London: Harcourt Assessment.

Horne, J.K., Singleton, C.H. and Thomas, K.V. (1999) *Lucid Assessment System for Schools (LASS) 11 to 15.* Beverley, East Yorkshire: Lucid Research Ltd.

Miles, T. R. (1997) *Bangor Dyslexia Test Revised.* Wisbech, Cambs: LDA.

Nicolson, R.I. and Fawcett, A.J. (2003) *The Dyslexia Early Screening Test – Second Edition (DEST-2).* London: Pearson.

Singleton, C.H., Horne, J.K. and Thomas, K.V. (2002) *Lucid Adult Dyslexia Screening (LADS).* Beverley, East Yorkshire: Lucid Research Ltd.

Singleton, C.H. Horne, J.K., Thomas, K.V. and Leedale, R.C. (2003) *Lucid Rapid Dyslexia Screener.* Beverley, East Yorkshire: Lucid Research Ltd.

Singleton, C.H., Thomas, K.V. and Leedale, R.C. (1996) *Lucid CoPS Cognitive Profiling System.* Beverley, East Yorkshire: Lucid Research Ltd.

Thomas, K.V. Horne, J.K. and Singleton, C.H. (2001) *Lucid Assessment System for Schools (LASS) 8–11.* Beverley, East Yorkshire: Lucid Research Ltd.

Turner, M. (2008) *Dyslexia Portfolio.* London: GL Assessment.

Turner, M. and Smith, P. (2004) *Dyslexia Screener.* London: GL Assessment.

CHAPTER 14

STANDARDISED ASSESSMENT OF READING

Chapter Overview

This chapter will enable the reader to:

- have knowledge of some commonly used standardised tests for assessing reading;
- understand their main uses and limitations.

Standardised tests can assess a range of different reading skills including: single word recognition (reading out of context), reading accuracy, reading comprehension (aloud or silent), reading speed and fluency, and decoding (e.g. non-word reading and basic phonic skills). No single test will assess all these skills and teachers must choose the test(s) that best suit the purpose. This book focuses on identifying and assessing learners with dyslexia or dyslexic-type difficulties which requires the use of individual reading tests that can reveal important information about strengths and weaknesses that lead to appropriate teaching. There may be some different considerations in selecting a test for individuals than for regular monitoring of progress and standards across a school.

Most reading tests used in schools in England have UK norms. One exception to this is the Wide Range Achievement Test 4th edition (WRAT-4), which has US norms but is widely used in the assessment of dyslexia and is now found in a number of UK schools. WRAT-4 assesses two aspects of reading: single word reading and comprehension (see Table 14.1). Comprehension is assessed using a series of sentences that grow in length as opposed to a passage of continuous prose, as may be found in other tests. A major disadvantage is that it does not assess speed/fluency or non-word reading, both of which have become of increasing importance in the assessment of dyslexia. However, WRAT-4 includes an assessment for single word spelling (see Chapter 15) and mathematics computation (see Chapter 18). It also offers parallel forms (blue and green), which can be useful to monitor progress.

WIAT-II[UK]-T also originated in the US but it has UK norms for the school population (see Table 14.2). It offers a test of single word reading which in its earliest levels tests decoding skills of letters (as does WRAT-4 single word reading test), but also rhyme, recognition of first sounds and blends, which are useful diagnostically as particular aspects can then be followed up in more detail. The WIAT-II[UK]-T test of reading comprehension includes both sentences and passages. The sentences must be read aloud to provide a reading accuracy score but a learner can choose whether to read the passages for comprehension aloud or silently. As the passages are also used to assess reading speed, the learner must notify the assessor when they get to the end of the passage if they have chosen to read silently. A further advantage of this test is that the manual helps the assessor to interpret results qualitatively and make appropriate recommendations. Like the WRAT-4, it includes an assessment of single word spelling although it does not include mathematics. It does not have parallel forms but this may not be important as the test's main purpose is the diagnosis of dyslexic-type difficulties.

The Diagnostic Reading Analysis (DRA) (Table 14.3) assesses a number of reading skills based on reading passages aloud. It provides scores for reading accuracy, fluency/reading rate and comprehension. Both fiction and non-fiction passages are included. An interesting aspect of this test is that it assesses listening comprehension to establish the starting point for testing reading. For most learners this will be appropriate and may be an advantage for those with general literacy difficulties who are

Table 14.1   Wide Range Achievement Test 4 (WRAT-4)

Name of Test:			
Wide Range Achievement Test (WRAT) 4			
Author: Wilkinson, G.S and Robertson, G.J.	**Publisher:** Psychological Assessment Resources, 2006	**Age Range:** 5–94	**Date of Norms:** 2005

Standardisation Sample: US

A sample of 3,000 5–94-year-olds with appropriate representation of race and ethnicity from across the USA. Sample size of 100–150 in each of 19 age groups

Purpose/Function:

To consider a range of academic skills and attainments. It measures the skills of word reading, sentence comprehension, spelling and maths computation. Particularly useful in giving an overall academic profile. The parallel forms can be used to monitor progress.

Test Description:

Comprises four subtests. There are two parallel forms (blue and green).

Administration time:	Reliability:	Validity:	How scores are reported:	Confidence intervals:
15–25 minutes for children aged 5–7 years. 30–45 minutes for 8+ and adults	Internal consistency at least 0.9 for all tests except maths (0.89) Test–retest 0.73-0.8 (5–6-year-olds), 0.77 (maths), 0.85–0.89 (literacy) (7–18 years olds)	Correlations with WIAT-II subtests varies from 0.6–0.8 for literacy, 0.84–0.92 for maths	Standard scores Percentiles Age and grade equivalent Stanines Rasch scaled scores	85% 90% 95%

Subtest Information: (as stated in manual)

1. Word Reading measures letter and word decoding through letter identification and word recognition.

2. Sentence Comprehension measures an individual's ability to gain meaning from words and to comprehend ideas and information contained in sentences through the use of a modified cloze techniques.

3. Spelling measures the ability to encode sounds into written form through the use of a dictated spelling format containing both letters and words.

4. Maths Computation measures the ability to perform basic mathematics computations through counting, identifying numbers, solving simple oral problems, and calculating written mathematics problems.

Comments:

A comprehensive manual is provided which gives full details of test development and psychometric properties. Clear information is given about administration and scoring at school level in three-monthly intervals. Separate scores can be found for word reading and comprehension but a reading composite score is also given.

Table 14.2   Wechsler Individual Achievement Tests Second UK Edition for Teachers (WIAT-II^{UK}-T)

Name of Test:			
Wechsler Individual Achievement Tests Second UK Edition for Teachers (WIAT-II^{UK}-T)			
Author: Wechsler, D.	**Publisher:** Pearson, 2006	**Age Range:** 4 – 16y 11m	**Date of Norms:** 2004
Standardisation Sample: UK			
892 children aged between 4 and 16 years 11 months including different racial/ethnic groups. US norms available from 17 to 85 years.			
Purpose/Function:			
To assess word reading, reading comprehension, reading rate and spelling, not only to give comparison with individuals but also to gain detailed information particularly in relation to word reading and spelling			
Test Description:			
There are three subtests which are individually administered.			

Administration time:	Reliability:	Validity:	How scores are reported:	Confidence intervals:
Varies depending upon age	Split-half 0.94–0.97 Test–retest 0.94–0.99 (US sample)	Mainly related to use of US tests	Standard scores Percentiles Age equivalent Stanines	90% 95%

Subtest Information:

1. Word Reading assesses phonological awareness and decoding skills including letter identification, letter sound awareness and automaticity and accuracy of word recognition.

2. Reading Comprehension tests literal, inferential and lexical comprehension, reading rate and oral reading accuracy and fluency and word recognition in context.

3. Spelling evaluates letter sound correspondence, spelling regular and irregular words and includes contractions and high frequency homonyms.

Comments:

The statistics in the manual should be read carefully to be able to distinguish which statistics relate to the UK and which to the US. There is a chapter on access arrangements which is useful (but please note you always need to read the current regulations). The manual gives clear details of how to score the subtests and provides frameworks for analysing strengths and weaknesses and in the case of spelling gives suggestions for intervention.

often asked to begin a reading assessment using passages that are too difficult. However, for readers with dyslexic-type difficulties whose listening comprehension may be very good, this could lead to asking them to start reading a passage well beyond their decoding ability. This then means that they are faced with working backwards through the passages to establish a basal level.

The test is popular in a lot of schools because of its reasonable cost, the fact that it yields standardised scores for three different aspects of reading and has parallel forms. However, as Table 14.3 shows, the standardisation sample is small. This is because it was normed mainly on children with literacy difficulties (chosen from the bottom quartile of the reading ability range). The manual notes that this means that the test norms are 'more representative of the pupils the test was actually designed for, rather than a general school population' (Crumpler and McCarty, 2007: 59). As this is a biased sample, they used a procedure called 'equating' to develop the norms by comparing the scores on this test to a group reading test with a large standardisation sample.

Another test produced by the same authors as DRA is the Access Reading Test (see Table 14.4). This test was standardised on a much larger sample and covers an age range up to 20+. It assesses four aspects of reading comprehension and is particularly useful when applying for Access Arrangements (see Chapter 20) because it is a timed comprehension test and built into it is an opportunity to show the difference that giving 25% extra time makes. Because of its age range it could be used for both primary and GCSE/A level Access Arrangements.

The York Assessment of Reading Comprehension (YARC), as the name suggests, is designed particularly to assess comprehension but also assesses reading accuracy and rate. Both the primary and secondary tests have two sets of parallel passages. There are more questions for the secondary passages. The passage reading can be analysed using miscue analysis to assess decoding skills, although in the secondary version this applies only to the supplementary passages as the others are read silently. The primary version includes an Early Reading section, which assesses alphabet knowledge, single word reading and phoneme awareness (see Table 14.5). This is a similar approach to the way in which early decoding skills are assessed in WIAT-II^{UK}-T and is particularly useful for the early identification of children at risk of dyslexia. YARC Secondary (see Table 14.6) includes two supplementary passages for poorer readers, which should be read aloud in order to identify decoding difficulties. These passages were developed for learners with a reading age of 8–9 years and whilst they are therefore appropriate for some students at secondary school they may not be appropriate for assessing learners who enter with even lower reading ages.

YARC is increasingly being used in schools and is often seen as a replacement for Neale Analysis of Reading Ability II, which was popularly used but now has fairly old norms and has a ceiling of age 12.11, which is inappropriate for secondary schools.

Whilst the tests described above target particular areas of reading, none of them includes a test of non-word reading (although the version of WIAT-II^{UK}-T used by educational psychologists does contain a test of pseudowords, as noted in Chapter 21). As

Table 14.3   Diagnostic Reading Analysis Second Edition

Name of Test:			
Diagnostic Reading Analysis			

Author: Crumpler, M. and McCarty, C.	Publisher: Hodder Education, 2007 (2nd edn)	Age Range: 7–16	Date of Norms: 2004

Standardisation Sample: 633 with Form A and 474 with Form B. Over 1,100 in total

Purpose/Function:

To assess listening comprehension and reading (accuracy, fluency/reading rate, comprehension and comprehension processing speed)

Test Description:

A listening comprehension task and assessment of reading using both fiction and non-fiction passages. Two parallel forms for reading

Administration time:	Reliability:	Validity:	How scores are reported:	Confidence intervals:
Untimed but each assessment takes up to about 15 minutes	Test–retest for listening comprehension 0.64–0.78 Split half 0.7 Parallel forms: reading accuracy 0.93; reading comprehension 0.68	No psychometric data given. A link is claimed between reading ages and NC levels.	Reading Accuracy: Standard scores Percentiles Reading ages Reading Comprehension and Reading Fluency: Five bands of standard scores	Not provided

Comments:

Gives good details for analysing errors and therefore is useful for diagnosing difficulties. Includes a checklist for recording test behaviour.

stated earlier in this book, non-word reading often indicates phonological processing difficulties in reading and most screening tests for dyslexia contain a test of non-word reading (see Chapter 13), as does PhAB (see Chapter 17). There are not many published single tests of non-word reading. One such is the Nonword Reading Test (Table 14.7), published in 2004. This was standardised at the same time as the Diagnostic Reading Analysis discussed above and on the same children. Although the standardised scores originally would not have been representative of the general population because it was designed for use with children presenting reading difficulties, the authors claim these

Table 14.4   Access Reading Test

Name of Test: Access Reading Test			
Author: McCarty, C. and Crumpler, M.	**Publisher:** Hodder Education, 2006	**Age Range:** 7–20+	**Date of Norms:** 2005
Standardisation Sample: 4092 between the ages of 7 and 25			
Purpose/Function: To provide a standardized assessment of reading attainment and reading skills used to extract meaning from a text			
Test Description: 60 questions based on 11 varied pieces of reading material. Assesses four reading skills of: literal comprehension, understanding of vocabulary, comprehension requiring inference or prediction and opinions, comprehension requiring analysis. Two parallel forms devised as a group test but can be used for individuals.			

Administration time:	Reliability:	Validity:	How scores are reported:	Confidence intervals:
30 minutes or less	Internal consistency 0.95	Only age standardisation provided: 0.713 (Form A) and 0.633 (Form B)	Standard scores Reading ages Percentiles	Not provided

Comments: Can be used for evidence of access arrangements. Learners who have not completed in 30 minutes can be given 25% extra time (i.e. 7.5 minutes) and the point reached at 30 minutes is marked and a different coloured pen used for the extra time. Test must be completed in a single session. User friendly manual for scoring.

have been equated with a normal population. It is more up to date than Turner's Nonword reading test, which is still commonly used, and it can be used diagnostically as it provides a detailed analysis of errors. Another test of non-word reading can be found in the Test of Word Reading Efficiency, 2nd Edition (TOWRE-2, Torgesen et al., 2011). This revised version was published in 2011 after being re-normed in 2008–9 on a sample of 1,700 for ages 6 to 24.11. However, it has American norms. There are two subtests: sight word efficiency (single word reading) and phonemic decoding efficiency (phonemically regular non-words). Each of the subtests contains alternate forms. It is extremely quick to administer and test–retest reliability is over 0.9. The test is widely used in the assessment of dyslexia, but it is expensive.

Another American-normed test that is often used in the assessment of dyslexia is the Gray Oral Reading Test, 5th Edition (GORT-5) (Wiederholt and Bryant, 2012). This

Table 14.5   York Assessment of Reading for Comprehension
(Primary Edition)

Name of Test:			
York Assessment of Reading for Comprehension (Primary Edition)			
Author: Passage Reading (PR): Snowling, M.J. et al. Early Reading (ER): Hulme, C. et al.	**Publisher:** GL Assessment, 2009	**Age Range:** PR: 5–11 ER: 4–7:11	**Date of Norms:** 2008

Standardisation Sample: PR: 1,376, (14.02% known to have EAL) ER: 662, (over 16% were known to have EAL). Both samples included regional and ethnic representation.

Purpose/Function:

PR: to assesses accuracy, rate and comprehension of oral reading skills

ER: to assess alphabetic knowledge, single word reading and phoneme awareness

Test Description:

PR: comprises of two parallel sets of graded passages (A and B) for reading aloud. Each passage has eight comprehension questions tapping literal and inferential comprehension skills.

ER: four tests: Letter Sound Knowledge, Early Word Recognition, Sound Isolation, Sound Deletion

Administration time:	Reliability:	Validity:	How scores are reported:	Confidence intervals:
PR: 10–15 minutes ER: up to about 20 minutes but can be given over several sessions	Internal consistency (PR) reading comprehension 0.48–0.77, parallel forms for reading accuracy 0.75–0.93 and reading rate 0.9–0.95; 0.88–0.98 (ER)	PR: content/face: comparison made with other tests. Concurrent validity for Form A 0.79 (SWRT), 0.75 for accuracy, 0.78 reading rate and 0.62 comprehension (NARA). Form B slightly lower correlations ER: criterion 0.55–0.87	Standard scores Percentiles Age equivalent	95%

Comments:

Detailed error analysis. Can be used diagnostically. User-friendly manual. The authors make the comment that reliability estimates for reading comprehension are lower than those for reading rate and accuracy but suggest that this reflects the fact that comprehension is multifaceted and point out that the estimates of it are based on a small number of comprehension questions for each passage.

Table 14.6   York Assessment of Reading for Comprehension
(Secondary Edition)

Name of Test:			
York Assessment of Reading for Comprehension (Secondary)			
Author: Stothard, S.E., Hulme, C., Clarke, P., Barmby, P. and Snowling, M.J.	**Publisher:** GL Assessment, 2010	**Age Range:** 11.00–16.00	**Date of Norms:** 2009

Standardisation Sample: 1,230 students in 39 UK schools, from 10 regional centres covering a range of types of schools and socio-economic status, including children with a statement of SEN and those with EAL from different ethnic minority backgrounds

Purpose/Function:

To assess decoding (reading accuracy), reading rate, reading fluency and text comprehension (literal and inferential meaning)

Test Description:

Passage Reading: comprises two parallel sets of graded passages (A and B) for silent reading; each passage has 13 comprehension questions and a 'summarisation question'. There are two supplementary passages for use with poor readers, which are read aloud. In addition there is a test of reading fluency and a single word reading test.

Administration time:	Reliability:	Validity:	How scores are reported:	Confidence intervals:
20–30 minutes	Reading comprehension: internal consistency >0.8, supplementary test 0.76.	Concurrent validity: 0.6–0.75 based on comparison of summarisation and reading comprehension questions Supplementary test: 0.52	Standard scores Percentiles Age equivalent	95%

Comments:

Can be used diagnostically (supplementary passages only), for access arrangements and for measuring progress. User-friendly manual. At each level the student reads a fiction and non-fiction passage. Pictures are only in non-fiction passages and are similar to those found in a secondary text book. Reading Comprehension passages can be read aloud if the student is more comfortable with this but it may produce a slower reading speed. It offers two ways of looking at reading speed: reading rate (time taken to read a passage silently) and reading fluency (number of words read accurately divided by the time taken) on a passage that is read aloud. It gives some short case studies of sample profiles including two which are particularly consistent with specific learning difficulties/dyslexia.

Table 14.7   Nonword Reading Test

Name of Test:			
Nonword Reading Test			

Author: Crumpler, M. and McCarty, C (UK edition)	**Publisher:** Hodder Education, 2004	**Age Range:** 6–16	**Date of Norms:** 2004

Standardisation Sample: 401 pupils (UK norms)

Purpose/Function:

It assesses decoding accuracy and speed.

Test Description:

Two parallel forms. Test booklet contains non-words with six per page in Sassoon font. The test materials include record sheets for the teacher to score the test.

Administration time: 5–10 minutes	**Reliability:** Test–retest: 0.96 (form A) and 0.95 (form B). Parallel forms: >0.9, internal consistency 0.96 (Australian version). Parallel forms UK: 0.51- 0.96	**Validity:** 0.9 when correlated with Coltheart and Leahy Nonword Reading (Australian version)	**How scores are reported:** Standard scores Percentiles Age equivalent	**Confidence intervals:** Not provided

Comments:

Clearly based on phonic skills but also includes morphemes such as 'ed' 'epi' 'ion'. It is very useful diagnostically as it provides a detailed diagnostic analysis of errors. It has a durable test booklet with good legibility. Manual has clear instructions for administration but lacks some of the details of standardisation. It was originally an Australian test and most of the information about reliability and validity is based on that sample from 2001 which was adapted and re-standardized in 2004 in UK but only on 401 learners. There are very small numbers in the standardisation sample for some ages. Age 10–10:11 has the largest number (77) but there are only nine in the sample of 6-year-olds. Unlike the Australian version, it is not based on a normal population distribution but mainly on 'weak readers'. The basis for selection is not known.

measures oral reading fluency and comprehension covering the age range 6 to 23.11 and so is useful for secondary schools, but like TOWRE-2, this is an expensive test. It also has American norms. In the UK, both TOWRE-2 and GORT-5 are used particularly for assessment for Disabled Student Allowance (DSA) and Access Arrangements for A-level rather than for general diagnostic assessment at school level. They are particularly useful because of their upper age limits.

Issues of Linguistic and Cultural Diversity

A number of issues relating to language and cultural diversity in the assessment of reading were raised in Chapter 6. One of the differences between informal and formal assessment of reading is the choice of reading material. This is more within the assessor's control in informal assessment, as often a wide range of reading material is available. When using standardised reading tests the materials have already been selected by the authors of the test, for a specific population. In using a test with a different population this is a major consideration. Not only should the learner have sufficient proficiency in English (if they have EAL) but the test chosen should have pictures and passages that are culturally appropriate and within their experience.

Summary

In this chapter we have given an overview of some of the most commonly used tests for assessing the reading difficulties of learners' dyslexia and dyslexic-type difficulties. In choosing tests of reading, assessors must ensure that they can cover a range of different aspects of reading including accuracy, speed/fluency and comprehension. Both single word and passage reading should be included, as should non-word reading.

Further Reading

Snowling, M. J. and Hulme, C. (Eds) (2005) *The Science of Reading: A Handbook*. London: Blackwell.
A useful collection of reviews of reading research bringing together many theories and models that support both the assessment of reading and its associated underlying processes.

References

Crumpler, M. and McCarty, C. (2007) *Diagnostic Reading Analysis*, 2nd edn. London: Hodder Education.
Torgesen, J.K., Wagner, R.K. and Rashotte, C.A. (2011) *TOWRE-2: Test of Word Reading Efficiency*, 2nd edn. Austin, Texas: Pro-Ed.
Wiederholt, J.L. and Bryant, B. (2012) *GORT-5 Gray Oral Reading Tests*, 5th edn. Austin, Texas: Pro-Ed.

CHAPTER 15

STANDARDISED ASSESSMENT OF SPELLING AND HANDWRITING

Chapter Overview

This chapter will enable the reader to:

- have knowledge of some commonly used standardised tests for assessing spelling and handwriting;
- understand their main uses and limitations.

As pointed out in Chapter 7, there is a strong relationship between spelling and hand-writing and the assessment of both is necessary to any consideration of literacy diffi-culties. However, it is not necessarily the case that someone who is poor at spelling has poor handwriting and vice versa.

Assessing Spelling

Informal assessment for diagnostic purposes normally considers analysing errors in free writing, testing of single words (both phonically regular and irregular words), and sometimes dictation, as described in Chapter 7. Standardised tests of spelling are usually tests of single words, graded for difficulty and including both regular and irregular words. Many standardised spelling tests are group tests (e.g. Young Parallel Spelling Tests, 2nd Edition, Young, 1998; Single-word Spelling Test, Sacre and Masterson, 2000; Diagnostic Spelling Test, Crumpler and McCarty, 2006; Graded Word Spelling Test, 3rd Edition, McCarty and Crumpler, 2006; British Spelling Test Series, Vincent and De la Mare, 2009), which are often used in schools to identify those who have spelling difficulties by making comparisons with peers. In addition to giving standard scores and spelling ages, many of these tests offer advice in the manual on how to examine the results for spelling errors thus pro-viding useful information for intervention. For example, the Single Word Spelling Test explains how to classify spelling errors as 'phonological errors', which are described as 'spellings that are incorrect but nevertheless conform to the phoneme–grapheme conversion rules or higher order rules imposing constraints on the inclusion and position of letters', and 'visual errors', which the manual describes as 'usually composed of the correct letters but in the wrong order in a word' (Sacre and Masterson, 2000: 18). The third edition of the Graded Word Spelling Test (McCarty and Crumpler, 2006) also provides Spelling Analysis classifications for particular year groups, allowing teachers to review the spelling patterns of pupils in their class, and the Diagnostic Spelling Test (2006), by Crumpler and McCarty, has an optional diagnostic facility too, using photocopiable marking grids provided in the manual.

Many group tests suggest that they can be used with both individuals and groups. However, it should be noted that group spelling tests have not usually been stand-ardised for use with individuals. Two standardised tests that are commonly used by specialist teachers to obtain a standard score for individuals are the spelling tests contained in WRAT-4 (Wilkinson and Robertson, 2006) and WIAT-II^{UK}-T (Wechsler, 2006). Summaries of both these tests can be found in Chapter 14 (Tables 14.1 and 14.2) as both of them also assess reading. The WRAT-4 spelling test asks the learner to write certain individual letters in response to the letter name, prior to the single word spelling. The words are graded in length to include a range of phonic skills, leading to polysyllabic tricky words, e.g. necessity, occurrence. WIAT-II^{UK}-T has more items but includes the spelling of some single sounds, blends and digraphs before the single words. It also includes homonyms such as 'too', 'right', and 'ceiling', and the use of contractions, e.g. couldn't and they're. The test has been developed for use in the UK with UK norms for the school population but some of the words appear to be based on American pronunciation. For instance it highlights 'they're' as a homonym but in English it is distinguishable from 'their' and is not normally considered a homonym. The issue of pronunciation should always be taken into account when using tests that originate in the USA. WIAT-II^{UK}-T does, however, provide a useful categorisation for analysing the spelling difficulties that can be used diagnostically in drawing up intervention.

In contrast to the individual spelling tests discussed above, the British Spelling Test Series, 2nd Edition (BSTS2) considers spelling at word, sentence and continuous writing level. It offers a mixture of questions and tasks to assess ability to spell in different contexts, including requiring a pupil to draw on their own vocabulary. There are two parallel forms. The variety of approaches keeps learners engaged even when they are poor spellers. However, BSTS2 is a group test (although the authors suggest that it can be used individually as part of a diagnostic battery for the assessment of individuals with learning difficulties). Moreover, teachers will still need to draw on their own knowledge of spelling in order to interpret it qualitatively.

Assessing Handwriting

Currently, the most useful test for assessing handwriting is the Detailed Assessment of Handwriting (DASH) (Barnett et al., 2007), as it provides standard scores for a school population of 9–16 years and is concerned with speed of handwriting in both free writing and copying situations (see Table 15.1). Slow handwriting can affect performance in examinations (see Connelly et al., 2006) and also compositional skills (see Connelly et al., 2006; Kelly and Phillips, 2011). This test can be used, therefore, to identify learners who write slowly in order to provide appropriate teaching and support. It is particularly used when applying for access arrangements (see Chapter 20). The test also includes an optional test of graphic speed which is especially useful to see whether or not there may be the possibility of a visual motor co-ordination difficulty.

DASH could be followed up by the use of the Beery Visual Motor Integration Test (BVMI), 6th edition, (Beery et al., 2010). This test requires the subject to copy geometric forms using a pencil or pen. The full form of visual motor integration can be followed up by two supplementary tests designed to give more information about the two aspects of visual perception and motor integration (see Table 15.2). The manual suggests that none of these tests is sufficient to identify a major difficulty but could indicate the need for other professionals to be involved in further assessment. The manual also includes some information about the teaching of handwriting, suggesting

Table 15.1   Detailed Assessment of Handwriting (DASH)

Name of Test:			
Detailed Assessment of Handwriting (DASH)			
Author: Barnett, A., Henderson, S.E., Scheib, B. and Schultz, J.	**Publisher:** Pearson, 2007	**Age Range:** 9–16	**Date of Norms:** 2006
Standardisation Sample: 546 in 34 primary/middle and 22 secondary schools in the UK			
Purpose/Function: To provide measures of handwriting speed, to identify learners with handwriting difficulties, and provide a description of handwriting performance			
Test Description: Consists of five different tasks including both copying and free writing			

Administration time:	Reliability:	Validity:	How scores are reported:	Confidence Intervals:
About 20 minutes	Inter-rate: 0.9 except graphic speed 0.8. Test–retest: above 0.7 (14–15year-olds) and over 0.8 (9–10-year-olds) except copy best (0.6) and copy fast (0.5). Internal consistency: 0.8	Concurrent validity for DASH free writing compared to Allcock 0.63	Standard scores Percentiles Scaled scores	SEM is given for each age group so that confidence bands can be calculated

Subtest Information:
Copy Best: copying a sentence in best handwriting for two minutes
Alphabet Writing (continuous): write the alphabet in lower case in correct sequence for one minute
Copy Fast: copying a sentence quickly for two minutes
Free Writing: on Topic 'My Life' for 10 minutes
Graphic Speed: drawing 'x's in circles for one minute (an optional non-language based test)

Comments:
Can be used as either an individual or group test. The manual suggests some aspects of what you might look for in analysis of handwriting but it does not give the detail provided in Chapter 8 for informal assessment. Free writing is time marked every two minutes to allow speed to be compared. Good detail of how to count words (e.g. numbers, abbreviations etc.) is given.

Table 15.2   The Beery–Buktenica Developmental Test of Visual–Motor Integration (Beery VMI)

Name of Test:			
The Beery–Buktenica Developmental Test of Visual-Motor Integration (Beery VMI) 6th edn			

Author:	Publisher:	Age Range:	Date of Norms:
Beery, K.E., Buktenica, N.A. and Beery, N.A.	Pearson, 2010	2–18	2010

Standardisation Sample:

A national sample of 1,737 aged 2–18 (2010) and 1,021 adults (2006)

Purpose/Function:

To identify difficulties in integrating or co-ordinating visual perceptual and motor (finger and hand movement) abilities

Test Description:

Group or individual, pencil and paper test in which they copy shapes. The 5th edition (2004) contained Beery VMI full form of 30 items which could be used with two supplemental tests: visual perception and motor co-ordination. These are administered as a follow-up to the Beery VMI. Children under 7 years use a short form which has 21 items. In the 6th edition the forms have been integrated with the adult forms.

Administration time:	Reliability:	Validity:	How scores are reported:	Confidence intervals:
BVMI Untimed (approx 15 minutes)	Internal consistency: 0.88. Test–retest: 0.9 Inter-scorer: 0.9+	Concurrent validity with other tests between 0.5 and 0.7	Standard scores Scaled scores Percentiles	SEM given by age so that confidence bands can be calculated

Supplemental Test Information:

Two supplemental tests can be given:

Visual Perception – 30 items, the first three for very young children asking them to point to parts of the body and 27 items requiring matching of geometric forms. They have to match as many geometric forms as they can in three minutes by pointing to their choice.

Motor Co-ordination – 30 items, the first three require very young children to climb on a chair, hold a pencil with their thumb and fingers and hold the paper as they mark it, the next 27 require them to trace a stimulus form with a pencil without going outside double lined paths. From the seventh item they have only five minutes to complete as many as they can. The manual points out that visual perceptual demands cannot be entirely eliminated but have been reduced by giving starting dots and paths in the motor co-ordination.

Comments:

The test is useful to see if there appears to be a problem in visual motor integration but the manual itself emphasizes that it only screens for difficulties and further detailed assessment needs to be carried out if the test identifies a problem in visual-motor skills, e.g. by an occupational therapist who may look for signs of DCD (dyspraxia). The manual refers to teaching strategies including those developed by the authors that would include teaching writing skills.

that early identification of visual-motor integration problems is important in terms of developing and teaching handwriting. They emphasise the need to move quickly from copying of shapes to the writing of letters and words. Although this is not a direct assessment of handwriting it is nevertheless relevant to the assessment of handwriting, particularly where teachers have noted a learner presenting poor letter formation, inconsistency of size and shape, difficulty writing on the line and difficulty in spacing.

Currently, the only test of handwriting in the UK that provides standard scores is DASH (Barnett et al., 2007). Two other tests of speed of handwriting have been used in the past 15 years. These are the Hedderley Sentence Completion Test (Hedderley, 1995) and the Handwriting Speed Assessment (Allcock, 2001). Hedderley can be used with both primary and secondary learners whereas Allcock is for secondary students, 11–16. The Hedderley test asks for 10 minutes of writing, as does the DASH free writing subtest. The Allcock test is based on free writing but requires 20 minutes of continuous writing. All three tests quote words per minute (wpm) for the relevant age groups. However, there are discrepancies in the average number of words quoted. This is a particular concern in the case of the Allcock test, which provides an average handwriting speed of 16.9 wpm for Year 11 whereas the average for Year 11 in Hedderley is 20 wpm and in DASH the mean is 24 wpm at age 16 and a speed of 19 is below average.

Issues of Cultural and Linguistic Diversity

Aspects mentioned elsewhere, particularly of vocabulary and experience, will affect results and the methods of teaching used with learners will affect performance in both spelling and handwriting. In spelling, familiarity with the words and their meanings may affect quality of spelling and could affect speed of handwriting, especially in free writing where proficiency in English is clearly relevant.

Summary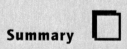

This chapter gives an overview of some of the most common forms of standardised spelling tests used in schools and by specialist teachers. Both group and individual spelling tests are discussed, some of which give useful guidance on how to analyse spelling errors as a basis for planning intervention in addition to standardised scores, spelling ages and/or percentiles. The chapter also considers issues of differences in what is considered to be 'average' writing speed for a given age in different tests used in schools. This is a particularly important issue for specialist teachers in making recommendations for examination arrangements as the test used may affect the outcome for the learner in terms of any additional time granted.

Discussion Point

- Discuss what might be the possible reason for discrepancies in 'average writing speed' in the DASH, Allcock and Hedderley tests.

Follow-up Activity

Obtain a copy of a spelling test used in your school and consider the extent to which you could analyse spelling errors using one of the frameworks for informal assessment of spelling proposed in Chapter 7.

Further Reading

Kelly, K. and Phillips, S. (2011) *Teaching Literacy to Learners with Dyslexia*. London: SAGE.
Includes chapters on spelling and handwriting development including the debate about whether to teach handwriting or keyboarding skills to learners with dyslexia.

References

Allcock, P. (2001) *Handwriting Speed Assessment*. www.patoss-dyslexia.org
Barnett, A., Henderson, S.E., Scheib, B. and Schultz, J. (2007) *Detailed Assessment of Handwriting (DASH)*. London: Pearson.
Beery, K. E., Buktenica, N.A. and Berry, N.A. (2010) *The Berry-Buktenica Developmental Test of Visual-Motor Integration (Berry VMI), 6th Edn*. London: Pearson.
Connelly, V., Campbell, S., MacLean, M. and Barnes, J. (2006) 'Contribution of lower-order letter and word fluency skills to written composition of college students with and without dyslexia', *Developmental Neuropsychology*, 29: 175–196.

Crumpler, M. and McCarty, C. (2006) *Diagnostic Spelling Test*, London: Hodder and Stoughton.

Hedderley, R. (1995) 'Sentence completion test', *Dyslexia Review*, 7: 2.

Kelly, K. and Phillips, S. (2011) *Teaching Literacy to Learners with Dyslexia*. London: SAGE.

McCarty, C. and Crumpler, M. (2006) *Graded Word Spelling Test* (*Vernon's Spelling Test, 3rd edn.*), London: Hodder and Stoughton.

Sacre, L. And Masterson, J. (2000) *Single Word Spelling Test*. Slough: NFER-Nelson.

Vincent, D. and De la Mare, M. (2009) *British Spelling Test Series, 2nd Edn*. London: GL Assessment.

Wechsler, D. (2006) *Wechsler Individual Achievement Tests Second UK Edition for Teachers (WIAT-II^{UK}-T)*. London: Pearson.

Wilkinson, G.S. and Robertson, G.J. (2006) *Wide Range Achievement Test (WRAT) 4*. Lutz, FL: PAR (Psychological Assessment Resources).

Young, D. (1998) *Parallel Spelling Tests, 2nd Edn*. Oxon: Hodder Education.

CHAPTER 16

THE ASSESSMENT OF UNDERLYING ABILITY

Chapter Overview

This chapter enables readers to:

- appreciate some of the issues involved in defining the concept of underlying ability;
- use this understanding when choosing a test of underlying ability and interpreting the results of such tests.

One of the most contentious areas in educational assessment is the issue as to whether there is a general underlying cognitive ability which is, in fact, an 'aptitude for learning'. For many years psychologists have attempted to structure and measure a general intellectual ability. Early attempts to describe this construct used the terms 'mental capacity' and 'intelligence'. A major problem with this latter term is that it became associated with the concept of 'innate' intellectual capacity which was 'fixed', and suggested that someone who shows good problem-solving skills in certain tasks will perform at the same level in all problem-solving situations. Clearly, this is not the case! Many people who achieve academically may not perform well in practical situations. In education, tests of intelligence/ability were used to judge whether children were 'underachieving' or could be dyslexic because their attainments (e.g. in mathematics or literacy) were lower than their scores on intelligence tests. Similarly, it was argued that some children presenting learning difficulties had 'general learning difficulties' if their scores for 'ability' as measured on intelligence matched their literacy attainment. These views are no longer accepted (see Chapter 1 of this book and also Kelly and Phillips, 2011). Nevertheless, at the time of writing, a full 'diagnostic' assessment for dyslexia usually involves the assessment of underlying ability, and it is required for an assessment for the Disabled Student Allowance. It is useful, therefore, for teachers/assessors to appreciate some of the background to the development of concepts and tests of underlying ability in order to be able to appreciate the purposes and limitations of the assessment procedures used.

Background to the Development of Tests of Ability

The first tests of 'mental capacity' for children were developed by Alfred Binet in Paris. (They were devised for the negative reason of deciding which children should not attend infant school because their low mental functioning meant they would not be able to learn.) Children were given a series of the sort of activities that were at that time carried out in infant schools, and observations were made of the range of ways in which children of various ages responded to them. Teachers helped to judge the 'average' performance. The majority (75%) were seen as 'average and above' for their age. Advances in statistics and factor analysis allowed a more rigorous approach to the study of the nature of intellectual ability. In 1904, Charles Spearman developed the concept of 'g' or a general intelligence, present in all cognitive abilities, but where a special factor 's' might also be found, related to the nature of a specific task. (This was known as Spearman's Two Factor Theory.) The concept of 'g', particularly as a non-verbal underlying ability, has strongly influenced later test development. In the 1930s, Thurstone, also using factor analysis, identified seven factors of ability, although they were later found not to be completely independent of each other. He considered, however, as many psychologists have done since, that a view of a single form of ability based largely on tests of reasoning is insufficient to explain individual strengths and weaknesses in the range of abilities demonstrated by individuals (e.g. musical, artistic).

Cattell (1971) proposed that 'g' comprised two major factors, which he called 'fluid' and 'crystallised' intelligence. He saw fluid intelligence as a general ability to think and solve problems in new/unfamiliar situations and see relationships. Crystallised intelligence is the ability to draw on knowledge, learning and experience. Whereas 'fluid' intelligence/ability is normally assessed using non-verbal tasks (usually involving visuo-spatial abilities), crystallised intelligence is usually assessed by vocabulary tests and the use of general knowledge.

By this time there was general acceptance that 'intelligence' was manifest in an ability to solve problems and to reason, and there was a need also to assess both verbal and non-verbal aspects. Wechsler (1949), in developing intelligence tests for children (and adults), adopted a similar approach to Cattell, proposing two major intelligences, each assessed by a series of sub-tests. Results of the sub-tests can be combined to give a Verbal IQ (Intelligence Quotient) and Performance IQ, which are further combined to produce a Full-Scale IQ.

Note: The term IQ tends not to be used now and was a legacy from the way tests were previously scored. Standard Scores (SS) are now quoted, although sometimes still termed IQ.

A version of the Wechsler Intelligence Scale for Children (WISC-4R) with UK norms is widely used by educational psychologists (see Chapter 21). Whilst the sub-test scores are not, in themselves, very reliable, they are useful to provide a profile of differing strengths and weaknesses. A statistical analysis of intellectual ability was also used by Elliot (1986) to produce the British Abilities Scale (BAS) for use by educational psychologists. A third version was published in 2011 and claims to produce a measure of 'intellectual functioning'. Like WISC-4R, it contains a number of sub-tests, verbal and non-verbal. It is interesting to note that the term 'abilities' is used in the title rather than intelligence.

A somewhat different approach from analysing factors involved in a range of intellectual tasks lies in the information-processing model, which attempts to identify the mental *processes* underlying 'intelligent'/reasoning behaviour. According to this model, differences in the ability to perform any task will depend on the specific processes an individual deploys in the task and their speed and accuracy in using them. This approach can be seen in the work of Sternberg (1985). Sternberg considered a range of different abilities, not just intellectual functioning. However, we are concerned here only with that aspect and his 'componential' model of the processes involved in problem solving. In the case of verbal analogies (a sub-test found in many assessments of verbal reasoning ability), Sternberg considered that the way in which the words are *encoded* (involving retrieval of meanings/attributes from long-term memory) and the *comparisons* formed are the major components. He concluded that high performers on these tasks may spend longer on encoding but thereby form more accurate representations than low performers. In particular, however, they are faster in forming comparisons even when equally accurate. (Spearman had considered this the ability to 'educe correlates' and saw it as a significant aspect of general ability observed in both verbal and non-verbal tasks.)

Both these approaches are important in identifying a learner's strengths and weaknesses. Models of ability based on factor analysis identify broad areas of strength and weakness, e.g. good verbal comprehension but weakness in verbal reasoning (and/or non-verbal reasoning). However, information-processing skills may provide a better profile of the processes accounting for some of the discrepancies in the behaviour/ attainments of learners, including those with dyslexic-type difficulties. These may relate to difficulties in knowing/using appropriate strategies to employ to tackle a problem. Such difficulties are often considered in themselves to indicate 'low ability', but may be reflecting what they have learned. An implication, therefore, is that meta-cognitive strategies can be taught. Similarly, they may have difficulty or be very slow in retrieving information from long-term memory or have difficulty in learning new concepts or facts (the acquisition component) because of their difficulty in processing. Although Sternberg did not explore his theory in relation to dyslexia/literacy difficulties, it is clear that processes such as phonological awareness, working memory and speed of processing are involved in cognitive tasks and any (or all) of these may impact on learning *and*, indeed, may affect performance on tests of 'underlying ability' (particularly tests of verbal ability). It is important, therefore, to include the assessment of cognitive processing skills in any diagnostic assessment. Many diagnostic assessment reports may not require (and do not contain) the use of tests of underlying ability/intelligence, preferring to rely on cognitive processing.

Sternberg, among others, argued that most tests of ability (or, at the time intelligence) primarily tap 'academic intelligence' thereby ignoring the 'practical' intelligence required to adapt flexibly in everyday life. Gardner (1983) argued that there are multiple intelligences, identifying six (and later nine) intelligences, suggesting that they operate independently. Three of these (linguistic, logico-mathematical and spatial) are measured by established tests of general ability but musical, bodily-kinaesthetic and personal-social are not, although he considers them of equal value in society. Many critics of 'intelligence'/ability-testing note that Western society places a higher 'value' on 'cognitive intelligence' tests and also on 'speed' of response. However, whereas ability tests *tend* to be reasonably good predictors of educational attainment (as indicated earlier, this is what they were originally designed to do) they are less valid in predicting job-success/career progression where other factors may play a more important role.

A comprehensive account of the development of tests of 'intelligence' (underlying cognitive ability) may be found in the manuals of both the Wide Range Intelligence Test (WRIT) and Raven's Progressive Matrices. What has been generally agreed, however, is that there are two important aspects of abilities to reason and problem solve: verbal and non-verbal. In carrying out and reporting assessments, we prefer to use the term 'underlying ability' or 'abilities' and point out that these should be seen as only *two* aspects of the behaviours contributing to learning, although they may contribute important information about these areas. The term 'underlying ability' is also recommended by Backhouse and Morris (2008) offering guidance on reporting on assessment for diagnosing dyslexia.

'Ability' and Dyslexia

For many years, dyslexia was associated with a discrepancy between general underlying ability (or intelligence) and literacy attainment (particularly measured by reading [decoding] attainments). This was based on the assumption referred to earlier, that a test of intelligence would show that a learner was 'capable' of learning, yet not achieving at that level in their acquisition of literacy. (It was sometimes also argued that a discrepancy between non-verbal reasoning ability and verbal reasoning ability could reflect the 'reason' for this.) The 'discrepancy' theory has not been held for some time (although some schools and LAs find it very attractive as an 'administrative' criterion). A discrepancy between verbal and/or non-verbal ability scores is not sufficient 'evidence' of dyslexia, although these variations can be a useful part of a profile. A very low score (2 SDs or a Standard Score below 80) in either (or both) and low attainments may suggest the need to refer to an educational psychologist. Although not all assessments *require* a test of underlying ability it may be appropriate to carry out an assessment. It is also useful, in terms of verbal ability, to distinguish between expressive and receptive verbal ability, particularly as measured in vocabulary tests (such as BPVS-III described below).

Tests of underlying ability which teachers can use

The WRIT, although an American standardised test, is widely used in the UK by specialist teachers. It includes four sub-tests of ability (two non-verbal and two verbal), as described in Table 16.1. WRIT uses the terms 'fluid' (non-verbal) and 'crystallised' (verbal) intelligence, following Cattell's definitions described earlier in this chapter. Crystallised intelligence is the product of experiences (cultural and educational) in *interaction* with fluid intelligence, and the manual provides a good overview of this theory and rationale for development and nature of test items. The test is popular with teachers because the two sub-tests of fluid/visuo-spatial abilities offer two differing approaches to non-verbal assessment:

- **Matrices** – where the testee has to reason which item correlates/completes a pattern of varying complexity; and
- **'Diamonds'** – where the testee has to manipulate diamond-shaped tiles to copy a pattern.

These tests do not require a testee to speak or write. The use of colour and the two forms of assessment give variety and interest to the testing procedure and most learners of both primary and secondary age enjoy them. Both tests are timed. The assessor observes closely as well as recording, as test behaviours yield insights into a learner's strategies. The 'Diamonds' sub-test, because it requires fine motor co-ordination skills, may not be an appropriate measure for some learners who have co-ordination difficulties. In some cases, however, problems in manipulation/handling the tiles (whilst not being used to score as a valid test of visuo-spatial ability) may suggest the need for referral to another professional (e.g. an occupational therapist) for assessment, where other evidence (e.g. from handwriting, design technology etc.) corroborates a possible specific difficulty such as Development Co-ordination Disorder (dyspraxia). The verbal subtests require the ability to deduce relationships and form correlates (which Spearman considered a major aspect of underlying ability).

Raven's Progressive Matrices and Vocabulary Scales (RPM-VS) test, on the other hand, as can be seen in Tables 16.2 and 16.3, are standardised on a British sample and have more recent norms than WRIT. They comprise a non-verbal matrices test (which in the standard edition is in black/white only) and an expressive vocabulary test (e.g. the Mill Hill Test). The Matrices test draws heavily on Spearman's theory of a 'general underlying intelligence'/ability 'g' and the manual claims that the test is a very valid and reliable test of 'g'. It is possible to use the Matrices test without the Vocabulary test if another test of verbal ability is selected, just as it is possible to use the WRIT fluid/non-verbal test alone. However, it must be remembered that 'overall', composite scores are only valid when used with their respective verbal tests. The Mill Hill Test assesses the ability to define certain words, as does the Vocabulary sub-test of WRIT. As such, it clearly reflects understanding of words and also a learner's experiences to date. To that extent, it also assesses 'verbal knowledge'. However, it does not assess the use of verbal analogies, which could tap into different aspects – one of classification and reasoning.

Concerns have been raised about some of the vocabulary in WRIT (e.g. 'gasoline' in the Vocabulary Test, and the vocabulary and knowledge required in the Verbal Analogies Test, e.g. 'termites' and 'beavers'). The publishers have authorised 'Anglicisation' of some items and these can be obtained from Patoss (see the Patoss website). Similarly, some assessors are concerned that learners with visual stress or tracking difficulties have problems using the new response sheets for Raven's Matrices, although at the time of writing, teachers have not reported this to us.

Another test of matrices is the Naglieri Nonverbal Ability Test (NNAT) (Naglieri, 2003), which is an American test of non-verbal reasoning. More recently (2007), a second edition of a group administered test (NNAT-2) has been published and an on-line version became available in 2008. The author claims that this is particularly useful for children with EAL and from different cultures. We know of some schools and local authorities who have made use of it because of that claim and also because at the time of its publication in England, the alternative (Raven's Matrices) had old norms. However, it seems not to be in common use now in the UK. Some users have found both it and Raven's were not reliable for use with learners from linguistically and ethnically diverse backgrounds, and under-identified those who might be 'gifted' (Lohman et al., 2008). However, that study used the older forms of Raven's and Naglieri. They also pointed out that NNAT has a higher SEM than Raven's, which affects reliability of scoring.

Table 16.1   Wide Range Intelligence Test (WRIT)

Name of Test:			
Wide Range Intelligence Test (WRIT)			

Author:	Publisher:	Age Range:	Date of Norms:
Glutting, J., Adams, W. and Sheslow, D.	Wide Range Inc. /Psychological Assessment Resources (2000)	4–85 years	2000

Standardisation Sample:

2,285 across the USA

Purpose/Function:

It assesses verbal (or crystallised) intelligence and visual (or fluid) intelligence and also gives a score for general intelligence.

Test Description

It consists of four subtests, two for verbal and two for visual, and begins with a non-verbal subtest (Matrices). The subtests alternate from visual to verbal.

Administration time:	Reliability:	Validity:	How scores are reported:	Confidence intervals:
30 minutes or less	Split half: above 0.9	Verbal and visual correlation: 0.75	Standardised scores	90%
	Test–retest: 0.7+	Correlation with WISC III: 0.9+	Percentiles	95%
	Inter-scorer: 0.98-0.99			

Subtest Information:

- Matrices (visual) – learner selects a picture or pattern from several alternatives in order to complete an implied visual perceptual relationship

- Verbal Analogies – the learner is asked to provide a word that best completes a verbally presented analogy such as 'Cat is to kitten as dog is to ….'

- Diamonds (visual) – the learner is asked to reproduce a two- and three-dimensional pattern using tiles shaped as single or multiple diamonds

- Vocabulary – the learner is required to define an orally presented word

Comments:

The verbal sub-tests assess both receptive and expressive vocabulary, and differences between these may be particularly useful in building a profile of a learner. The Diamonds sub-test is timed which can disadvantage learners with DCD (dyspraxia) or other motor difficulties. In some cases this can be seen in a discrepancy between the Diamonds sub-test score and that for the Matrices.

Table 16.2   Standard Progressive Matrices Plus Version (SMP+)

Name of Test:			
Standard Progressive Matrices Plus Version (SMP+)			
Author: Raven, J.	**Publisher:** Pearson, 2008	**Age Range:** 7–18 years	**Date of Norms:** 2008
Standardisation Sample: UK			
926 aged 7 – 18y 11m. The sample was demographically representative of the UK population. All were fluent English speakers.			
Purpose/Function:			
A non-verbal measure of general ability which can be administered to a group or on an individual basis, providing 'a fairer measure of ability for children from diverse populations with different language and cultural backgrounds'. Sometimes used to determine potential for achievement. In combination with the Mill Hill Vocabulary Scale (MHV) it can be used to measure the difference between verbal and non-verbal aspects of general ability.			
Test Description:			
Comprises a set of 'diagrammatic puzzles exhibiting serial change in two dimensions simultaneously', presented as five sets of 12 problems. Each set starts with easy items and increases in difficulty so the examinee should be encouraged to attempt all five sets.			

Administration time:	Reliability:	Validity:	How scores are reported:	Confidence intervals:
45 minutes (approx)	Split-half 0.936 N = 924 Test–retest 0.833 N = 105	Concurrent validity with SPM –C is 0.797 N = 109	Standard scores Percentiles Age equivalents	85.6% 94.2% 99.8%

Comments:
The test is easy to administer and score. Information is given for administration to both groups and individuals. The test instructions are scripted and include information about guessing. Scoring is done using an acetate sheet placed over the examinee's record form. The assessor should note that confidence intervals are calculated using raw scores rather than standard scores and then converted to standard scores. **Note:** Standard Progressive Matrices Plus (SMP+) and Mill Hill Vocabulary Scale (MHV) were designed to be used together as a screening measure for general ability although they can each be used independently.

Verbal ability is also assessed by a test of receptive vocabulary. The British Picture Vocabulary Scale test, now in its third edition (BPVS-3) (see Table 16.4) is commonly used to discover learners' understanding of words. It is useful because it makes no

Table 16.3 Mill Hill Vocabulary Scale (MHV)

Name of Test:			
Mill Hill Vocabulary Scale (MHV)			
Author: Raven, J.	**Publisher:** Pearson, 2008	**Age Range:** 7–18 years	**Date of Norms:** 2008

Standardisation Sample: UK

926 aged 7 – 18y 11m. The sample was demographically representative of the UK population. All were fluent English speakers. This was the sample used for standardizing Raven's SPM+.

Purpose/Function:

A verbal measure of general ability that can be administered to a group or on an individual basis. It assesses verbal skills 'involving familiarity with a culture's store of explicit, largely verbal, information'.

Test Description:

It contains a list of words that examinees are asked to define. There are 88 words arranged in two sets, one set requiring a written description of words and the other based on multiple choice of word definition. There are two forms: Form 1, set 1, requires open-ended definitions and set 2 is multiple choice. In Form 2 this order is reversed.

Administration time:	Reliability:	Validity:	How scores are reported:	Confidence intervals:
35 minutes (approx)	Test–retest 0.916 N = 177	Construct 0.63 with verbal ability and 0.69 with general ability (1990)	Standard scores Percentiles Age equivalents	80.7% 94.1% 99.5%

Comments:

The test is easy to administer and score. Information is given for administration to both groups and individuals. The test instructions are scripted and include information about guessing. The manual contains the answers and full details for scoring. The assessor should note that confidence intervals are calculated using raw scores rather than standard scores and then converted to standard scores.

Note: Mill Hill Vocabulary Scale (MHV) and Standard Progressive Matrices Plus (SMP+) were designed to be used together as a screening measure for general ability although they can each be used independently. As some reading and writing is required for this test, care should be taken in deciding its appropriateness for the learner to be assessed.

demands on a learner's spoken language and the new edition uses colour, which makes it attractive to testees. Its standardisation sample included learners with EAL. The test is often used to indicate what a learner can understand in school (e.g. when a teacher is talking) as it is an indicator of how much vocabulary they have learned. Such an assumption may not be useful – it can only compare with what peers in the standardisation sample have acquired in relation to these words. We suggest that tests of **both** expressive and receptive vocabulary be given as they may provide differing results. It is often useful to compare results on a test of receptive vocabulary with those from an expressive vocabulary test. These results can also be compared with reading/listening comprehension and with the vocabulary used in written work. A comparison can also be made with the difference between vocabulary used when describing an event orally or in discussion and their written vocabulary. This blend of formal and informal assessment is useful in drawing up a profile and making links between varying aspects of performance.

As noted earlier, verbal (crystallised) ability will reflect cultural and educational experiences. It also places demands on memory and retrieval. Both verbal and non-verbal tests make demands on cognitive processing skills and point to the need for assessment of these skills, as discussed in the next chapter.

Although a general or composite score for underlying ability is more reliable and valid than any sub-test score, it is important, in the case of underlying ability, to look at the separate scores for verbal and non-verbal ability. This is *not* to use a discrepancy between the two to imply dyslexia, but it may suggest a need for:

- further investigation, e.g. verbal/language processing/speed of processing/visual perception;
- different approaches to be used in teaching, e.g. a need to develop vocabulary through experiential learning; greater/less use of diagrams/visual approaches;
- ensuring strengths are built on and extended;
- different approaches to recording work where good verbal ability is not represented in written work because of handwriting and/or spelling difficulties;
- greater use of teaching using manipulative skills/spatial abilities;
- different profiles and abilities in different areas of the curriculum may be reflected in underlying ability scores.

These need to be taken into account particularly when dyslexia is identified as a result of the *total* assessment process and is considered so severe that a recommendation is made for 1:1 specialist teaching. This provision is normally on a withdrawal basis and therefore should take into account the areas where strengths in underlying abilities may be supporting high achievement. There should be minimal disruption to those lessons. The frequency of withdrawal and the length of time over which withdrawal is used should also be considered where possible.

Issues of Cultural and Linguistic Diversity

The concept of intelligence, and in particular the use of 'intelligence testing', is one of the most contentious issues in education. Much research in the USA from 1960 to the 1980s showed that African-American children score significantly below white children.

Table 16.4   The British Picture Vocabulary Scale, Third Edition (BPVS-3)

Name of Test:			
The British Picture Vocabulary Scale, Third Edition (BPVS-3)			
Author: Dunn, L.M. and Dunn, D.M. et al.	**Publisher:** GL Assessment, 2009	**Age Range:** 3 – 16y 11m	**Date of Norms:** 2009

Standardisation Sample:

3,278 between 3 and 16 years in eight age ranges across England, Wales, Scotland and Northern Ireland

Purpose/Function:

Designed to measure receptive (hearing vocabulary) for standard English. An achievement test since it shows the extent of English vocabulary acquisition. It can be used as indicator of 'verbal ability or verbal intelligence' or as one element in the assessment of cognitive processes but only when English is:

- the language of the home and community, and

- is/has been the primary language used at school.

Test Description:

A multiple choice test comprising 14 sets of 12 test items. Each item in the test consists of four colour illustrations on a page. The task is to select the picture that best illustrates the meaning of a given word spoken by the assessor. It requires no reading or written or verbal responses.

Administration time:	Reliability:	Validity:	How scores are reported:	Confidence Intervals:
Untimed (normally about 10 minutes)	Built into the confidence bands	Construct validity: correlated with CATS verbal battery 0.72 with overall CATS scores 0.61	Standard scores Percentiles Age equivalent	95%

Comments:

It is easy to use although practice is needed with the plates. It is based on the American Peabody Picture Vocabulary Test (PPVT) which has been found to predict reading comprehension. It is often used as a predictive measure of language skill. However, caution should be exercised in using it for this purpose or in making inferences about general ability, and this is made clear in the manual.

This 'fact' was, at times, used to reinforce a belief that intelligence is 'innate' and largely genetic in determination. This often fuelled a debate about 'institutional racism'. However, distributions of scores overlap and many African-Americans score much higher than white children. Further, consideration of the nature of intelligence test items and performance reveals the importance of the social and educational backgrounds of children and the relationship between *how* intelligence is measured and a child's own culture. What is relevant to and important in one culture may not be in another. Anthropological studies showed that tasks such as categorising objects differ in different societies, as does the value put on 'speed'. In some societies 'the wise are *slow* to respond'.

It is now generally accepted that all tests will show a culture-bias despite efforts to devise those which are 'culture-fair'. This is particularly true of verbal comprehension questions. Peer and Reid (2001) point out that when asking a child 'What do you do if you find a purse lying on the pavement?', the expected 'correct' answer of 'Pick it up and hand it to the police' might *not* be the response of a child in a country/city where it might contain an explosive device. (Yet knowing this could be the case indicates an ability to adapt to their environment – one aspect of underlying ability!)

Non-verbal items, such as contained in Matrices (e.g. Raven's Standard Matrices, WRIT's Matrices and Copying Patterns – Diamonds, Cattell's Culture Fair Test) are often seen as more culture-fair in that they present all testees with an unfamiliar situation and are less dependent on a learner's experiences. However, they are open to the criticism that children who are familiar with jigsaw puzzles and looking at abstract patterns, including geometric diagrams, will be at an advantage over those who are not. When testing is conducted with very young children, their early experiences may put some of them at an advantage over others, e.g. where children have attended nursery education and initiatives such as Sure Start.

Tests of verbal ability (both expressive and receptive) are highly dependent on a learner's language proficiency and experiences relating to vocabulary. There may well be great differences between the vocabulary used/spoken by a child and their understanding of those words. They may appear to use a word correctly in context yet not be able to define it. A verbal test seeking definitions is a useful indication of this but it does not necessarily imply a poor underlying ability. As noted earlier in the book, children for whom English is an Additional Language may 'underperform' on tests of verbal ability, particularly at an early stage of English acquisition.

When tests of underlying ability are administered to learners from different ethnic and language backgrounds and to children from white socially disadvantaged groups, caution should be exercised in relying too much on *scores*. These must be seen in the light of observations and performance in other forms of assessment – both formal and informal. It is important to note the composition of the standardisation sample and date of standardisation to ensure that learners similar to the testee were included. In addition, the test manual may show an analysis of results from sub-groups and there may be information with which a 'better' comparison can be made than with the whole group.

Assessment using tests of underlying ability should still be undertaken as they can provide useful information about test behaviours, strengths and weaknesses. They will point to areas for the standardised assessment of underlying processes and also identify areas requiring more detailed analysis of behaviours based on informal diagnostic testing. However, caution should be exercised in interpreting scores.

Summary

This chapter discussed some of the ways in which underlying cognitive ability may be assessed. It provided an overview of the development of models of 'intelligence' as the basis of approaches used to measure underlying ability in relation to educational attainment with particular reference to the diagnosis of dyslexia. Attention was drawn to some of the tests most commonly used for this purpose. However, although measures of underlying ability are still seen as an important part of full diagnostic assessment, their contribution must be seen in the light of all the information from other tests and observations. A preferred approach is to consider the underlying verbal and non-verbal abilities as just *two* aspects of underlying abilities/ skills, contributing to the overall profile of learning.

Points for Discussion

- Discuss with colleagues some of the ways in which ability tests can be used and misused.
- If we no longer accept a 'discrepancy' definition of dyslexia (i.e. difference between underlying ability and reading/spelling attainment), discuss whether you consider there is any need to assess underlying ability.

Further Reading

Good accounts of the concepts of ability and intelligence can be found in the manuals for Wide Range Intelligence Test (WRIT) and Raven's Progressive Matrices. Many general texts on psychology also contain accounts.

Nolen-Hoeksema, S., Fredrickson, B.L., Loftus, G.R. and Wagenaar, W.A. (2009) *Atkinson and Hilgard's Introduction to Psychology*, 15th edn. Andover: Wadsworth Cengage.

References

Backhouse, G. and Morris, K. (2008) *Dyslexia: Assessing and Reporting: The Patoss Guide.* London: Patoss.

Cattell, R.B. (1971) *Abilities: Their Structure, Growth, and Action.* Boston, MA: Houghton Mifflin.

Elliot, C.D. (1986) 'The factorial structure and specificity of the British Ability Scales', *British Journal of Psychology*, 77: 175–85.

Gardner, H. (1983) *Frames of Mind: The Theory of Multiple Intelligences*. New York: Basic Books.

Kelly, K. and Phillips, S. (2011) *Teaching Literacy to Learners with Dyslexia: A Multi-sensory Approach*. London: SAGE.

Lohman, D.F., Korb, K.A. and Lakin, J.M. (2008) Identifying academically gifted English-language learners using non-verbal tests: A comparison of the Raven, NNAT and CogAT, *Gifted Child Quarterly, 52*: 275–96.

Naglieri, J.A. (2003) *Naglieri Nonverbal Ability Test*. London: Pearson.

Peer, L. and Reid, G. (eds) (2001) *Dyslexia: Successful Inclusion in the Secondary School*. London: David Fulton Publishers.

Sternberg, R.J. (1985) *Beyond IQ: A Triarchic Theory of Intelligence*. Cambridge: Cambridge University Press.

Wechsler, D. (1949) *Manual for the Wechsler Intelligence Scale for Children*. New York: The Psychological Corporation.

CHAPTER 17

STANDARDISED ASSESSMENT OF COGNITIVE PROCESSING SKILLS

Chapter Overview

This chapter will enable the reader to:

- have an awareness of standardised tests that can be used to assess cognitive processing skills;
- appreciate the issues raised by these standardised tests.

The same aspects of cognitive processing that were discussed in Chapter 10 can be assessed using standardised tests. It could be argued that some aspects can be better assessed by standardised tests (particularly speed of processing, short-term and working memory) as there is a norm with which to compare performance.

Phonological Processing

As stated in Chapter 10, poor phonological processing is often considered a major contributor to literacy difficulties. Whereas informal approaches can give useful indicators of specific areas of weakness in phonological processing, a standardised test enables a teacher to discover if there is a deficit or not compared to a 'typical' learner and indicates severity. However, there are only a relatively small number of published tests. The three most common tests are the Comprehensive Test of Phonological Processing (CTOPP) for ages 5–24 (Wagner et al., 1999 although since writing, a second edition has been published,2013), the Test of Auditory Processing Skills (TAPS-3) for ages 4–18 (Gardner, 2005) and Phonological Assessment Battery (PhAB) for ages 6–14 (Frederickson et al., 1997). The first two have American standardisations. The latter was developed in the UK but standardisation samples were smaller and the norms would now be considered to be dated.

One of the considerations in choosing a test is that it should include a range of sub-skills so that qualitative information is also yielded, which will form the basis of any necessary intervention. It is important to note that a task to assess phonological processing may require the use of other processing skills. For example, tests of phoneme manipulation (as in 'say frog without the /r/' or 'say pat backwards') rely on working memory as well as phonological awareness. This relationship is acknowledged both in theories of phonological deficit and in the development of standardised tests, which often include subtests that assess more than one of the three aspects of phonological processing (phonological awareness, phonological memory and rapid naming).

As its title suggests, CTOPP is a comprehensive test that contains a number of subtests which can be combined to give composite scores for Phonological Awareness, Phonological Memory and Rapid Naming (see Table 17.1). The test is quick to administer and the range of sub-tests keeps learners engaged, but some children find the American accent on the CD-Rom off-putting.

CTOPP has a good range of sub-tests of phonological awareness, including segmenting and phoneme reversal, but does not include a test of rhyming or auditory discrimination. A Rhyme Test is included in PhAB (1997) and a test of auditory discrimination (word discrimination) is included in TAPS-3 (2005), e.g. 'Are the words the same word or different words … compute [pause] commute?' TAPS-3 includes nine sub-tests presented in order of level of difficulty and one optional sub-test of auditory figure-ground presented on CD. Gardner (2005) suggests that this sub-test may be

Table 17.1   Comprehensive Test of Phonological Processing (CTOPP)

Name of Test:

Comprehensive Test of Phonological Processing (CTOPP)

[NB. A second edition (CTOPP-2) has been published 2013. The data here refers to the first edition.

Author:	Publisher:	Age Range:	Date of Norms:
Wagner, R.K., Torgesen, J.K. and Rashotte, C.A.	Pro-Ed, Austin, TX (1999)	5–24	1997–98

Standardisation Sample: 1,656 people in 30 states

Purpose/Function: Assesses phonological awareness, phonological memory and rapid naming

Test Description:

There are two versions, the first for 5–6-year-olds and the second version for 7–24-year-olds. There are 13 subtests split into core and supplemental. A supplemental subtest allows the examiner to assess and obtain more detail about phonological strengths and weaknesses.

Administration time:	Reliability:	Validity:	How scores are reported:	Confidence Intervals:
Individual 30 minutes	Internal consistency 0.7–0.9	Criterion prediction for reading 0.4–0.8	Percentiles Standard scores Composite scores	Not quoted

Subtest Information:

V1 = 5–6-year-olds, V2 = 7–24-year-olds

- Elision – measures the extent to which an individual can say a word and then say what is left after dropping out designated sounds (V1 & V2)
- Blending Words – measures ability to combine sounds to form words (V1 & V2)
- Sound Matching – measures the extent to which an individual can match sounds (V1)
- Memory for Digits – measures the extent to which an individual can repeat a series of numbers ranging in length from two to eight digits (V1 &V2)
- Non-word Repetition – measures ability to repeat non-words that range in length from 3 to 15 sounds (V1 & V2)
- Rapid Colour Naming – measures speed with which an individual can name the colours of a series of different-coloured blocks printed on a page (core V1, supplemental V2)
- Rapid Object Naming – measures speed with which an individual can name a series of objects printed on a page (core V1, supplementary V2)
- Rapid Digit Naming – measures speed with which an individual can name numbers printed on a page (V2)
- Rapid Letter Naming – measures speed with which an individual can name letters printed on a page (V2)
- Blending Non-words – measures ability to combine speech sounds to make words (supplemental V1 & V2)
- Segmenting Words – measures ability to say separate phonemes that make a word (supplemental V2)
- Segmental Non-words – measures ability to say separate phonemes that make a non-word (supplemental V2)
- Phoneme reversal – measures the extent to which an individual can reorder speech sounds in non-words to make a real word (supplemental V2)

Comments:

Record sheets give full instructions for administering subtests. The subtests can be combined to give composite scores for phonological awareness, phonological memory and rapid naming. However, CTOPP does not assess working memory. A CD-Rom is provided and is essential for some subtests (American pronunciation).

used to assess whether the learner 'has sufficient attentional and hearing capability' to undertake the other sub-tests. The nine main subtests are: Phonological Segmentation, Phonological Blending, Number Memory Forward (like Digit Span in CTOPP), Number Memory Reversed (i.e. a test of working memory), Word Memory (retaining and manipulating sequences), Sentence Memory (where sentences increase in length and complexity), Auditory Comprehension and Auditory Reasoning. The final two sub-tests provide useful information about language comprehension. The test of Auditory Reasoning assesses understanding including the use of inferences and ability to make logical conclusions which are higher order processing skills. However, as in any test of listening comprehension, short-term memory is an important factor. This aspect concerning language structure and meanings of words is not included in either CTOPP or PhAB.

PhAB (1997) contains three tests of phonological awareness (Alliteration, Rhyme Test and Spoonerism Test), fluency tests (two assess retrieval of phonological information from long-term memory, and one assesses semantic fluency), naming speed (pictures and digits) and a non-word reading test. It is unusual to include non-word reading in a test of phonological processing but this shows an application of phonological skills to the reading process (although it is normally seen as a test of decoding rather than phonological processing). Two of the sub-tests identified here (i.e. non-word reading and rapid naming) are found in many screening tests, as described in Chapter 13.

Working Memory

The most common test for assessing working memory is digit span reversed order. This is included in TAPS-3 (number memory reversed). Some dyslexia screeners, however, include the digit span reversed as a sub-test, e.g. Dyslexia Portfolio (Turner, 2008), Dyslexia Screening Test (DST-J and DST-S) (Fawcett and Nicolson, 2004a; Fawcett and Nicolson, 2004b). Visual memory is less frequently included in assessing learners' difficulties, perhaps because it has often been seen as an area of strength. However, a test of visual memory can be found in Lucid COPS (Singleton, 1996), LASS 8–11 (Thomas et al., 2001) and LASS 11–15 (Horne et al., 1999), and because the learner has to manipulate the mouse to drag the correct object to its correct position some may consider it a test of working memory. The Automated Working Memory Assessment (Packiam-Alloway, 2007) for ages 4–22 is also a computerised assessment that contains 12 sub-tests assessing a range of working memory skills including auditory and visual memory. An on-line version is now available for 5- to 79-year-olds. These give a more comprehensive assessment of working memory than just a digit span test but at an additional cost. They should not be confused with the Working Memory Rating Scale (Packiam-Alloway et al., 2008), which is an observation checklist of behavioural characteristics.

Speed (

As mentioned in Chapter 10, Rapid Naming is the most common test of speed of proc... ing although it also affects rate of reading and writing speed (see Chapters 16 and 17 for appropriate tests of speed). Rapid Naming is recognised in dyslexia research as a significant factor. Snowling (2000) proposes that poor rapid naming is characteristic of dyslexia and one aspect of a phonological deficit, whereas Nicolson and Fawcett (2008) attribute problems in speed of retrieval of information (including rapid naming) more to automaticity deficit. Some screening tests (Dyslexia Portfolio, DEST-2, DST-J and DST-S) include rapid object naming and in addition DEST-2 (Nicolson and Fawcett, 2003) for 4- to 6-year-olds includes rapid naming of letters and numbers. Rapid naming tests can also be found in CTOPP, which tests rapid colour naming and object naming for 5- to 6-year-olds, whereas for 7- to 24-year-olds it uses rapid digit naming and letter naming, although rapid object naming and colour naming can be given as a supplement. PhAB has a naming speed test that includes Object Naming and Digit Naming. One of the differences between object naming in PhAB and CTOPP is that CTOPP uses colour and PhAB uses black and white. There is also a difference in the way that Rapid Digit naming is presented. In CTOPP, digits are well spaced following a similar format to rapid object naming whereas in PhAB the learner is asked to name a row of 50 digits split into groups of five with a very small space between each. It may be more difficult for a learner to keep their place in the PhAB Digit Naming Test and numbers may accidentally be repeated or omitted.

A difficulty in naming speed may offer an explanation for slow rate of reading and lack of fluency due to slow or inaccurate labelling of letters, which results in poor decoding and encoding skills (in reading and spelling). Lack of automaticity in retrieval of letter names, sounds and shapes can lead to increased error in activities that involve multi-tasking, such as writing a story or assignment. Where spelling is not automatic then the effort taken to retrieve the required information can affect the ability to concentrate on content, letter formation, punctuation and grammar. Lack of automaticity can also affect tasks such as copying from a book or the board as the learner has to identify a word or combination of letters, a series of numbers or shapes, and then hold them in working memory long enough to reproduce them. Poor labelling reduces the number of items that can be held in working memory, requiring the learner to refer to the source more frequently thereby slowing down the process and potentially leading to more errors.

Slow processing speed can also offer an explanation for sequential or temporal order processing difficulties. When spoken information is given at a rate that is too fast for the learner to process, then the order in which they have heard the sounds may become confused (because they are still processing one item when another is received) or some sounds may be omitted (because they are still processing an earlier item when another one is offered). Slow processing speed provides an alternative explanation of the transposition of letters or omission of letters in words in spelling or repetition of a word to those offered by working memory or phono-logical awareness difficulties. Temporal processing can be assessed in young children using the 'Sound Order' subtest of DEST-2 which asks the learner to decide which sound (of two) they hear first. The gap between the two sounds is gradually reduced, requiring the child to process rapidly to determine the order. This type of test is not included in screeners for older learners. However, tests of phonemic awareness such as sound blending (found in most dyslexia screeners and tests of phonological processing) assess the ability to order sounds (although not rapid processing).

Visual Stress/Scotopic Sensitivity

Stein (2008) continued to draw attention to visual processing difficulties in relation to the magnocellular theory of causation of dyslexia. The behavioural characteristics of visual processing difficulties might be that print appears to move around on the page, headaches, sensitivity to bright light, difficulty scanning text for specific information, omitting letters or words when reading, spelling or copying, and depth perception. Some of these presenting characteristics may have been observed by a teacher and may have been reported by a learner when describing the reading process. Whilst these characteristics may indicate other problems, difficulties in visual processing should nevertheless be considered. Teachers who have undertaken a specific training course such as the Irlen Screening would be provided with a pack of assessment materials which would enable them to carry out assessment for coloured overlays but they would still need to refer on to an ophthalmologist for further assessment for coloured lenses. Alternatively there are published materials that do not require specific training. Lucid Visual Stress Screener (ViSS) for ages 7 to adult assesses 'Meares–Irlen Syndrome' through a computerised assessment in the form of a Wordsearch game which takes 20–30 minutes. The ViSS manual gives guidance on appropriate action after screening, which might include referral to an optician or eye specialist. The Visual Stress Assessment Pack is a paper-based form of assessment that allows teachers to screen for coloured overlays, although it not as detailed or as long established as the Irlen Screening.

Issues of Cultural and Linguistic Diversity

Issues of standardisation of the sample must be considered, as noted in Chapters 12 and 13. The PhAB manual includes reference to a special study of 50 Bengali/Sylheti speakers aged between 10 and 12 years, who were fluent English speakers and had been educated in England since the age of 5. They are reported separately and included in the test norms. Clearly this is somewhat limited in range but at least shows that there was a consideration of whether or not the test could be used with children who had been at an English primary school for at least five years and had EAL. In the American tests cited in this chapter the sample included individuals from a range of multiethnic and linguistic backgrounds and the proportion is fairly representative of the American school population but is less representative of the UK school population. It also has to be borne in mind that the statistics about ethnicity represent different groups from those in England.

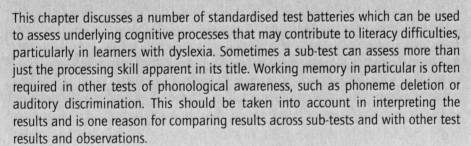

Summary

This chapter discusses a number of standardised test batteries which can be used to assess underlying cognitive processes that may contribute to literacy difficulties, particularly in learners with dyslexia. Sometimes a sub-test can assess more than just the processing skill apparent in its title. Working memory in particular is often required in other tests of phonological awareness, such as phoneme deletion or auditory discrimination. This should be taken into account in interpreting the results and is one reason for comparing results across sub-tests and with other test results and observations.

Points for Discussion

- Consider three sub-tests and discuss the extent to which they assess more than one area of cognitive processing.
- Discuss what seem to you to be issues of cultural and linguistic diversity in the tests outlined in this chapter.

Follow-up Activity

Research the extent to which tests of phonological awareness are good discriminators in older learners (i.e. secondary age and adults) using journals and/or tables from test manuals.

Further Reading

Nicolson, R.I. and Fawcett, A.J. (2008) 'Learning, cognition and dyslexia', in G. Reid, A. Fawcett, F. Manis and L. Siegel (eds), *The SAGE Handbook of Dyslexia*. London: SAGE. pp. 192–211.
This chapter discusses research into automaticity deficits and the implications for speed of processing.
Wilkins, A., Huang, J. and Cao, Y. (2004) 'Visual stress theory and its application to reading and reading tests', *Journal of Research in Reading*, 27: 152–62.
This paper considers the implication of the theory of visual stress for the testing of reading and suggests that more attention needs to be paid to visual stress when designing reading tests.

References

Fawcett, A.J. and Nicolson, R.I. (2004a) *The Dyslexia Screening Test-Junior (DST-J)*. London: Harcourt Assessment.
Fawcett, A.J. and Nicolson, R.I. (2004b) *The Dyslexia Screening Test-Secondary (DST-S)*. London: Harcourt Assessment.
Frederickson, N., Frith, U. and Reason, R. (1997) *Phonological Assessment Battery*. Windsor: NFER–Nelson.
Gardner, M. (2005) *Test of Auditory Processing Skills-3*. Ann Arbor, MI: Academic Therapy Publications.
Horne, J.K., Singleton, C.H. and Thomas, K.V. (1999) *Lucid Assessment System for Schools for 11 to 15 year olds*. Beverley: Lucid Creative Ltd.
Nicolson, R.I. and Fawcett, A.J. (2003) *The Dyslexia Early Screening Test – Second Ed. (DEST-2)*. London: Harcourt Assessment.
Nicolson, R.I. and Fawcett, A.J. (2008) 'Learning, cognition and dyslexia', in G. Reid, A.J. Fawcett, F. Manis and L.S. Seigel (eds), *The SAGE Handbook of Dyslexia*. London: SAGE. pp. 192–211.
Packiam-Alloway, T. (2007) *The Automated Working Memory Assessment (AWMA)*. London: Pearson.
Packiam-Alloway, T., Gathercole, S. and Kirkwood, H. (2008) *The Working Memory Rating Scale*. London: Pearson.
Singleton, C.H. (1996) *COPs – Cognitive Profiling System*. Beverley: Lucid Research Ltd.
Snowling, M.J. (2000) *Dyslexia*, 2nd edn. Chichester: Wiley–Blackwell.
Stein, J. (2008) 'The neurobiological basis of dyslexia', in G. Reid, A. Fawcett, F. Manis and L. Siegal (eds), *The SAGE Handbook of Dyslexia*. London: SAGE. pp. 53–77.
Thomas, K.V., Horne, J.K. and Singleton, C. H. (2001) *Lucid Assessment System for Schools for 8 to 11 year olds*. Beverley: Lucid Creative Ltd.
Turner, M. (2008) *Dyslexia Portfolio*. London: GL Assessment.
Wagner, R.K., Torgesen, J.K. and Rashotte, C.A. (1999) *Comprehensive Test of Phonological Processing*. Austin, TX: Pro-ed.

CHAPTER 18

IDENTIFYING SPECIFIC LEARNING DIFFICULTIES IN MATHEMATICS, INCLUDING DYSCALCULIA

Chapter Overview

This chapter will enable the reader to:

- consider some of the problems and issues in identifying dyscalculia;
- understand the ways in which standardised mathematics tests can be used.

The term 'dyscalculia' is used to describe specific difficulties with mathematics:

> Dyscalculia is a condition that affects the ability to acquire arithmetical skills. Dyscalculic learners may have difficulty understanding simple number concepts, lack an intuitive grasp of numbers, and have problems learning number facts and procedures. Even if they produce a correct answer or use a correct method, they may do so mechanically and without confidence. (DfES, 2001)

Discrepancy theory is often applied to dyscalculia and the difficulty is not seen as being due to low general cognitive ability or lack of appropriate educational experiences but rather due to 'distinct difficulties in mastering the basics of mathematical thinking' (Hannell, 2005: 2). Butterworth and Yeo (2004) point out that there are probably as many learners with severe difficulty in learning about numbers and arithmetic procedures (dyscalculia) as there are with literacy difficulties such as dyslexia. They note prevalence estimates of between 3.6% and 6.5% and suggest that poor numeracy skills may present more problems in the workplace than poor literacy skills. They also argue that there are many reasons for having difficulties in mathematics, including 'inappropriate teaching, behavioural problems, anxiety and missing lessons' which makes 'identifying a specific condition difficult' (Butterworth and Yeo, 2004: 1). As there are many reasons why a learner may underachieve in a specific area of mathematics the use of a standardised test alone is not sufficient to identify dyscalculia. The results should be followed up by further diagnostic assessment, observation and appropriate questioning, as discussed in Chapter 11.

What then are the advantages of using a standardised test as part of the assessment procedure? Standardised tests allow large-scale screening of groups of learners to identify those who are underachieving and need to be assessed more thoroughly. They enable comparisons to be made with aspects of literacy development such as reading accuracy, reading comprehension and spelling as part of the process of identifying a specific learning difficulty in mathematics. They are also useful in measuring progress and determining if a certain level of proficiency needed for particular tasks or vocations has been achieved. Some standardised tests allow profiles to be built up of an individual's performance on different aspect of mathematics and identify strengths and difficulties as a basis of planning intervention. In this chapter, we outline tests commonly used in UK schools to assess mathematics and discuss how they might contribute to the process of identifying a specific learning difficulty in mathematics, including dyscalculia.

Wide Range Achievement Test (WRAT-4)

The WRAT-4 is intended to be used as a quick and simple assessment of basic numeracy (and literacy) skills in order to assess learners who may have a learning difficulty. The results are intended to be used as part of a comprehensive assessment that includes additional assessment and psychometric data of cognitive functioning, background history, behavioural observations and informal diagnostic assessment that will contribute to the identification of a specific learning difficulty such as dyslexia or dyscalculia. WRAT-4 has four subtests: Word Reading, Sentence Comprehension, Spelling and Maths Computation.

The Maths Computation subtest has two sections: oral maths (15 items), which assesses counting ability, number recognition, number relationships and simple mental calculations; and computation (40 items), which assesses the four basic rules. In this section the problems become progressively harder and later items include decimals, fractions, percentages and algebra. Test instructions are scripted for both sections. The oral maths must be administered individually but the computation section can be administered in small groups for learners aged 8 and older and is a timed test (15 minutes). A comprehensive manual is provided which gives full details of test development and psychometric properties and these are summarised in Chapter 14 (see Table 14.1). The manual also provides tables for comparing the results of the Maths sub-test to those in the Word Reading, Sentence Comprehension and Spelling sub-tests, enabling the assessor to see if there is any statistically significant difference between mathematics and literacy scores. This is useful in highlighting learners who may be underachieving in mathematics due to a specific learning difficulty. For example, if a learner had a standard score of 105 in word reading but only 88 in maths computation, the difference in standard scores would be 17 points, which is significant at the 0.5 level (blue form). This degree of difference was found in only 20% of the standardisation sample. A difference of 21 points (e.g. a standard score 102 in word reading and 81 in maths computation) is significant at the 0.01 level and this degree of difference was found in around 10% of the standardisation sample. Where there is a statistical difference in scores (i.e. significant at the 0.5 or 0.1 level), the learner may have a specific learning difficulty in mathematics and further assessment is needed. A very large difference in scores could be a possible indication of dyscalculia. In the standardisation sample, only 1% had a difference of 40 points (e.g. a standard score of 112 in word reading and a standard score of 72 in maths computation). As specific learning difficulties can be co-morbid, however, not all learners with dyscalculia will show this kind of discrepancy, as some may also have literacy difficulties.

Dyscalculia Screener

Butterworth (2003) notes three main features of dyscalculia as being:

- difficulty learning and remembering arithmetic facts (e.g. number bonds to 10);
- difficulty in executing calculation procedures;
- difficulty counting and detecting counting errors.

He suggests that it is possible that all these difficulties stem from a lack of conceptual understanding of basic ideas of numerosity (such as a set of objects has a number and that numerosities can be ordered by size, e.g. three is bigger than two). Another related hypothesis discussed by Butterworth is that learners with dyscalculia may have slower processing speed and this is measured in three of the sub-tests of the Dyscalculia Screener, which includes computer-controlled item-timed tests involving counting, number recognition and calculation to assess the main features described above (see Table 18.1) as well as a simple reaction test that 'allows the examiner to take into account individual differences in speed of processing' and decide if the learner responds slowly to the questions in the item-timed tests or is simply a slow responder. It could be argued that a learner with dyscalculia is likely to respond normally on the reaction time test but be slower on the item-timed tests, whereas a learner with more generalised learning difficulties is likely to be a slower responder on all subtests (although this is not made explicit in the manual). Butterworth (2003) proposes that general speed of processing deficits do not explain dyscalculia.

Butterworth (2003) argues that a dyscalculia screener is needed because general maths tests usually test a range of abilities, including spatial and verbal abilities, and often only when a learner substantially underachieves on a standardised test is dyscalculia considered. He points out that individual items are not usually timed on general maths tests and therefore do not highlight a learner who takes significantly longer than his/her peers to answer particular questions. He suggests that these tests may miss some learners with dyscalculia who manage to answer questions but may be using inappropriate strategies for their age (e.g. finger counting rather than recalling facts from memory). Observation of test behaviour must play an important part in administering tests and should be considered in interpreting the results. Screening for dyscalculia often follows whole-class testing on a general maths test for learners who are underachieving in mathematics or who have a significant difference between literacy and maths scores. However, we have known teachers to report that as the items on the screener are very simple, some children find them easy and do well on the test and yet still experience difficulty in maths due to the possible impact of another specific learning difficulty such as dyslexia or dyspraxia. A test that gives a profile of strengths and weaknesses can be useful here.

Mathematics Assessment for Learning and Teaching

Mathematics Assessment for Learning and Teaching (MaLT) is a test developed by Manchester University for Hodder Murray (published in 2009) and was standardised in 2005 on a nationally representative sample of 12,591 children aged between 5 and 14 from 111 schools (Williams et al. 2005). It can be used for screening, monitoring and tracking the progress of children. The test is available in both pencil and paper and interactive computer-adaptive (CAT) formats and is designed to highlight errors

Table 18.1   Dyscalculia Screener

Name of Test:			
Dyscalculia Screener			
Author: Butterworth, B.	**Publisher:** GL Assessment, 2003	**Age Range:** 5–16	**Date of Norms:** 2002

Standardisation Sample:

Stratified random sample of 549 pupils across 21 infants, primary, junior and secondary schools in England

Purpose/Function:

Computer-based assessment to help to identify 6–14-year-olds with dyscalculic tendencies

Test Description:

A diagnostic tool is designed to diagnose dyscalculic tendencies and is not a test of general mathematical achievement. It consists of four subtests given continuously.

Administration time:	Reliability:	Validity:	How scores are reported:	Confidence intervals:
30–35 minutes	Not given	Correlations of dot enumeration, number comparison, addition and multiplication are between 0.334 and 0.426. Correlation with mental maths is between 0.131 and 0.369	Standard age scores Stanines	N/A

Subtest Information: (as stated in manual)

Four subtests – three computer-controlled item-timed tests and a reaction time test

- Simple reaction time – pupil presses a key in response to stimulus
- Dot enumeration – pupil compares the dots on one half of the screen with the numeral on the other half
- Number comparison – the pupil selects the larger of two numbers
- Arithmetic achievement test (addition and multiplication)

Comments:

The assessment is easy to administer and many children are motivated to work on the computer. Sample profiles and sample reports are provided. It can be used to screen whole year groups. Low correlations may reflect the fact that different skills are being assessed in the sub-tests.

and misunderstandings, providing whole-class profiles of weaknesses, common misconceptions and errors. The computerised adaptive assessment (Williams, 2011) provides individual reports on pupil performance for 8- to 14-year-olds. Report 1 gives details of performance in relation to standard score, national curriculum level and percentile rank. Report 2 gives a breakdown of individual answers indicating type of error, national curriculum level and time taken to answer. Similar reports can be generated for the pencil and paper tests (5–14 years) using the Scorer/Profiler CD-Rom provided (but without the times for individual answers). Thus diagnostic information is given that can feed directly into teaching. A 'Performance Map' can be produced for each pupil that shows any unusual pattern of errors (e.g. any 'easy' questions they got wrong and any 'difficult' questions they got right), which may be useful in identifying a specific learning difficulty in mathematics.

Progress in Maths

This series of 11 tests is designed to provide ongoing assessment in maths for 4- to 14-year-olds. The questions assess aspects of the National Curriculum and cover Number, Algebra, Shape and Space, Measures, and Data Handling. The tests have been standardised nationally and one of their strengths is the large number of pupils from each year group included in the standardisation. Raw scores can be converted into standard scores and National Curriculum levels. The results of the test as a whole, therefore, give an indication of the learner's overall attainment at a given point in time but analysis of responses to individual questions can also 'shed light on aspects of their understanding and use of specific skills and concepts'. Skills and concepts in four process categories are assessed: knowledge of facts and procedures, using concepts, solving routine problems and reasoning (see Table 18.2).

A further advantage of the test is the analysis of responses to individual questions provided in the test manuals and suggestions for teaching/intervention. One example from the number relationships category is:

> To reinforce their understanding of the concept of division and of its relationship with multiplication, pupils might find it useful to practise finding the second-edge length of a rectangle, given one length and the area. (Progress in Maths 12 Teacher's Guide: 22)

Many learners with dyslexia find the language of mathematics difficult (see Chinn, 2011 and Clayton, 2005) and struggle with specific areas of mathematics such as algebra. There is advice in the manual on teaching the concept of equality, which is a key algebraic concept essential to understanding equations, e.g. by using the image of a balance scale. Fractions, ratios and percentages are often problematic for learners with dyspraxia (see Dixon and Addy, 2004). Difficulty in these aspects of mathematics can again be highlighted by analysing responses to individual questions and the manual gives examples of mathematical models that might be helpful, such as the use of

Table 18.2   Progress in Maths

Name of Test:			
Progress in Maths			

Author:	Publisher:	Age Range:	Date of Norms:
Clausen-May, T., Vappula, H. and Ruddock, G.	GL Assessment, 2004	4–14	2004

Standardisation Sample:

Sample size varies with age group but around 2,000 per year group taken from a random selection of schools on the national register

Purpose/Function:

Tests a pupil's mathematical skills and concepts. Highlights strengths and weaknesses to help teachers to address areas of concern

Test Description:

Available in both paper and digital formats. A group test that covers primary and secondary phases. It is produced as a series of tests with tests for 6–11-year-olds covering number, shape and data handling, with algebra being introduced at age 10. For 6–8-year-olds questions are given orally.

Administration time:	Reliability:	Validity:	How scores are reported:	Confidence intervals:
30–60 minutes	Above 0.9, e.g. Maths 12 (test–retest 0.93) Maths 14 (test–retest 0.94)	Concurrent validity with Maths 5–14 series is 0.8	Standard scores Stanines	90%

Test Information: (as stated in manual)

The tests have two sections which can be taken successively or in two sessions on consecutive days. In section one calculators are allowed but not in section two. Questions have been designed to operate at different levels using concepts and skills in four process categories:

- Knowing facts and procedures (e.g. recalling mathematical facts)
- Using concepts (assesses pupils' ability to make connections between different areas of mathematical knowledge)
- Solving routine problems (involves selecting and applying learned procedures)
- Reasoning (e.g. analysing a pattern in a number sequence)

Comments:

Tables are given which show the relationship between the raw score on the test and National Curriculum levels. Helps to identify areas of mathematics that are insecure. The manual gives examples of common errors on test items and implications for teaching/intervention. Clear instructions for marking and scoring are provided. A scoring and analysis service is also available but at an additional cost. Although a group test it is useful diagnostically.

hundred squares (Progress in Maths 12: 24) or Slavonic abacus (Progress in Maths 14: 22) for teaching the relationship between fractions and percentages and the complements to 100 that are needed to calculate parts of 100%. This link between test responses and implications for teaching is an important aspect of assessment that is not always addressed by standardised tests and is clearly a major strength of these materials. To be used effectively by specialist teachers, knowledge of the characteristics of different specific learning difficulties in mathematics (as outlined in Chapter 11) is useful.

Summary

Assessing a pupil for specific learning difficulties in mathematics is a complex procedure. There are many factors that contribute to underachievement in mathematics (such as attendance, quality of teaching, motivation) that must be taken into account before dyscalculia or the impact of another specific learning difficulty (e.g. dyslexia or dyspraxia) can be considered. Standardised maths tests can be used in different ways:

- to identify underachievement in mathematics,
- to highlight learners who need further assessment,
- to show a discrepancy between literacy and mathematical attainment,
- to screen for typical dyscalculic behaviours,
- to identify strengths and weaknesses,
- to plan intervention,
- to measure progress.

However, the use of a standardised test alone is not sufficient to identify dyscalculia; it should be followed up by further diagnostic assessment, careful observation and appropriate questioning.

Points for Discussion

- How useful is it to compare scores on literacy and numeracy tests in trying to identify a specific learning difficulty?
- What kind of test behaviours would it be useful to note during the assessment procedure?

Follow-up Activity

Evaluate the tests and assessment procedures used to identify learners who are underachieving in mathematics in your setting and reflect on the different ways in which the assessment data can be used.

Further Reading

Butterworth, B. and Yeo, D. (2004) *Dyscalculia Guidance*. Slough: NFER–Nelson.
Describes developmental dyscalculia and gives general guidelines and teaching strategies for supporting learners with dyscalculia.
Haylock, D. (2006) *Mathematics Explained*, 3rd edn. London: SAGE.
A general text that gives a comprehensive guide to teaching mathematics in ways that deepen learners' understanding.

References

Butterworth, B. (2003) *Dyscalculia Screener*. London: GL Assessment.
Butterworth, B. and Yeo, D. (2004) *Dyscalculia Guidance*. London: NFER–Nelson.
Chinn, S. (2011) *The Trouble with Maths*, 2nd edn. London: RoutledgeFalmer.
Clausen-May, T., Vappula, H. and Ruddock, G. (2004) *Progress in Maths 4–14 Series*. London: NFER–Nelson.
Clayton, P. (2005) *How to Develop Numeracy in Children with Dyslexia*. Cambridge: LDA.
DfES (Department for Education and Skills) (2001) *The National Numeracy Strategy: Guidance to Support Pupils with Dyslexia and Dyscalculia*. London: DfES.
Dixon, G. and Addy, M. (2004) *Making Inclusion Work for Children with Dyspraxia*. London: RoutledgeFalmer.
Hannell, G. (2005) *Dyscalculia*. London: David Fulton Publishers.
Wilkinson, G.S. and Robertson, G.J. (2006) *Wide Range Achievement Test (WRAT-4)*. Lutz, FL: PAR (Psychological Assessment Resources).
Williams, J. (2011) *Mathematics Assessment for Learning and Teaching (MaLT) 8–14*. Computer-adaptive CD-Rom. www.hoddereducation.co.uk
Williams, J., Wo, L. and Lewis, S. (2005) 'Mathematics assessment for learning and teaching: an overview of the age standardisation model ages 5–24', *Proceedings of the British Society for Research into Learning Mathematics*, 25 (3): 93–8.

PART IV

CONDUCTING ASSESSMENT

The final part of the book is concerned with both the process of carrying out assessment (whether formal, informal or a combination). There is an emphasis on writing reports, and a model for report-writing is offered. This can be used for 'diagnostic' assessments, i.e. where a learner's profile of strengths and difficulties will form the basis for recommendations for intervention. In some cases this may imply targeting specific areas, but where teaching can be carried out in the normal classroom or where a learner can be supported within a dyslexia-friendly environment. In other cases, more formal, detailed assessment may suggest that a learner will benefit from direct teaching by a specialist teacher using a structured, multi-sensory programme. (A range of possible interventions may be suggested as a result of assessment, in relation to the nature and severity of the difficulties.) Some learners may have specific difficulties that mean they will only be able to 'show what they can do' in examinations if they have special arrangements made. Writing reports for such 'Access Arrangements' is therefore included in the chapter on report writing.

The last chapter in the book acknowledges that, in some cases, further assessment, by another professional, is required. There are brief descriptions of the roles of the main professionals likely to be involved in the area of dyslexia, together with mention of the main tests they use. Greater detail is given about educational psychologists as they are the main professional, other than a specialist teacher, involved in the assessment of dyslexia and other specific learning difficulties.

CHAPTER 19

CONDUCTING ASSESSMENT

Chapter Overview

This chapter will enable the reader to:

- appreciate some of the ethical considerations involved in assessment;
- plan and manage the assessment process.

The main purposes of carrying out assessment for learners with dyslexic-type difficulties relate either to diagnostic assessment to investigate the nature and severity of difficulties or to monitor progress following an intervention. This is particularly important where there has been little or no progress, in order to determine if there is a need for further support or assessment by other professionals. In some cases assessment is carried out for Access Arrangements, as discussed in Chapter 20. Whatever the purpose of the assessment, there will be a number of ethical considerations to take into account.

Ethical Considerations

Ethical considerations are necessary not only to protect human rights but also to avoid compromising the validity and reliability of the assessment, which might seriously affect outcomes for a learner. The following points are relevant to teachers and other professionals working with learners with dyslexic-type difficulties:

1   The assessor must have theoretical and practical knowledge of the nature of dyslexia in order to understand the areas that need to be assessed.
2   Assessors should be appropriately qualified and have good knowledge of how to construct and use informal tests, as well as a sound understanding of psychometrics when using standardised tests. They must also be practised in whatever form of assessment they are conducting. (Teachers carrying out formal assessments should make sure that they are covered by professional indemnity insurance if they are undertaking assessments in a private capacity.)
3   Materials used should be relevant to the culture and age of the learner and in the case of formal tests should also be appropriate in terms of standardisation sample, with recent norms.
4   Parental permission and the consent of the learner is necessary.
5   All assessment data must remain confidential. Raw data must be stored securely in a place where no-one other than the assessor has access. Electronic data, including the assessment report, should not be removed from the premises and the computer should have secure passwords. Data should not be stored on discs or memory sticks, which are easily lost. It should be made clear prior to assessment who will have access to the data and the appropriate permission obtained (see Data Protection issues in Chapter 3). It is important to follow a school's policy. Practitioners working privately should check with the Information Commissioner's Office (ICO) to see whether they should register with them.
6   Care should be taken not to subject the learner to more assessment than is sufficient to make appropriate decisions about the nature of the difficulties.
7   Consideration should be given as to which lessons or activities the learner is missing while the assessment is being conducted and his/her view of this.

8   It is important to give appropriate feedback to the learner and parents and to ensure that the parent has a copy of the report. Good practice would take this further and ensure that there is an opportunity to discuss the report.

Preparation for Assessment

The assessor must be clear about the purpose for the assessment as this will aid selection of relevant procedures. Assessment should not be undertaken unless there is a commitment to follow up the results, i.e. knowing that the outcomes will be acted on.

In planning the schedule for assessment the assessor needs to consider whether it will take place in one session or over several shorter sessions. Where shorter sessions are used they should occur within a short time frame (of no more than two weeks) for the results to be comparable. The dates of an assessment must always be recorded and it might also be useful to note the particular day and time as these might affect performance. If assessment is to take place in one session it is important to allow time for breaks. In planning the order of the tasks, the type of activities should be considered and the demands they place on the learner, e.g. practical activities can be alternated with written tasks; reading tasks can be scattered throughout the session. Planning should also take into account the organisation of materials and any additional resources needed, such as a stop watch, pencil or eraser.

Carrying Out the Assessment

Assessment should take place in a quiet room without interruption by people or telephones and with as few distractions as possible. Care should be taken to cover any visual prompts (e.g. spelling banks, alphabet chart). Physical conditions such as temperature should be taken into consideration. These are sometimes reported as the 'test conditions'.

Any assessment session usually begins by establishing an appropriate relationship between assessor and testee to help the learner feel comfortable with the situation. This is particularly important where a specialist teacher or SENCO is carrying out an assessment of a learner who is not known to them. In situations where the assessor is well-known to the learner (e.g. their teacher) there may be a need to establish the fact that the teacher is now in the role of an assessor and cannot supply answers or support. The purpose of the assessment should be explained clearly to the learner. The assessment session and breaks between testing and activities offer an opportunity for the assessor to find out more about the learner's views.

Before starting the assessment it is important to consider the seating arrangement. In informal assessment it is customary to sit beside or cornerwise to a learner. However, some standardised tests prescribe seating arrangements and the manual should always be consulted. The assessment materials and record sheets should be arranged so that a learner is not able to see how their responses are being recorded. Where an oral response is being made it is good practice to write down the response rather than appear to be making ticks and crosses. Instructions should always be given clearly and in the case of standardised tests the instructions given in the manual must be followed. It is not appropriate to rephrase the instructions unless the manual indicates this is allowed.

Observations of behaviours during assessment should be noted, e.g. degree of engagement, concentration on the task, any indication of anxiety, lowering of voice, strategies used, such as using fingers to count in mental arithmetic. It should also be noted if performance deteriorates over time. A high level of anxiety and disengagement in the testee suggests that the assessor should stop testing.

Scoring and Interpreting

In the case of informal assessment, an appropriate form of recording and analysis should have been decided at the planning stage (e.g. as in carrying out a miscue analysis of reading or spelling) and a consistent approach should be used. Where standardised tests have been used it is crucial to convert raw scores into derived scores accurately (double checking is advised). Scoring, interpreting results and writing up qualitative analyses should be carried out as soon as possible after the procedure, whether informal or formal assessment has been used.

All the information should be collated, looking particularly for discrepancies and consistencies between the results. Where standardised tests have been used, significant discrepancies between standard scores (e.g. of more than 1 SD) should be commented on. Some manuals provide a table to allow comparison between subtests which indicate the level of statistical significance of any discrepancy and may give the percentage of population where that discrepancy can be found. The record sheets of many formal tests provide a means of plotting the scores to present a visual profile. A variety of formats is used, e.g. vertical or horizontal bar chart, normal distribution curve, graph of standard scores, or chart showing deviation from the mean. However, these only record the subtests of one assessment instrument. Assessors may wish to produce a diagrammatic profile of performance across *all* the tests (subtests) used in their assessment and attach this to the end of the report following the table of technical data. Two common approaches can be seen in Figures 19.1 and 19.2.

Making a 'Diagnostic' Decision

An appropriately qualified person can offer an opinion based on formal assessment as to whether or not the testee has dyslexia and may comment on its severity. However, someone who has used only informal testing or is not appropriately qualified may only

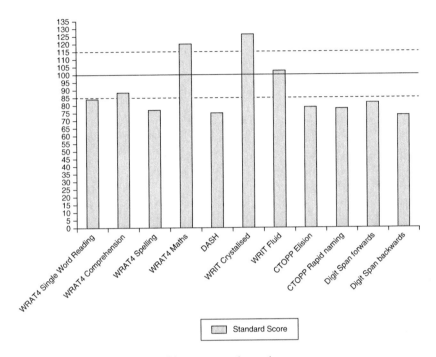

Figure 19.1   Presenting a profile using a bar chart

go so far as to suggest that there may be some dyslexic-type tendencies and state whether there is a need for formal assessment. In order to make a decision that a learner has dyslexia, a teacher would have to hold Associate Membership of the British Dyslexia Association (AMBDA) and preferably an Assessment Practising Certificate (APC) or have ATS and have taken a Certificate of Competence in Educational Testing (CCET) accredited by the British Psychological Society and an APC. A course is now also available through Patoss which can lead to APC following ATS or AMBDA taken some years ago, when the BDA did not offer APC. (See SASC website for details, www.sasc.org.uk).

There is no single set of criteria for deciding if someone has dyslexia. Rather, the assessor has to make a decision based on their knowledge and experience of dyslexia. It is generally considered that learners with dyslexia exhibit a 'spiky' profile. This can imply, for example, variations in attainments in different aspects of the curriculum (e.g. higher attainment in mathematics and/or science than in literacy) or discrepancy between listening/language comprehension and decoding in reading and/or spelling. As these differences may have other explanations (such as EAL, Emotional and Behavioural Difficulties, teaching styles) such profiles need further investigation. This might include comparing scores on attainment tests with those on tests of underlying verbal

Test	−3SD SS 55–69	−2SD 70–84	−1SD 85–100	+1SD 101–115	+2SD 116–130	+3SD 131–145
WRAT-4:						
Single word		x				
Sentence comprehension			x			
Spelling		x				
Maths					x	
DASH:						
Free writing speed		x				
WRIT:						
Verbal				x		
Non-verbal					x	
CTOPP:						
Elision			x			
Rapid naming		x				
Dyslexia Portfolio:						
Digits forward		x				
Digits backward		x				

Figure 19.2   Table showing profile by standard deviation

and non-verbal ability to see if they are consistent. A comparison of verbal and non-verbal scores could also be considered. In particular the results of tests of cognitive processing skills should be scrutinised to see if there are difficulties in any of the major areas associated with dyslexia, e.g. speed of information processing, working memory, phonological processing and in some cases visual processing. Where difficulties in processing skills are consistent with underlying ability (i.e. the learner has a flat profile) it is unlikely that the learner has dyslexia. However, as they are presenting considerable difficulties in learning which need to be addressed, the assessor might use the phrase 'shows some dyslexic-type difficulties' and make appropriate recommendations for teaching and support.

Note: It is worth noting that occasionally scores on tests of ability can be so severely depressed due to the effects of cognitive processing skills (such as very poor working memory or extremely slow processing speed) that they have suggested a flat profile which has been disputed in a later assessment.

In order to have sufficient evidence on which to base a decision it is important that a full range of assessments is conducted and reported on, as suggested in the following chapter. In reaching a decision all the assessments must be considered in relation to the age of the learner and the opportunities they have had for formal schooling in English.

Writing Recommendations

The recommendations made in an assessment report should relate directly to the summary of the nature of the learner's difficulties and strengths and might include:

- a recommendation for teaching and intervention indicating whether a specialist programme is needed in a 1:1 or small group situation, and who might carry this out, e.g. specialist teacher or teaching assistant (in the case of the latter this should be supervised and monitored by a dyslexia specialist);
- detailed recommendations for intervention, including specific targets that can inform an individual learning plan;
- the need for on-going monitoring by a specialist teacher, stating the frequency of review;
- a recommendation for support that can be carried out in the classroom by a trained teaching assistant under the supervision of a specialist teacher;
- suggestions as to how a classroom/subject teacher can make the curriculum more accessible;
- indications of suitable technical aids, computer software, and low-tech aids such as coloured overlays, reading ruler, sloping desks;
- a recommendation for referral to another professional or professionals for further assessment (as indicated in the flow chart of assessment in Figure 2.1), e.g. an occupational therapist;
- recognition of the part that parents could play in supporting the learner; these should normally only be made following discussion with parents.

Individual Learning Plans

Any recommendations for specialist teaching should form the basis of an Individual (personalised) Learning Plan (ILP). This is different from an Individual Education Plan (IEP). One of the main differences is that IEPs usually have 'general' cross-curricular targets but a maximum of four, whereas an ILP may have a larger number of targets but they are closely linked to the cognitive areas that have been assessed (e.g. phonological processing, working memory, speed of processing) in relation to the acquisition of literacy and/or numeracy. Sometimes an ILP could be written with very few targets,

INDIVIDUAL LEARNING PLAN

Name:
Date of birth:
Areas of concern:
Date of ILP:
External agencies involved:
Class teacher:
Other staff involved in support for reaching the targets:
Long-term aims:

Class teacher:
Year group:

Year group:
Chronological age:
Review date:

Current Level of Achievement	Targets	Success Criteria	Strategies/Resources (including named staff)	Evaluation

Pupil's contribution:	Signed:	Date:
Parental contribution:	Signed:	Date:

Figure 19.3   Example of pro forma for ILP

Photocopiable
Assessment of Learners with Dyslexic-Type Difficulties © Sylvia Phillips, Kathleen Kelly and Liz Symes, 2013 (SAGE).

e.g. where informal assessment has identified a specific difficulty in spelling, the ILP may target particular spelling rules. Others may have targets in the area of study skills.

In all cases, ILP targets should be SMART targets, i.e. Specific, Measurable, Achievable, Realistic and Time-bound. An example of a target for handwriting might be 'John will form the letters "c", "a", and "o" correctly in cursive writing using appropriate joining strokes.' A 'fuzzy' target would be 'John will learn to write in cursive writing.' It is very important to state the criteria by which achievement would be recognised (often called the 'success criteria'). In the example cited this could be 'correct formation of the letters "c", "a" and "o" with appropriate joins will be used consistently in three consecutive pieces of writing'. The plan will have to take into account frequency of the teaching in order to set the targets and the time limit in which they are to be achieved. Usually an ILP suggests appropriate resources and who will be carrying out the teaching activities (see Figure 19.3). Good practice would suggest that they should be reviewed at least once per term and half-termly if possible. Sometimes an ILP will be devised in relation to 1:1 teaching on structured, multi-sensory programmes, but it could be written to target a very specific area of difficulty, e.g. at a secondary school targeting particular spelling rules.

Summary

This chapter has given an overview of some of the issues to take into account when planning and conducting assessments. It has particularly drawn attention to the need to consider the ethics in testing as currently there is no written ethical code for teachers carrying out assessments in schools. In reading this chapter the assessor must draw upon knowledge and understanding derived from earlier chapters. This chapter should be used in conjunction with the next one when writing reports and recommendations.

Discussion Points

- Discuss the practical and resource implications of some of the recommendations suggested in this chapter. What other recommendations may result from assessment?
- What are some of the issues raised by a recommendation for specialist 1:1 teaching? Discuss the pros and cons.

Further Reading

Dyslexia Action (2007) *The Dyslexia Guild Practising Certificate: Code of Practice*. http://training. dyslexiaaction.org.uk/sites/default/files/sharedfiles/PCCodeofPractice.pdf
Suggests an ethical code that should be followed by specialist teachers undertaking assessment of learners who may have dyslexia.

CHAPTER 20
WRITING AN ASSESSMENT REPORT

Chapter Overview

This chapter will enable the reader to:

- appreciate the main types of reports written by teachers conducting assessments of learners with dyslexia and dyslexic-type difficulties;
- appreciate the main types of format these reports can take.

This chapter considers three main types of assessment and how these might be reported. These are:

- an assessment based mainly on observation and informal teacher-made assessment as a basis for planning intervention for learners with dyslexic-type difficulties, which could include direct teaching either in a small group or 1:1 situation;
- a diagnostic assessment carried out using mainly formal standardised tests, possibly supplemented by informal assessment, in order to identify formally dyslexic difficulties and their severity, perhaps leading to more intensive specialist support and intervention (this will have greater resource implications than an informal assessment);
- an assessment for learners with specific learning difficulties/dyslexia who may need special concessions to be made in external examinations (Access Arrangements) in order to demonstrate what they know.

In the case of students over the age of 16 continuing into Further and/or Higher Education, assessment may be carried out to determine eligibility for a Disabled Student Allowance (DSA). This is similar to a full diagnostic assessment report as described below but may be carried out only by an educational psychologist or specialist teacher holding an Assessment Practising Certificate. This is not discussed further as it is outside the remit of the book.

Characteristics of a 'Good' Assessment Report

A good report will be clearly presented and well-written, using a good standard of grammar, spelling and punctuation. It will be written with a sense of audience, that is, recognising the range of people who will read it, such as teachers, educational psychologists and teaching assistants etc., parents and, in the case of older learners, the young person being assessed. The use of sub-headings to indicate areas assessed helps a reader to understand the process of an assessment. A report should be relatively jargon-free and where specific terminology is used, examples should be given from the learner's performance to illustrate meaning. This is particularly useful for parents but is also relevant to professionals as it gives them a clearer picture of what the learner does: for example, in discussing a learner's decoding strategies in reading, a report may state – 'Isabella substituted "back" for "book"'.

An assessment report must state the reason the assessment is being carried out as this will determine and indicate the limits of its future use. Similarly, the purpose of each form of assessment or test used should be stated and a brief explanation given of any activity the learner was required to do. The chronological age of the learner at the time of the assessment and the date of that assessment must be given as this enables the reader to understand the analysis provided and conclusions drawn as well as the currency. There should also be information about behaviours and attitudes during each test session and some information about the environment in which the assessment was conducted. The latter is usually reported as 'test conditions'. Where formal tests are used they must be scored accurately and an explanation given of what the score means. The possible implications for the effects on learning of any of the difficulties identified should be stated. This will lead to a summary and recommendation for practice. Where standardised tests have been used these should be listed in a summary table appended to the report. Any report should be signed by the assessor, whose role and qualifications should be specified.

Although there is a recommended format for writing a report for a Disabled Student Allowance (see the SpLD Assessment Standards Committee (SASC) website) there is no single recommended format for any other form of assessment report for specific learning difficulties. However, criteria for what makes a good report are set out in relation to Assessment Practising Certificates. Practising certificates can currently be given by Patoss, Dyslexia Action and the BDA. The recommendations that they suggest would lead to reports very similar in format to the example given on the SASC website for DSA.

Suggested Format for an Assessment Report

The example provided in Figure 20.1 is based on that provided for the DSA assessment report. It is particularly appropriate when carrying out formal assessment using standardised tests but can be adapted for use with informal teacher-made tests.

Informal assessment report

The suggested format may be adapted in the case of an informal assessment that is to be used mainly to inform teaching. This kind of report may be written by a classroom teacher, a SENCO, learning support or specialist teacher. In this case:

- there is no need to put information about the assessor or provide a summary at the beginning of the report; these must, however, be included at the end of the report;
- instead of using the term 'test conditions' a heading such as 'assessment situation' could be used; it is important, however, to report on the conditions in which testing took place, as suggested in Chapter 19;
- the 'Note about Assessment' referring to interpretation of standardised testing is not applicable (this section should be omitted);
- the method used to assess each area should be clearly described with examples of responses made and interpretation of these – this is particularly important in informal reports as the reader cannot refer to a published test for further information (recommended approaches can be found in Part II of this book);
- the heading 'Underlying Ability' should be omitted as it is not relevant;
- speed of processing will not be included under the heading 'Cognitive Processing' as Rapid Naming requires the use of a formal test;
- results can be listed in an appendix using the format in Example 1 in Figure 20.1 but is not essential if the report gives sufficient detail elsewhere.

ASSESSMENT REPORT

Name: **Date of assessment:**

Date of birth: **Age at assessment:**

Home address: (optional)

School:

Class/Year:

Name of author of this report: (please print)

Signature: **Qualifications:**

Date of report:

Reason for assessment:
Brief statement to indicate why this assessment was carried out.

Summary:

This should state what the findings of the assessment indicate with a summary of the evidence on which it is based. There should be a brief summary of the effects of these difficulties (SpLD) on the learner's literacy/ study skills/school life, taking account of strengths. There should be a clear statement as to whether or not, according to their performance in these assessments, taking account of and incorporating any background information, the learner may have a specific learning difficulty.

(N.B. In the case of professionals with AMBDA, and using appropriate standardised tests, this section may include whether the learner has been found to have dyslexia.)

Background information:

This might include:
- *attainment/progress in general as well as difficulties in literacy (and maths if applicable)*
- *family, developmental, educational and language history, relevant medical information (usually from parents: some from teachers)*
- *in the case of learners with EAL, there should be reference to home language, parents' first language and the learner's proficiency in English*
- *summaries of previous assessment reports (if any)*
- *SATs results (and dates) where applicable: make it clear if these are teacher-assessments*
- *previous educational support, examination access arrangements (where applicable)*

The learner's views: *(personalise – use name)*
- *perceptions of difficulties/strengths: interests in and out of school – ambitions*
- *what helps/hinders them learning successfully*
- *what they feel about the assessment*

Test conditions:
A brief statement about the test environment, comfort, interruptions as well as health of learner, attention, motivation, anxiety and his/her response to these. Any factors in the test situation that might have affected results should be noted.

Note about assessments:
This section only applies if standardised tests are being used (and this is expected in the case of candidates for AMBDA). The following statements (or equivalent) should be included so that teachers/parents/carers can understand the terms used. It may be that only standardised scores are given in the report, in which case only the first definition should be given here and the three definitions placed at the end where there are details of the tests given with all three pieces of information.

- Standardised score: A score which shows how a learner is performing in relation to others of the same age. Standardised scores of 85–115 are within the average range for most standardised tests.
- Percentile score or rank: This score shows a learner's position in relation to 100 learners of the same age. A score or rank of 45 indicates that 45 learners out of 100 learners of the same age would score at that level or below. Percentiles of 16–84 are within the average range.
- Confidence bands/intervals: This is the range of standard scores within which a 'true score' lies. A 95% confidence band gives a range of scores within which we can be 95% confident that the learner's 'true score' lies.

(Continued)

Assessments

Reports of performance in individual tests/activities should be prefaced by a brief statement about the attainment or cognitive function which the assessment is designed to examine (i.e. its purpose) and a description of the requirements of the procedure for the learner (what the learner is asked to say/do).

Attainments in Literacy

Reading:

Text reading – *decoding/accuracy, reading comprehension (aloud or silent) speed/rate of reading*

Single word reading – *word recognition*
Phonics – *checklist/graded (teacher made)*
Non-word – *e.g. TOWRE-2 or teacher-made, phonics-based*
Reading speed – *of passage and/or single word reading*
Summary *(of reading profile)* – *implications for classroom behaviours/performance*

Spelling:

Single word spelling test

Spelling in free writing/dictation *(state time given)*

Phonics – knowledge in spelling *(dictated words/informal)*

Summary *(qualitative analysis of errors)* – *implications for classroom behaviours/performance*

Writing:

Free writing –

- Organisation/style – to cover vocabulary, grammar, complexity of sentence structure, organisation/coherence of writing (cogency of argument in the case of older readers)
- Legibility/letter formation/legibility/print-cursive etc.
   Handwriting speed in free writing
   Handwriting speed for copying

Copying untimed 'best' writing *(if appropriate)*

Summary – *implications for classroom behaviours/performance*

Underlying Ability

Verbal and non-verbal (not relevant in an informal report)

Cognitive Processing

Phonological awareness – *list of subtests with information for each*

Memory

Visual memory – *STM/working memory (usually informal or subtest of screener)*
Auditory memory – *STM/working memory*

Speed of processing – *test of rapid naming*

Visual discrimination ⎫
Auditory discrimination ⎬ optional

Summary of cognitive processing skills – *implications for classroom behaviours/performance*

Alphabet Knowledge *(where appropriate)*

Names *(upper and lower case)*
Sounds *(upper and lower case)*
Sequence

Optional sections: *Mathematics/Numeracy; Motor Skills. These should be conducted if referral or other tests suggest they are relevant.*

(Continued)

Summary (Conclusion)

A brief summary of strengths and weaknesses must discuss links/discrepancies between the results on the tests. This should include the nature of the difficulties and likely impact on schoolwork. If appropriate, it should make a statement about whether further assessment is required and whether other professionals should be involved. It can state, where the assessor is appropriately qualified, whether difficulties are 'of a dyslexic-type/specific learning difficulties/dyslexia'.

Recommendations *(as appropriate)*

- For the class teacher/subject teachers/SENCO
  - ○ *(3 to 5 points maximum)*
- For home/parents/carers *(following discussion with them)*
  - ○ *(2 to 5 points maximum – **never** more than for the teachers – particularly 'fun' activities)*
- For the specialist teacher

*NB: It may be that you are designing a programme for someone else to carry out (e.g. for support teacher/ TA) in which case you should insert a separate heading, **ending** with specialist teacher (i.e. your role).*

Name: ....……............................   **Signed:** ……....……….............................

Position/role: ....   **Date of report:** ....

Qualifications: ....……..

[NB. This is the usual format for informal reports and it is good practice to sign all reports at the end. However, the name and qualifications of the assessor would normally be found at the beginning of a report for DSA or formal assessment.]

Appendix: Assessments used and summary of scores/results (on separate page(s))

Example 1: Appropriate for informal assessment

Assessments used	Results	Date

Example 2: Where standardised tests are used

Date	Test/Assessments used with date of publication	Standard score	Confidence band (95%)	Centile

Italics have been used to indicate guidance for content.

Figure 20.1   Assessment report pro forma

Photocopiable

Assessment of Learners with Dyslexic-Type Difficulties © Sylvia Phillips, Kathleen Kelly and Liz Symes, 2013 (SAGE).

Formal assessment report/diagnostic assessment report

The format provided in Figure 20.1 is particularly appropriate for a formal assessment report. This form of assessment should be carried out by a specialist teacher holding AMBDA and/or an Assessment Practising Certificate or an educational psychologist and could lead to a formal diagnosis of dyslexia. It will be based on the types of tests discussed in Part III of this book and may be supplemented by the use of informal assessment. Particular considerations in writing up this kind of report are:

- The 'Note about Assessments' is important so that readers understand the meaning of scores. This could be placed as suggested in Figure 20.1 or could be written on a separate page in the appendix where the results of the assessment are listed. Good practice would insert at least the definition of a standard score in the body of the report.
- Tests should use side headings to show the area being assessed and should always give the full name of the standardised test used together with any abbreviation and reference to the edition. For example, Wide Range Achievement Test 4 (WRAT-4) could be listed under single word reading and under reading comprehension. Under each test there should be a statement about what it assesses and how.
- The account of each test should give a score and if confidence bands are used, should show the range. The terms used to describe the scores should be explained (see Chapter 12). Qualitative information is also required to show the nature of difficulties.
- In the section 'Underlying Ability' tests should be divided into non-verbal and verbal assessments with separate scores given and discussed for each. A composite score should be given if available. Distinction should be made between verbal reasoning ability (as in WRIT) and verbal ability as measured by expressive vocabulary (e.g. Mill Hill), and receptive vocabulary if given (e.g. BPVS-3).
- Where there is a significant discrepancy, i.e. more than one standard deviation (1 SD), between verbal and non-verbal scores (or expressive/receptive vocabulary) such discrepancy should be discussed and in the final summary this should also be discussed in relation to other test results.
- If the assessor is appropriately qualified and/or has access to appropriate software such as LUCID Visual Stress Screener (ViSS) then visual processing would be included in the section on cognitive processing. If neither applies but there is some concern about visual processing then the observations giving rise to concern should be noted here (e.g. losing place when reading/copying; saying the print jumps; rubbing eyes a lot). The report's final summary should, in this case, recommend there should be further assessment by an appropriately qualified person.
- All tests results should be listed in an appendix, as suggested in Example 2 in Figure 20.1. Where a confidence band is quoted this should show the range of scores and the related confidence level (as this may not always be 95%).

An example of extracts from a formal assessment report is given in Figure 20.2.

Example of an assessment report

This extract is based on an assessment report conducted by a specialist teacher. It demonstrates how an assessment justifying **specialist teaching** can be made without subjecting a learner to too much testing. (It is not intended to be a full assessment leading to a diagnosis of dyslexia. The real name of the pupil and certain other facts within the original report have been changed to preserve anonymity.)

As there had not previously been an individualised intervention programme, a first step was to investigate the nature of the difficulties and provide appropriate teaching. If there is little or no progress then further assessment may be carried out.

The actual report is, of course, dated and signed and accompanied by a table giving the test results (also quoting percentiles and age equivalent scores), as shown in Figure 20.1. We have added an 'Endnote' after the report to show there was some progress following intervention.

Name: Jack

Date of birth: 30 March 2004

Date of report: 20 September 2012

Date of assessment: 14 September 2012

Age at assessment: 8 years 5 months.

Reason for assessment:

Jack's parents and the school were concerned about his difficulties in acquiring literacy skills. It was agreed that the Learning Support Service (LSS) would assess the nature and level of these difficulties.

Summary:

The assessment and information from the parents and school indicate that Jack has severe and persistent difficulties in acquiring literacy skills which will have a significant impact on his ability to access the curriculum. In lessons that do not rely on reading and spelling Jack contributes well and performs at an average level. A full diagnostic assessment was not considered necessary at this stage as the testing carried out established that he would benefit from an individual intervention programme where progress will be monitored closely.

Background information:

Information from his mother and the headteacher of the school (who had consulted Jack's class teacher) showed that they had been concerned about Jack's literacy difficulties for some time. Jack has not received any specific, targeted intervention to help develop his literacy skills, although because he is in a class with a small number of pupils, he has benefited from small group work. The headteacher described Jack as a very polite boy who is confident, chatty and popular with other children. Jack has been part of a small group within the school working on developing self-esteem and this was believed to have improved. Some concern had been expressed about his fine motor skills

Jack's mother reported that his eyes had been recently tested and he has been prescribed glasses which will have blue-tinted lenses but will not require magnification. He has previously had grommets in his ears but these have now been removed. Jack has previously attended speech therapy but has now been discharged.

His current attainment levels (teacher's estimate are):

Reading: 2c
Writing: 1a
Speaking and Listening: 2c

Attainment overall is considered:

English: 1a
Mathematics: 2a

(Continued)

Figure 20.2   (Continued)

Jack's views:
Jack appeared confident in talking to me although he is concerned about his poor reading, writing and spelling, where he seemed to have very low self-esteem. He talked very confidently and freely about his hobby, which is snowboarding. (There is an indoor centre locally where he goes with his family.) He feels he always takes too long to do written work and 'Can't keep up with some people'.

Test conditions:
Jack was assessed in the morning in a quiet room in his school with no interruptions. He participated well and was willing to attempt all the tasks given. He became increasingly tired towards the end of the session, which lasted 2 hours with a short break in the middle.

Note about assessments:
In the report below, reference is made to standardised scores. This is a score which shows how a learner is performing in relation to others of the same age. Standard Scores of 85–115 are within the average range for the tests used. A table of all the test results can be found attached to this report.

Assessments
Attainments in Literacy

Passage Reading:
The York Assessment of Reading Comprehension (YARC) was administered to gain a better understanding of Jack's reading accuracy, rate of reading and understanding of text. This requires the child to read a passage aloud and then answer questions to find out what he understands. He began with the 'Beginner Passage'. Jack read 24 of the 26 words correctly, and was supported with words he did not know. He 'sounded out' most words. He answered 7 of the 8 questions correctly.

The second passage was more difficult for him. He answered 2 of the 8 questions correctly, supplying his answers in very short sentences of 1 to 2 words. He was less confident in this test than in later assessments. His reading comprehension was clearly affected by his difficulties in decoding. His Standard Score for Reading Accuracy was 77; Rate of Reading and Reading Comprehension scores were both 78. These scores are below average and suggest that his reading comprehension is affected both by his ability to decode (pronounce words correctly) and his rate of reading. The 'sounding out' method also slows down his reading and hinders comprehension.

These difficulties will affect all areas of the curriculum where he has to read. Jack should be encouraged to read for meaning, by asking him what he is reading about, asking him to predict the endings to stories and engaging him in conversations about the book.

He will also benefit from texts being read to him, as his comprehension will not be affected by the effort he has to make in decoding.

Sentence Reading:
The new (2011) Salford Reading Test (Form A) was given to explore his reading accuracy and comprehension further. This requires a pupil to read a series of sentences of graded difficulty followed by literal and inferential questions to check comprehension. Jack's Standard Score was below 70 in both reading accuracy and comprehension. This is well below average. Jack could read the CVC (consonant–vowel–consonant) words (such as 'bed') and the early, high-frequency words (such as 'the'). He struggled with words of two syllables which affected his ability to read the sentences. Jack's decoding skills are very weak and he has difficulty with any unfamiliar words. He would benefit from targeted work to improve his phonic skills (knowledge of letter-sound correspondence). Currently, he tends to sound out letter-by-letter which is not always appropriate. He would also benefit from work on building up his sight vocabulary in addition to continuing to read from his 'reading book'.

Non-word Reading:
The non-word reading test from the Phonological Assessment Battery (PhAB) was given to assess the way Jack draws on phonological processing skills and knowledge of letter-sound relationships. It was not formally scored, as it is a sub-test of a battery of tests. In this test the pupil is asked to read words which are not 'real' (so that they are not able to rely on a sight vocabulary or visual memory) although they follow regular phonic rules (e.g. 'tib'). Jack successfully decoded CVC words but struggled with two-syllable words. This test confirmed the results of other reading assessments.

(Continued)

Figure 20.2   (Continued)

Summary:

Further assessment of reading was not conducted as it was clear from the above that decoding was a major area of weakness. Jack will have difficulty in any area of the curriculum where he is required to read (from a book, worksheet, interactive whiteboard etc.). Targeted teaching of phonic skills and building sight vocabulary will be necessary to improve his decoding skills. Support could include having a 'reader' for some areas of the curriculum. He also needs support to help develop his reading comprehension.

Spelling:

Young's Parallel Spelling Test

Jack's spelling was assessed using Young's Parallel Spelling Test which requires pupils to spell words of increasing difficulty after hearing them in isolation and then within the context of a sentence. The words used represent common spelling structures and are drawn from the vocabulary used by children. His Standard Score of 87 is in the low average range and higher than his decoding ability in reading. It suggests that he is at a stage where he understands that sounds are represented by letters but that he is more able to apply this knowledge in his spelling. This often occurs when children are first learning to write and spell and this knowledge is then normally transferred to reading.

Spelling in free writing

Jack made several spelling errors in his writing but showed that he understands the need to match sounds to letters, and appreciated the length of words. However, his knowledge of grapheme-phoneme (letter–sound) correspondence is insecure and he is unsure of spelling choices. He usually correctly identifies the phoneme at the beginning and end of words, although occasionally he makes an incorrect spelling choice (e.g. he wrote 'lefd' for 'left'). He has particular difficulty with words containing vowel digraphs (such as 'ea' and 'oa') or more complex spelling choices (e.g. he wrote 'bowt' for 'boat' and 'wudn' for wooden'). However, he was clearly representing each sound.

Jack's spelling will be helped through systematic teaching of synthetic phonics as part of a programme to improve his reading. Within normal lessons he can be helped to learn specific rules and practise writing these. His attainment in spelling is within the average range for his age.

Handwriting:

He wrote freely for just over five minutes about an event during his summer holiday.

Jack has a good pencil grip and secures the paper well with his left hand. Setting the paper or exercise book at an angle so that he is writing away from his bodyline might help to improve writing and also enable him to see what he has written. He produced 34 words in that time, with some crossings out. His letter formation is poor and inconsistent. He prints and the letters are very small. He needs to enlarge his writing and this will help him to feel the movement he makes as he writes each word.

Jack would benefit from learning to write using a cursive style. In learning a new skill, he can start to form letters consistently and of an appropriate size. Using cursive writing will help Jack to write more quickly because it does not require a pen/pencil lift between letters. This will increase automaticity and fluency which will also help improve his spelling.

Underlying Ability

British Picture Vocabulary Scales 3

This test is designed to assess receptive vocabulary, i.e. a child's comprehension of words they hear. It is sometimes used to show an underlying verbal ability because it demonstrates the meanings children give to words they have heard. It must be seen in relation to a child's language experiences up to the time of assessment.

Jack was asked to look at pictures presented in sets of four and asked to choose the picture that represents the meaning of a given word. He enjoyed this activity, which is presented visually and requires no reading or spelling. He achieved a Standard Score of 103, which is average for his age. This suggests that Jack can understand instructions and information given orally at an age-appropriate level. When given a word, he responded fairly quickly as the test did not require him to recall/name the word.

Cognitive Processing

Phonological Processing:

The **Phonological Assessment Battery** was used to assess Jack's phonological processing skills because many pupils with difficulties in reading have some underlying difficulties processing sounds. This assessment comprises several sub-tests which were given to provide more detailed information about Jack's processing skills.

The **Alliteration Test** assesses the ability to isolate the first sounds in single-syllable words. The pupil listens to three words and has to identify the two with the same first sound. Jack correctly identified 8/10.

The **Naming Speed Test** assesses speed of naming a set, first of pictures, then of digits (numbers). His Standard Scores in these tests were 92 for Picture Naming and 87 for Digit Naming. These are in the moderately and low average range. He struggled at times to process the name and retrieve information.

The **Rhyme Test** assesses the ability to identify the rhyme in single-syllable words. Three words are given, two of which rhyme. Jack was able to do this successfully, although when given a single-syllable word and asked to supply a rhyming word, he could not.

The **Spoonerisms Test** assesses the ability to replace the first sound of a word with a new sound, e.g. 'cot' with a /g/ gives 'got' and then to 'swap' the first sounds in a pair of words, e.g. 'King John' becomes 'Jing Kon'. Jack struggled with these tasks, which are timed, and did not complete the tasks. Testing was discontinued when he was clearly finding it hard.

The **Fluency Test** asks a pupil to say as many words of a particular type as they can in 30 seconds. It requires retrieval of words from long-term memory. Three types of word retrieval are asked for: by semantic category (e.g. 'animals'), by alliteration (e.g. starting with the /k/ sound) and by rhyme (e.g. rhyming with the word 'bat'). Jack found all of these tasks difficult because they required him to process information quickly.

Summary

The tests of phonological processing suggest that Jack has difficulty processing information quickly. One implication of this in the classroom is likely to be that he is slower to process information and answer questions quickly, particularly those requiring retrieval from long-term memory. He may also be slower in free writing because he may take some time to organise his thoughts and find the words he needs. The use of word-lists may be helpful to support both his composing of stories/writing and also his spelling. His difficulty in manipulating sounds in words may also undermine retrieving letter–sound correspondence in reading and writing.

Memory:

Jack's short-term and working memory skills were assessed. His auditory memory skills were assessed by asking him to repeat strings of letters presented orally. He was able to recall a string of 5 letters forwards and 4 when asked to recall a string in reverse order. When presented with a card with letter strings printed on them (visual memory) he could recall 5 items (forwards and reverse order). Jack should be encouraged to use this strength and build on it during the learning of spellings. It suggests this is not a particular reason for difficulty in reading or spelling. Games such as Kim's Game can help maintain and develop this strength further.

Alphabet knowledge
Sequencing the alphabet:

Jack was asked to place wooden capital letters of the alphabet in alphabetical order. He was very slow in carrying out this task, although he was largely accurate. His strategy was always to return to 'A' and 'start again'. He placed 'L' between 'T' and 'U' and also reversed the order of 'X' and 'Y' (i.e. Y/X/Z). The 'J' was placed with wrong orientation.

Letter sounds and names:

Jack knew the sounds of all the letters and knew all letter names except 'u' and 'k' where he first said 'y' and hesitated over 'k', before getting it correct.

There is still some insecurity of alphabetic knowledge, particularly in sequencing, and this area should be addressed to ensure automaticity. Not placing the alphabet quickly in correct sequence may also be a sign of his slow processing speed in retrieving information.

Summary

The above assessment shows that Jack may have a specific difficulty in acquiring literacy skills. His language comprehension assessed by his understanding of vocabulary is average but his reading is well-below average. His slow speed of processing information may be affecting his ability to recall letter-sound correspondence sufficiently automatically to aid reading accuracy. His 'sounding out' of letters does not help this. Jack's visual and auditory memory skills are average for his age and are strengths which can be built on.

Jack's reading difficulties will have a significant impact on his ability to access the curriculum without substantial differentiation. Differentiated activities will give him greater opportunities for success and encourage his independent

(Continued)

Figure 20.2   (Continued)

learning. His slow processing speed means he will require extra time to complete tasks, particularly those involving handwriting. However, he may also need time to process questions and instructions in class. His literacy difficulties suggest that he will benefit from a multisensory approach using a structured literacy programme in order to acquire automaticity in decoding. This should incorporate the teaching of handwriting. Because of the severity of his reading difficulties, such a programme should be individualised and delivered at a pace to meet his learning needs.

Jack is highly motivated to want to learn to read and co-operated well in all the tasks he was given.

Recommendations
For the school:
Jack should be given:

- access to a scribe;
- encouragement to use mind-maps, storyboards, flow charts, as alternatives to writing text;
- minimal copying from the board – if at all;
- differentiation and modification of all curriculum materials to support his learning;
- access to appropriate resources including IT programmes such as Word Shark or Lexia;
- access to age- and interest-appropriate reading material which is levelled to his ability – Catch Up books, Rainbow Readers, Barrington Stoke publish books with high interest/low reading age written specifically for children experiencing difficulties in literacy;
- regular reading sessions with an adult. It is very useful to undertake a preparatory read with a book to introduce new vocabulary and to have a discussion of the story prior to asking Jack to read. This will support his understanding of the text and help with prediction.

For the parents:
Parents should continue to support Jack at home and listen to him read materials sent home.

For a specialist teacher:
The specialist teacher will support the school by:

- discussing and explaining the implementation of the recommendations listed above;
- teaching Jack in a 1:1 situation using a cumulative, multisensory, structured literacy programme for one hour a week for 10 weeks in the first instance;
- monitoring and evaluating Jack's progress at the end of the 10 weeks; liaising with Jack's parents and school staff as appropriate and reporting progress at the end of the 10 weeks.

Figure 20.2   Example of an assessment report

Endnote

The above report was written in September, 2012. The specialist teacher reported that after implementing a 10-week intervention programme, Jack showed major improvements in reading and most areas of phonological processing, including his use of alliteration, spoonerisms and non-word reading. His reading skills still gave cause for concern, but he had improved from a standardised score of 70 to 77, a rise from the first percentile to the sixth based on Salford Sentence Reading Test- Form B. His spelling remained at the same level (low average) and was still better than his reading.

Importantly also, Jack's self-esteem has risen – this was reported by his parents and the school. In school, staff noted he now believed he *could* learn to read and was more able to access the curriculum. The specialist teacher emphasised that the school had been extremely supportive and contributed greatly to his improved literacy. They carried out all the report's recommendations and provided a support assistant to observe the weekly session and to work with Jack every day to follow-up and reinforce the work given by the specialist teacher. The school will continue to provide support and monitor his progress carefully.

It is always worth remembering that assessment is only the **start** *of a process designed to help learners achieve!*

Access Arrangement Reports

Under certain circumstances, concessions may be requested for learners who experience special educational needs in order to demonstrate what they know in examinations. This requires assessment that leads to the third type of report listed above. This can, but does not need to, follow the format provided in Figure 20.1. It is likely to be shorter than a full diagnostic report because it only has to justify a specific request.

The main external examinations taken currently by learners in English schools are Key Stage 2 National Curriculum tests (SATs) in primary schools, General Certificate of Secondary Education (GCSE), AS and A2 (secondary or FE). Certain other examinations such as Basic Skills and Diploma may also be taken. All examinations are under review at the time of writing. The regulating bodies, the Standards and Testing Agency of the DfE in the case of SATs and the Joint Council for Qualifications (JCQ) for other qualifications, both prescribe the conditions under which Access Arrangements can be made. These conditions can change annually for a number of reasons, reflecting changes resulting from research and also changes in legislation (for example the 2012–13 JCQ regulations refer particularly to the Equality Act 2010). Before conducting the assessment the assessor should, therefore, always refer to the current guidelines.

What access arrangements can be sought?

We indicate below the sorts of special arrangements that can be sought that are particularly relevant for learners with dyslexia.

JCQ regulations for GCSE, AS and A2

The main arrangements that can be requested which require assessment and are relevant to candidates with specific learning difficulties are:

- **Extra time**: for candidates who read, write, or process information very slowly. Normally this would be up to 25% but it is possible to ask for up to 50% additional time in examinations where processing speed is extremely slow or where a reader or scribe is not allowed (even though an assessment would indicate the need for one).
- **A reader or reading software**: where a learner has poor reading accuracy, speed and/or reading comprehension.

- **A scribe/voice-activated software**: for those who have a writing difficulty such as illegible handwriting, slow speed, poor grammar or considerable spelling difficulties.

Two other special arrangements that could be sought (particularly for learners with co-existing difficulties) are:

- **Oral language modifier**: usually where a learner has poor reading comprehension; a supporter can rephrase questions on request but must not change any technical language.
- **Practical assistant**: where a candidate has poor motor control, e.g. a physical difficulty or Developmental Co-ordination Disorder (Dyspraxia).

Under the current regulations a number of Access Arrangements can be provided that do not require formal application and assessment, provided that they reflect a candidate's usual way of working. These are as follows:

- The use of a **word processor**: this is preferable to a scribe or transcript but computers/lap tops must conform to the regulations so that only the word processing facility can be used.
- A **transcript**: can be made where writing may be difficult for an examiner to read and the use of a word processor is not the normal way of working or where spelling is so difficult to decipher that the examiner would benefit from a transcript.
- **Supervised rest breaks**: for those with a medical condition or very poor concentration. This may be common practice for some learners who cannot maintain sustained writing comfortably for any period of time.
- **Reading aloud**: permitted where reading comprehension is poor but understanding is improved sufficiently by reading aloud.
- A **prompter**: where the candidate is easily distracted and needs to be brought back to task.
- A **live speaker**: for pre-recorded components of an examination (e.g. MFL listening examinations) where the candidate can benefit from lip reading. It might also be considered for those with very slow processing speed who cannot keep with the speed of the recording (although this is not given as an example in the current JCQ guidance).
- A **bilingual translation dictionary** (without extra time) can be used in most examinations except English/English language, Irish or Welsh language, and MFL (for certain languages).
- **Coloured overlays/reading rulers**: for learners experiencing visual disturbance or visual stress when reading from texts in black print on white paper, as an alternative to photocopying the test/examination onto coloured paper.

Several of the above carry implications for how a centre organises accommodation and the provision of invigilators. These should not, however, be considerations for the specialist assessor, whose only concern is for the needs of the individual learner.

Key Stage 2 National Curriculum Tests

Currently the only formal application that needs to be made for Access Arrangements in written tests at the end of Key Stage 2 is for up to 25% additional time (no application is necessary for children with a statement of SEN). Criteria are set out on the DfE website and divided into two sections. Section A contains the criteria most likely to be used for assessing learners with dyslexic-type difficulties. Some choice is provided in terms of what is assessed, but the emphasis is on the use of standardised testing and can include discrepancy between cognitive ability and performance, e.g. between verbal and performance IQ, or between cognitive ability and attainment in literacy. An exception is that writing speed can be based on free writing conducted informally with a criterion of 10 words per minute or less. At least three of the criteria in section A must be met, which can require more testing to be conducted than for a request for extra time for GCSE. Section B is concerned with reports from other professionals for children who have medical or physical conditions or sensory impairments which will affect their ability to access the test in time. It acknowledges that there may be other exceptional circumstances.

Schools do not need to seek permission for the following Access Arrangements provided that they are based on normal classroom practices:

- Rest breaks
- Reader
- Scribe
- Transcript
- Word processor or other technical or electrical aid
- Photocopying onto coloured paper etc.
- Coloured overlays
- Prompter

How are applications for access arrangements made?

Applications for Access Arrangements for Key Stage 2 tests and for the JCQ examinations are made on-line by the school or centre concerned using the appropriate form using information based on standardised tests.

GCSE/GCE

For GCSE and A level examinations, applications should be made online using www.jcq.org.uk/exams-office/aao-access-arrangements-online. This should ensure that information is presented in the same way nationally and therefore can be regarded as good practice.

DIAGNOSTIC ASSESSMENT REPORT

(Candidate and Assessor information is provided on page 1 as indicated in Figure 20.1.)

Summary

Assessment with a range of diagnostic instruments suggests a profile consistent with that normally associated with a profile of strengths and weaknesses characteristic of dyslexia. Rachel's ability to think and solve problems is similar to most other people her age. However, underperformance in phonological processing and working memory appears to affect Rachel's literacy and learning. This means that some of her literacy attainments are not what would normally be expected from someone with her underlying ability.

Background information

Rachel was identified as 'potentially dyslexic' and perhaps requiring special arrangements for examinations, by the school's English teacher in Year 10.

Rachel reports that although she prepares well for examinations, her results are poor and she does not always understanding the questions. She feels that she is 'not good' at spelling, mixes up b/d and says her hand tires easily when writing. She finds it difficult to get ideas down on paper. She also says she is easily distracted in class, is forgetful and sometimes finds it difficult to find the right words for what she wants to say, often finding it hard to say new or long words. When younger, she found it difficult to learn to tell the time. She prefers to think in pictures rather than words.

Test conditions

Rachel was tested in a private office at school, free from distractions and interruptions. She appeared comfortable, concentrated well showing little anxiety, and co-operated well throughout.

ASSESSMENT RESULTS

Attainments in Literacy

Reading:

Rachel's ability to decode individual words out of context was assessed using the single word reading test from Wechsler Individual Achievement Test, Second Edition for UK Teachers (WIAT-II^{UK}-T). Her Standard Score of 87 lies within the average range but is at the low end. She tended not to attempt words that she was unsure of, although she responded speedily to words with which she was familiar.

She was then asked to read the WIAT passages which she chose to read aloud. Occasionally Rachel showed a tendency to lose her place and transpose sounds. Her ability to answer questions based on what she had just read is just outside the average range for her age (standard score 83). She always referred back to the text to answer the questions, but this strategy was not always effective. Rachel's ability to accurately decode words in context is not strong but her speed of reading for comprehension is well within the average range (standard score 106).

Spelling:

Rachel's ability to spell single words was assessed using WIAT-II^{UK}-T and was average for her age (Standard Score 94). She was able to spell a range of common words accurately. Her errors tended to be phonic representations of the target word, but showed uncertainty over spelling rules, e.g. double consonants (begining); wrong choice of homophones (their/they're); and vowel choice (princeple). In one case she missed a final letter (ceilin) and in another substituted a similar sounding word ('addiction' for 'edition'). The analysis suggests a possible underlying phonological/auditory difficulty.

Writing:

Rachel was assessed using the Detailed Assessment of Speed of Handwriting where she was asked to write on the topic of 'My Life' for 10 minutes. Her handwriting varied in style and legibility and some letters were unclearly formed e.g. 't' and 'x'. Capitals and punctuation were used inconsistently. There were ten crossings-out, including two false starts.

Her rate of writing was slightly above average (Standard Score 117). Her writing showed mistakes in choice of homophone (knew/new, drawer/draw); grammatical errors (wrote/written) and in one case substituted 'by' for 'my'. It may be that some of her errors including crossings out are because she is trying to write more quickly than she can accurately process information.

Underlying Ability

Rachel's ability to think and solve problems was assessed using all four sub-tests of the Wide Range Intelligence Test (WRIT) and found to be average in three out of four subtests. She performed best on the Verbal Analogies subtest, a measure of verbal reasoning ability, obtaining a Standard Score of 102.

However her expressive vocabulary score was significantly lower at 76. This is an unusually large discrepancy. Reading contributes significantly to vocabulary, and the WIAT-II^{UK}-T assessment suggested that reading presents a challenge to Rachel. This could mean that she has not developed her vocabulary as well as most students her age. This score may therefore not reflect her ability. Her scores for the non-verbal subtests of underlying cognitive ability were both in the average range. This means her ability to think and solve problems using logical visual reasoning is on a par with most other students her age.

Cognitive Processing

Working Memory:

Rachel's auditory short-term and working memory was assessed using the Recall of Digits subtests from Dyslexia Portfolio. She obtained a Standard Score of 89 for digits forwards but only scored 78 for digits backwards, which is below average. This suggests that her auditory working memory is poorer than short-term memory which will affect any task where she has to retain and manipulate information, such as decoding in reading, particularly of longer words, spelling and possibly compositional skills in writing assignments. The score for working memory is also low compared with general underlying cognitive ability which suggests that without support her performance will not reflect what she knows.

Phonological Processing:

Rachel's phonological processing skills were assessed using the Elision sub-test from the Comprehensive Test of Phonological Processing (CTOPP). This tests the ability to delete sounds from words. Rachel obtained a Standard Score of 70. Analysis of Rachel's errors suggests that accurate processing of medial phonemes (deleting a middle sound from a word as in 'say winter without the /t/') presents a particular challenge to her. Processing medial phonemes is the finest level of phonological discrimination and a common challenge for people with dyslexia.

Speed of Processing:

Rachel's speed of processing was assessed using two rapid naming sub-tests from CTOPP. She was asked to name digits presented randomly and then letters also presented randomly. She scored below average, with a composite score of 82. The implication of this is that she needs more time to process verbal information.

Conclusions

The evidence suggests a profile of strengths and weaknesses characteristic of dyslexia. Rachel's ability to think and solve problems is average for her age. However, difficulties in phonological processing, working memory and information processing speed appear to have a negative impact on her academic attainments, particularly in literacy. Her low average score for decoding together with a well-below average score for vocabulary contribute to her below average score for reading comprehension. However, the assessment of Rachel's underlying ability suggests that she has the potential to succeed both in school and beyond given appropriate tuition and learning strategies together with reasonable adjustments in examinations.

Recommendations for access arrangements

Rachel's rapid naming speed is below average, at Standard Score 82. The current JCQ regulations state that a cognitive processing speed score of 84 and below will support the application for up to 25% extra time. Given that she also has a below average score for working memory (Standard Score 78), the full 25% extra time should be sought.

Rachel's reading comprehension is below average (Standard Score 83) and this was probably affected by a low average reading accuracy and poor working memory. Under the current regulations she is eligible for a reader. In the case of elements of GCSE English, where she is not allowed a reader, consideration should be given as to whether requesting up to 50% extra time will enable her to improve her performance.

Rachel needs to be taught strategies of how to use extra time and have practice in using it. She also needs to have practice in using a reader. Both recommended arrangements should form part of her normal way of working.

Signed: **Date:**

(Attached to the report would be a table showing details of tests and scores. In addition, as the report itself does not contain information about the tests used a brief description of each test would be provided at the end of the report.)

Figure 20.3   Example of a report to support a request for access arrangements

The assessment information obtained from a specialist teacher is entered under Section C which uses the term 'the diagnostic report'. Where a specialist teacher has carried out a full assessment they are only required to report information on those aspects of difficulties that will enable the examinations officer to make an informed decision as to whether a particular access arrangement is justified. Section C may be completed by the specialist assessor or by the centre but in any case the signature and qualifications of the assessor is required to confirm that they conducted those assessments. It is important to check that the scores have been recorded accurately.

As there is an expectation that any access arrangement is based on normal practice, there is a need for early consultation between an examination centre and specialist teachers. This is to ensure that there is evidence that the arrangements requested facilitate the learner's performance to show what they can do. Indeed, specialist teachers can have a role in advising what the most appropriate access arrangements are for a particular individual. JCQ specify that a 'specialist assessor' should be a suitably qualified psychologist or specialist teacher (who in the case of dyslexia holds AMBDA and/or an Assessment Practising Certificate) or other professional who has undertaken appropriate training in psychometrics and the use of standardised tests and meets certain other additional criteria.

National Curriculum Tests (SATs)

Assessment for SATs can be conducted by a specialist teacher or SENCO who is familiar with the tests to be used. Application for extra time is made via the NCA Tools website of the Standards and Testing Agency (DfE) using the form provided. In the case of a scribe, a transcript and the use of a word processor/technical or electrical aid, for which permission is not necessary, a school must notify the Standards and Teaching Agency of any of these special arrangements used during a particular test using a form of notification. Guidance is given in the Key Stage 2 Assessment and Reporting Arrangements.

Producing an assessment report for access arrangements

The scores recorded on the forms requesting access arrangements are normally the result of formal assessment carried out by an appropriate assessor. Good practice would suggest that a formal report would be written and kept on file as evidence of the assessments undertaken. An example of a report written to advise an examinations centre for access arrangements in GCSE is given in Figure 20.3 where the student, Rachel, was aged 15.6. The first page of the report contained the basic information about the learner and assessor and the report was signed and dated at the end following the format described earlier in this chapter.

Summary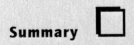

This chapter has outlined the main forms and indicative content of assessment reports. It has suggested a format for report writing based on that currently used for diagnostic reports in FE/HE but which can be amended and adjusted according to purpose. It has considered the current areas for which access arrangements can be made for examinations in some detail whilst acknowledging these could change. However, the list provides a useful reminder of the sorts of reasonable adjustments that can be made in schools so that learners with dyslexic-type difficulties can show what they know. Some of the recommendations could be put into informal and formal diagnostic assessment reports in order to make reasonable adjustments in the classroom.

Follow-up Activities

1 Obtain a copy of an assessment report written for a particular purpose and evaluate it in the light of good practice suggested in this chapter.
2 Read the guidelines for making access arrangements and note any points of difference with those cited here.

Further Reading

Jones, A. (ed.) (2011) *Dyslexia: Assessing the Need for Access Arrangements during Examinations: A Practical Guide*, 4th edn. Worcester: Patoss.
This book is particularly relevant for specialist teachers working in secondary and FE sectors.

CHAPTER 21

ASSESSMENT BY OTHER PROFESSIONALS

Chapter Overview

This chapter will enable the reader to:

- appreciate the roles of other professionals in the assessment of learners with dyslexia and dyslexic-type difficulties;
- appreciate the range of professionals involved in the assessment process.

A multi-professional approach to the identification and assessment of Special Educational Needs is recommended in the 2001 SEN Code of Practice (DfES) and the current reforms plan to strengthen this by making it a requirement rather than a recommendation. For learners with dyslexia the main professionals who may be involved are: educational psychologists (EPs), speech and language therapists (SALTs), occupational therapists (OTs) and sometimes physiotherapists. Others may sometimes be called upon, such as audiologists, optometrists or opticians. However, referral is usually made to individual specialists rather than a multi-professional team. Often a particular difficulty has been noted by a school or parent and it is believed that there is a need for additional expertise over and above that which the school can provide. Some of these professionals may have expertise and experience of dyslexia, but not all. Much depends on their initial professional training and subsequent professional development.

Educational Psychologists

The most common referral for learners where dyslexia is suspected is to an educational psychologist. Such referrals would normally be made when a learning difficulty has been identified by school or parent and is not responding to the intervention normally available within a school. EPs are usually employed by Local Authorities and may have a service agreement with schools, but some work independently. The picture is variable throughout Authorities, in that some schools have greater ease of access to an EP than others. Some parents feel it necessary to seek an assessment for their child from an independent EP because they have found it difficult to get a referral to an LA educational psychologist, either because the school considers it unnecessary or because they do not have ready access to an EP, and the parent is not aware that they have the right to request an LA assessment. This has a financial implication for families and assumes that they are aware that they can 'go privately' and have the money to afford it.

An educational psychologist is the professional who is always involved in Statutory Assessment under the current arrangements but the other professionals listed above may not be. Educational psychologists making a formal diagnosis of dyslexia, including for Disabled Student Allowance (DSA) should hold a Practising Certificate from the British Psychological Society (BPS) and follow the professional code from the Health and Care Professions Council (HCPC).

What form should an EPs report take?

Most reports will follow a similar pattern, and the pro forma suggested in Chapter 20 (based on a DSA report) is not dissimilar from that used by most educational psychologists.

A front cover provides basic information about the learner and the name, qualifications/ role of the assessor. In the case of EPs this might include a reference to certification by the HCPC (or their Code of Practice).

Assessment by an educational psychologist usually starts with observation of the learner in classroom situations, scrutiny of class work and discussion with teachers/ teaching assistants. They also review any reports or records written about the child. This normally includes information about attainments, difficulties, family and medical history. There is normally a consultation with parents and a separate interview with the child. This information is reported as 'Background Information'. Sometimes this is extremely lengthy and based purely on *reading reports* from others rather than inter- views and observations. Any account referring to reports/progress and intervention should make the chronology clear. A learner's views, interests and attitudes to school should be situated in this or a subsequent section, should be up-to-date and indicate whether this information was gained first-hand, i.e. from the learner, or whether it is summarising what parents/teachers have said.

If they decide to proceed with formal assessment they usually administer one of two tests of underlying ability. These are: Wechsler Intelligence Scales for Children – Fourth UK Edition (WISC-IV UK), published in 2004, and British Ability Scales: Third Edition (BAS3), published in 2011. As these are tests that teachers cannot use, they bring new information and interpretations which can be used to compare with the assessments a school/other teachers have conducted. Both tests provide 'Full'/Overall Scores and yield separate verbal and non-verbal scores. These tests are particularly useful for reporting on variations between scores on subtests, indicating areas of strength and weakness. Some of these sub-scores contribute to a composite score, which is referred to as an Index Score. In the WISC-IV UK, for example, there are four such indices:

- verbal comprehension;
- perceptual reasoning;
- working memory;
- processing speed.

This is a revised version of the earlier WISC and reflects research into how children learn rather than emphasising *only* verbal and non-verbal reasoning, although retaining subtests to assess these areas. It provides two 'Ability' Scores – Verbal and Performance.

A good report will quote not only scores but interpret these in the light of other scores commenting on both consistencies and inconsistencies. Either in the body of the report (or at the end in some cases), there should be an explanation of the test itself and each subtest, stating the purpose of the activity and what a testee was required to do. This helps parents and teachers to see the relevance to the learner's behaviour/score on this test and relate it to attainments and the demands of the school.

In the case of referral because of literacy and/or numeracy difficulties, most EPs will also carry out relevant assessments of attainment. Usually they now use the Wechsler Individual Achievement Test – Second Edition (WIAT-II^{UK}) (a version available to EPs, not the same as the WIAT-II^{UK}-T described in Chapter 14). In 2005 this replaced word-reading and number tests formerly used by psychologists (WORD, WOLD and WOND) and provides an assessment of reading, language and numerical attainment. It has been linked directly to the WISC-IV UK and used for comparisons of achievement and ability.

WIAT-II^{UK} includes:

Reading

- Word reading
- Reading comprehension
- Pseudo-word reading

Numerical attainment

- Numerical operations
- Mathematical reasoning

Language

- Written language

  o Spelling
  o Written expression

- Oral language

  o Listening comprehension
  o Oral expression

These sub-scores can be used to form composites and are normally used to develop a profile when compared with the composite scores and subtests of WISC. It can be very useful to have information based on 'unfamiliar' test situations, particularly for a learner who may have experienced many assessments (formal and informal) in school.

The British Ability Scales: Third Edition (BAS3) was published in November 2011. However, it is interesting to note that it was co-normed with YARC (Early Years/Primary) and YARC (Secondary), 'to provide evidence of discrepancies between cognitive ability and *comprehension* (our emphasis) of extended text.' It may well be that when YARC is used more widely, there may be greater use of BAS3. The BAS3, like earlier versions, contains a number of subtests, including verbal, non-verbal and number scales as well as providing an overall scale. An intriguing aspect of BAS3 is that the publishers offer a 'Scoring and Reporting Service' or 'create a customisable Psychologist or Parent Report'.

Whilst this could lead to greater consistency in reporting (currently EP reports vary considerably in length and quality of information as much as those of teachers or any other professional), it is to be hoped that this is not at the expense of qualitative discussion and recommendations that are individualised. Some reports we have seen have had lengthy lists of materials/technical aids/teaching programmes and schemes which, whilst relevant to the field of dyslexia, give no indication as to which are the most appropriate for the learner who has been assessed, or how they should be used.

Educational psychologists' reports quote *at least* Standard Scores and many provide percentiles. Usually, they include a note that any test can only provide an indication of behaviour on a particular test on a particular occasion. Many take care to include confidence bands as part of their discussion. As with any assessment report there should be a listing of all test results summarised in a table and a summary of conclusions with recommendations.

It can be seen from the above that the format of the report is very similar to that recommended for use by specialist teachers/SENCOs. What an educational psychologist brings to the assessment process is a greater knowledge of the psychological development of children and young adults together with the ability to use individual tests that can produce detailed profiles of their learning (some prefer to conduct dynamic assessment). They also have greater knowledge of psychometrics and how to interpret, integrate and discuss consistencies and differences in profiles, particularly in relation to underlying cognitive processing. In addition, they will have more skills and experience in identifying possible co-existing conditions and be able to advise schools where they need to refer to other specialist professionals. Because of these skills and the fact that they bring a different perspective and external view of the situation, educational psychologists have much to offer to schools and teachers.

Lindsay Peer has contributed a personal view of the benefits of securing an educational psychologist's report. An experienced EP, teacher and specialist in dyslexia, she was Education Director of the BDA from 1994 to 2003. Since that time she has worked privately as an educational psychologist specialising in specific learning difficulties. She draws attention to the need for early identification and assessment of both dyslexia and dyscalculia.

In an account written specifically for this book, she suggests that:

> Prior to formal assessment, reporting from a number of parties should ideally be secured. This will help inform the assessment process, e.g. teachers, SENCOs, TAs, therapists, parents/carers – and of course the learner whom we wish to 'buy into' the process. In such a way, the assessment process and subsequent report will reflect the input of those who work and live with the learner as well as the person themselves.

Following this, Peer notes:

> Observation should take place in school both within the classroom – ideally in a literacy-based lesson – as well as in the playground to observe interaction. In literacy lessons,

observation should be made as to where the learner is experiencing difficulties. For example:

Is the learner experiencing difficulties with the listening process, phonics and spelling or perhaps the acquisition of modern foreign languages?

Is this consistent with a history of or current suffering from 'glue ear' (otitis media)?

Does the learner experience difficulties related to vision of the printed word such as movement of letters, reversals or difficulty reading on a white background, on paper or on a computer screen?

Is the learner experiencing difficulties with the reading and writing processes?

Is the learner experiencing attention difficulties?

Is the learner fearful of reading out loud?

Is the learner disorganised?

In all such scenarios, the question has to be why and thereafter what should be done about it.

The next step is formal testing,

including cognitive functioning where comparisons can be made between strengths, weaknesses and overall ability levels. This should be measured alongside assessments of phonological skills and attainments (literacy, numeracy and listening). A comparison of results can then be made between a learner's chronological age as well as their measured cognitive ability levels. An evaluation of self-esteem and emotional functioning should also be made.

She also points to the need to assess processing skills (as described earlier in this book).

Importantly, she adds:

The educational psychologist will want to evaluate the effectiveness of programmes and strategies used to date – and then make suggestions for a future plan of action. Moreover, consideration will need to be given to the needs of the child in terms of the experience and qualifications of staff who will be delivering the dyslexia programme.

This has an implication for a school/SENCO to make sure that all information gathered so far, together with information about any intervention and evaluation of progress, is available for an EP to study.

An educational psychologist must also be able to offer suggestions as to:

how best to support the individual learner. Teachers should be given a list of helpful things to do – as well as a list of things not to do! Furthermore, within the secondary school sector, subject guidance should additionally be given to teachers to aid learners when they are attempting to access curriculum subjects.

Further:

> Advice will also focus on strategies to be used for the differentiation of the curriculum, appropriate levels of language and literacy needed – and perhaps technology which may be used to reinforce (but not replace) teaching. Where appropriate, examination provisions may be recommended. These tend to change on an annual basis; staff should therefore seek guidance from the JCQ website. In addition to advice for school staff, parents/carers may well need help as to how to reinforce the learning programme and use suitable techniques for the management of homework, coursework and revision for examinations.

As many teachers query whether an EP can offer advice or merely 'Tell us what we already know' about difficulties, Peer's emphasis on the advice and range of suggestions that can be made could be used as criteria by which to judge an assessment report received from any professional. It should not merely list strengths and weaknesses but offer pertinent and useful advice.

Peer presents an optimistic view and is confident that:

> Dyslexic learners in the right environment with appropriate teaching delivered by qualified staff have the potential to make very good progress and develop strategies to help them achieve in life. Early identification is very important. Nevertheless at whatever age the dyslexic learner is identified, much can be done. The educational psychologist has a significant role to play.

Speech and Language Therapists

Speech and language therapists (SALTs) are less frequently called in by schools when dyslexia is queried. However, many learners with dyslexia may have exhibited speech difficulties or delays in the pre-school years and a speech and language therapist may well have been involved through a referral from health visitors, parents, nurseries or in some cases through routine screening. The sorts of difficulties presented in these early years include delay in the development of specific speech sounds, putting sounds and/or syllables in the wrong order in certain words and difficulties in phonemic awareness. A high proportion of learners with dyslexia receive speech therapy pre-school, but have no follow-up and their dyslexia is not identified until much later.

Speech and language therapists tend to be called in to assess children of school age where poor speech or articulation difficulties are considered to be affecting phonological processing. The areas normally assessed by speech and language therapists are:

- speech – the ability to enunciate words clearly/ articulation;
- language – the ability to use and understand words and sentences;
- communication – the ability to use language (both expressive and receptive) in interaction with others.

It is the first of these areas which is considered particularly relevant to dyslexia, whereas children with specific language impairment may have more difficulty in the second and third areas. The main tests SALTs use in relation to investigating difficulties associated with dyslexia are Phonological Assessment Battery (PhAB) (see Chapter 17), Clinical Evaluation of Language Fundamentals – Fourth Edition UK (CELF-4UK) and the Test for Reception of Grammar 2 (TROG2). These would show understanding of language which could be compared with phonological difficulties. Because speech therapists have knowledge of phonetics and phonological development they are able to identify any specific problems in distinguishing and pronouncing sounds that might have a bearing on decoding. Like educational psychologists, SALTs follow a code of conduct laid down by the HCPC.

CELF4 is a comprehensive assessment of language difficulties and gives both expressive and receptive language scores. It is interesting to note that CELF4 offers composite scores in language structure, language content, language content and memory, and working memory. Subtests include phonological awareness, rapid automatic naming, digit span, and sequences. This testing may be seen as either unnecessary, if enough information in these areas has been gleaned from other assessments, or as further confirmation of dyslexic-type difficulties. Speech therapists often identify other possible difficulties and refer to other professionals. For example, they often refer to an audiologist where they believe there is a central auditory processing disorder or maybe a hearing loss. They often pick up on co-existing difficulties such as dyspraxic (DCD) tendencies and may refer to an occupational therapist for further assessment. Similarly they may refer to an EP where they consider a learner has an autistic spectrum condition, e.g. through their use of language, understanding of metaphor and poor theory of mind.

Occupational Therapists

Some occupational therapists (OTs) specialise in working with children and young adults. Like most speech therapists, OTs are employed by health services. They also must register with the HCPC and observe their professional code when carrying out assessments. Those who work with children can carry out a range of activities but those that are particularly relevant to the assessment of dyslexia and dyslexic-type difficulties are considerations of written work where a school or parent might be querying whether the child might be dyspraxic. Occupational therapists may assess for proprioception and sensory integration. Their assessments would include looking at fine motor skills and visual motor skills, sometimes using the Beery Visual Motor Integration Test, a test available for use by teachers (see Chapter 15 for details). Another test frequently used to assess fine and gross motor skills is the Bruininks–Oseretsky Test of Motor Proficiency. It contains a number of subtests that are presented as a series of games.

The eight subtests are:

- Fine motor precision, e.g. cutting out a circle
- Fine motor integration, e.g. copying a shape
- Manual dexterity, e.g. sorting cards, stringing blocks
- Bilateral co-ordination, e.g. jumping activities
- Balance, e.g. standing on one leg on a balance beam
- Running speed and agility, e.g. sideways hops
- Upper limb co-ordination, e.g. catching a ball
- Strength, e.g. doing sit-ups.

This can give composite scores as well as a total overall score and thus can offer a profile of different motor skills.

Occupational therapists are often involved in the assessment of co-existing specific difficulties such as dyspraxia and dysgraphia and use a number of handwriting assessments. They may make assessments as to whether an alternative form of recording rather than handwriting is needed, e.g. the use of a word processor and the teaching of keyboarding skills, or the use of speech-activated software. The tests of sensory integration are often used when there is consideration of an autistic spectrum condition. Occupational therapists can advise schools about intervention that may be appropriate to support learners with dyslexia but are rarely directly involved in intervention themselves. Parents can get a referral to an OT either through the school or their GP. In the past learners with dyslexia were sometimes referred to a physiotherapist prior to seeing the OT in order to build up their inner core strength, but this rarely seems to happen now.

Optometrist

Optometrists can assess for visual difficulties including visual stress/scotopic sensitivity. This is not part of a routine eye-test and the orthoptist or optometrist uses special equipment such as an intuitive colorimeter to determine the exact colour of lens that is to be prescribed to reduce sensitivity to glare sometimes experienced from black print on a white background. Coloured lenses are an alternative to the use of coloured overlays or coloured paper and have the advantage of enabling the learner to read material where an overlay cannot be used (e.g. notices, street signs), although some learners are very resistant to wearing glasses. However, where a learner is showing any indication of visual stress as described in Chapter 17 then it is worth considering referral to an optometrist. Where there are literacy difficulties it is always worth checking that the child has had a recent eye-test and if not refer to an optician.

Audiologist

An audiologist specialises in identifying, diagnosing and treating hearing and balance problems. Where children have severe phonological difficulties it is worth checking that their hearing has been tested. Audiologists can also check whether they can distinguish specific sounds in a noisy background. Hearing problems as a root cause of literacy difficulties should be ruled out at an early stage. However, it is possible to have a hearing loss and be dyslexic.

Summary

A range of professionals could be called upon to carry out assessment in particular areas of a learner's difficulty where specialist expertise is required. This chapter has focused on educational psychologists, who tend to be the main professionals involved and who also can identify co-existing difficulty. It is very rare for all the professionals mentioned in this chapter to be involved in the assessment of a particular learner with dyslexia or dyslexic-type difficulty. It is important for teachers to be aware of the range of professionals who could be called on because in so many cases dyslexia exists alongside other difficulties where assessment lies outside the expertise of a specialist teacher of dyslexia. An implication is that if a referral is not made other co-existing difficulties may not be properly addressed.

Point for Discussion

- Discuss your experiences of working with other professionals and the contributions they have made to assessment and intervention with learners presenting difficulties.

Follow-up Activity

Find out how to access appropriate professionals for your school and what services they offer.

Further Reading

Carroll, J.M. and Myers, J.M. (2010) 'Speech and language difficulties in children with and without a family history of dyslexia', *Scientific Studies of Reading*, 14 (3): 247–65.
A paper that considers the relationship between dyslexia and speech and language impairments.
Peer, L. (2005) *Glue Ear*. London: David Fulton.
Peer's research showed that a significant number of learners with dyslexia have suffered with glue ear at some time.

Reference

DfES (Department for Education and Skills) (2001) *The SEN Code of Practice*. London: HMSO.

APPENDIX 1

Appendix 1(a) Examples of teacher-made single word reading tests

Single Word Reading Test: Primary Example

This should be used only **after** the assessment of the first 100 words suggested in Letters and Sounds has been made.

school	there	said	day	have
saw	people	one	what	good
right	door	key	still	want
please	thought	horse	come	would
cried	etc.			

Single Word Reading Test: Secondary Example

park	said	where	new	would
cold	any	every	took	other
print	soft	fine	shelter	thought
vain	planet	source	method	triangle
climate	record	present	asked	practice
answer	science	global	change	model
addition	recognise	system	experiment	etc.

Notes: We suggest about 50 words (maximum).

Unless there is comparison across an age group, this information, whilst perhaps indicating how a learner fares when meeting these words, is of limited use diagnostically.

Appendix 1(b)   Example of teacher-made phonic skills reading test (real words)

PHONIC SKILLS READING TEST (REAL WORDS)

The words can be copied on to small cards or written in columns. The learner is asked to read them aloud and their response is recorded.

van	hum	big	fog	sit
top	led	rat	wet	but
milk	hand	sink	belt	bunk
wisp	loft	list	damp	rent
crab	plum	skip	smug	snap
spin	drop	trap	grin	step
chip	rich	ditch	shed	pack
with	thin	fish	whip	phone
pain	may	weigh	late	claw
torn	bore	roar	shout	clown
moan	bone	blown	chose	collar
colour	dream	field	meet	beat
wipe	light	try	pie	tube
root	stew	rule	hard	burst
shirt	dirty	curl	herd	though

Notes: These are suggested words; teachers may devise their own test, adopting the principles previously described.

The same words can be used to assess spelling, although the spelling test should not be given on the same day. A comparison of results will provide valuable information.

If a learner has many errors in the first two sets, discontinue. However, if they are successful in these and they then struggle, it is worth asking them to look carefully at other lines and words to see if they can read any of the others.

(Correct responses may reflect their phonic skills but *could* imply they have read them as 'sight' vocabulary.)

Photocopiable
Assessment of Learners with Dyslexic-Type Difficulties © Sylvia Phillips, Kathleen Kelly and Liz Symes, 2013 (SAGE).

Appendix 1(c)   Example of non-word reading test

NON-WORDS READING TEST

nid	fod	jud	tek	mab
kep	zid	hev	gan	rox
sta	spov	flet	trag	blen
plig	clum	snat	sked	grob
jund	vung	bilk	wist	famp
melf	yalp	masp	donk	sesk
chon	thid	whad	shev	mich
heth	kush	quon	hoth	frang
genned	junting	stibbed	fondwin	palkened
danlerwin	etc.			

Photocopiable

Assessment of Learners with Dyslexic-Type Difficulties © Sylvia Phillips, Kathleen Kelly and Liz Symes, 2013 (SAGE).

Appendix 1(d)   Examples of questions to assess comprehension

ASSESSMENT OF COMPREHENSION

1. **Literal**
   Recognition: Point to the words which show where the
                           action/event takes place

   Recall: What is the name of the main character?

                           What happened after/when ***?

                           How did X feel? (Assuming this is stated in the
                           passage)

2. **Reorganisation:**   Summarise the main points of the passage.

3. **Inferential:**   Why did 'X' do ***? (When reason was not
                           explicitly stated)

                           What sort of person is 'X'? (A character)

                           What do you think will happen next? Why?

                           How does *** compare to ***?

                           Why do you think the author included ***?

                           What is meant by (quote figurative description
                           or particular words?)

4. **Evaluation**:   Could this sort of event happen nowadays?

                           Do you think this is a true story?

                           What do you particularly like/dislike about this
                           book/passage? Why?

                           Is there enough information about 'X'?

5. **Appreciation:**   Is this a happy/sad/frightening book/story?

                           Why do you say this?

                           How do you think 'X' spoke when he said ***?

                           (Orally, ask 'Say what 'X' said', demonstrating
                           how s/he said it.)

Notes: These categories are based on Barrett's Taxonomy of Comprehension Questions (see Pettit, N.T. and Cockriel, I.W. (1974) 'A factor study of the Literal Reading Comprehension Test and the Inferential Reading Comprehension Test', *Journal of Literacy Research*, 6 (1): 63–75.

Despite the fact it dates from 1968, this taxonomy is still a useful guide for teachers setting questions.

Photocopiable
Assessment of Learners with Dyslexic-Type Difficulties © Sylvia Phillips, Kathleen Kelly and Liz Symes, 2013 (SAGE).

APPENDIX 2

Appendix 2(a)   Assessment of phonological awareness

Name: **Date of assessment:**

Date of birth: **Chronological age:**

1. Perception of Rhyme

Instructions:

a. Say, 'Listen to these two words and tell me if you think that they rhyme:

   cat – mat'

   (NB: Take care to say these words using normal intonation. Do not emphasise each sound.)

   If the learner answers incorrectly say, 'Listen to that one again:

   cat – mat'

   Make sure that the learner understand the instructions.

   Then say, 'Now try these'

Stimulus words	Learner's response
pen – hen	
fan – pin	
ball – fall	
boy – top	
speak – leak	

b. Say, 'Now listen to these three words and tell me which two words rhyme:

   tan – man - nap'

   If the learner answers incorrectly say, 'Listen to that one again:

   tan – man - nap'

   Make sure that the learner understands what to do.

   Then give these:

Stimulus words	Learner's response
sip – lip – pin	
fun – ten – sun	
nap – can – ran	
wit – sick – bit	

Note: Where performance on this subtest is poorer than the other two, it may suggest poor working memory.

Photocopiable
Assessment of Learners with Dyslexic-Type Difficulties © Sylvia Phillips, Kathleen Kelly and Liz Symes, 2013 (SAGE).

c. Say, 'Can you think of three other words that rhyme with the words I say?' Give example 'bat' but include this in the responses below.

Stimulus words	Learner's response
bat	
cot	
hall	
pen	

2. Phoneme Blending

Instructions:

'I am going to say some sounds that go together ('blend') to make words'

Practice items:

Say, 'I am going to say some sounds like a robot and I'd like you to tell me what word they make'

'/d/-/o/-/g/ What word do those sounds make?'

'Yes, good, /d/-/o/-/g/ makes the word, dog'

'What word do these sounds make? /r/-/a/-/t/'

If the learner makes a mistake, say, 'Listen again and have another go'

Stimulus words	Learner's response
t-i-p	
c-a-p	
s-i-t	
p-o-t	
s-n-a-p	
ch-i-p	
c-oa-t	
b-ir-d	
s-a-n-d	
s-t-o-p	

3. Phoneme Segmentation

Instructions:

Say, 'Listen to me as I say a word – top'

'Now I'm going to say the same word like a robot – /t/-/o/-/p/'

'Can you say the word *pit?*'

'Now can you say the word *pit* like a robot?'

'Now try these words'

(Continued)

Photocopiable

Assessment of Learners with Dyslexic-Type Difficulties © Sylvia Phillips, Kathleen Kelly and Liz Symes, 2013 (SAGE).

Appendix 2(a)   (Continued)

Stimulus words	Learner's response
pan	
step	
ship	
frog	
dish	
lost	

4. Phoneme Manipulation/Deletion

Instructions:

Practice item:

Say, 'Listen to me say the word 'dog'

Can you say the word 'dog' without the 'd'?'

If the learner does not respond correctly (-og) give another example

Then proceed, saying, 'Now try these'

Stimulus words	Learner's response
Say 'mat' without the /m/	
Say 'cat' without the /c/	
Say 'fan' without the /f/	
Say 'stop' without the /s/	
Say 'frog' without the /f/	
Say 'lost' without the /s/	
Say 'frog' without the /r/	

5. Syllable Segmentation

Instructions:

Say, 'Do you know what a syllable is?' (Give examples: 'It is part of a word which means we open our mouths to say it – like a beat.' Practise clapping for 'a beat' if necessary.)

Practice item:

Say, 'Can you tell me how many syllables there are in these names? –

'John', 'Megan'

When the learner understands, use names of children in the class using names with 1, 2 and 3 syllables, and then give: 'school, Saturday, playtime, giant, computer'. (Make sure you say the word with normal pronunciation, not stressing syllables!

Photocopiable

Assessment of Learners with Dyslexic-Type Difficulties © Sylvia Phillips, Kathleen Kelly and Liz Symes, 2013 (SAGE).

Names	Response in number of syllables
Other items	
school	
Saturday	
playtime	
giant	
computer	

For older learners, under 'other items', choose words such as:
perpendicular, impossibility, frightening, necessary, unkindly, generous, hospitality, etc.

6. Blending Syllables

Instructions:

Say, 'Now I am going to give you some parts of words that go together to make a word. I want you to guess what the word is. Listen carefully – '

Practice items:

snow – man

di – no – saur

When it is clear the learner understands, present the following, allowing about a one-second gap between each syllable:

(You can choose any words you consider appropriate. Some people might include non-words, e.g. proo – fan – tic - al.)

Stimulus words	Learner's response
clev – er	
nui – sance	
pho – to – graph	
cin – e – ma	
un – der – stand – ing	
su – per – mar – ket	
ce – re – mon – y	
gen – e – ros – i – ty	
se – quenc – ing	
meth – od – ol – og – ic – al	

Photocopiable

Assessment of Learners with Dyslexic-Type Difficulties © Sylvia Phillips, Kathleen Kelly and Liz Symes, 2013 (SAGE).

Appendix 2(b)   Assessment of auditory discrimination

Name: **Date of assessment:**

Date of birth: **Chronological age:**

Instructions:

The learner should face away from you so that there are no visual clues. (It is usual to stand *behind* the learner when giving this test.) Care should be taken not to emphasise particular phonemes where there are differences.

Say, 'I'm going to say two words to you and I want you to tell me if you hear two different words like "house" and "mouse" or two words that are the same said twice, like "pan" and "pan".'

Practice item:

Say, 'Are these words the same or are they different?: "flap", "clap"'

(The learner can say, 'same or different' or 'Yes' for same and 'No' for different.)

Stimulus words	Learner's response
rag - bag	
gate - cake	
sun - sun	
tap - pat	
nip - pin	
kind - kind	
sit - sit	
mug - hug	
chip - ship	
tin - tan	
no - no	
step - stop	
bog - dog	
in - on	
trip - trap	

Scores: Number correct *Same*   /4

 Number correct *Different*   /11

 Total correct   /15

Note any particular difficulties.

Appendix 2(c)   Assessment of visual discrimination

Name: **Date of assessment:**

Date of birth: **Chronological age:**

Instructions:

Give a copy of this sheet to the learner. It then becomes a record sheet. Ask the learner to look at the letter or word on the left and circle the letter or word that matches in the line on the right.

Practice item:

Point to the letter in the margin and ask the learner to look carefully at all the letters on the right to find the one that matches. Do not do it for the learner, so that this counts in the score.

1.	b	d	p	q	b	h	g
2.	f	t	l	f	j	k	d
3.	u	n	v	m	w	u	o
4.	a	e	a	u	o	i	c
5.	on	no	on	in	an	ou	oh
6.	saw	sam	wan	was	saw		man
7.	bus	sub	bus	sud	dus		ubs
8.	girl	gril	lirg	irig	girl		glir
9.	past	saps	pats	past	stap		taps
10.	little	kitten	litter	kettle	skillet		little

Photocopiable
Assessment of Learners with Dyslexic-Type Difficulties © Sylvia Phillips, Kathleen Kelly and Liz Symes, 2013 (SAGE).

Appendix 2(d)   Assessment of auditory sequential memory

Name: **Date of assessment:**

Date of birth: **Chronological age:**

Auditory sequential memory (short term)

For primary age children

Instructions:

1. When carrying out this assessment, items should be delivered at an even pace of about one item per second (which gives time to repeat a word/item **silently** before saying the next).

    Say, 'I am going to tell you some things that are in my shopping bag. I want you to say back to me exactly what I have said to you.'

    Practice item:

    Say, 'Sausages'. Pupil responds, 'Sausages'.

    Say, 'Now try two things: tea, jam. Say them back to me in the same order.'

    If correct, proceed (NB: you can choose your own items.)

ALWAYS WRITE DOWN EXACTLY WHAT THE LEARNER SAYS.

Series	Response (forwards)
1. apples, eggs 2. chicken, butter	
1. meat, sugar, cola 2. cake, spaghetti, milk	
1. beans, cheese, fish, pizza 2. oranges, chocolate, bread, peas	
1. grapes, flour, nuts, sugar, jam 2. eggs, crisps, peas, pears, jelly	

2. Explain that you are going to do the same thing using numbers this time. Give an example to practise: 7 – 2. Discontinue when learner has difficulties.

Series	Response (forwards)
3 – 7 4 – 8	
7 – 3– -1 4 – 8 – 6	
5 – 2- -6 – 1 1 – 4 – 9 – 2	
2 – 6 – 1 – 5 7 – 9 – 3 – 1	
4 – 9 – 2 – 3 – 6 6 – 4 – 3 – 6 – 8	

In the case of older learners only give the second test (digit span). Increase the number of digits to give two sets of six numbers and two sets of seven.

Photocopiable

Assessment of Learners with Dyslexic-Type Difficulties © Sylvia Phillips, Kathleen Kelly and Liz Symes, 2013 (SAGE).

Auditory sequential memory (working memory)

Reverse order

For primary age children give both: use second example only for older learners.

1. *Instructions:*

   Say, 'I am going to tell you again some things that are in my shopping bag.
   I want you to say back to me what I have said, **but this time** can you say them
   backwards?'

   'So if I say, "chops, chocolate", you will say, "chocolate, chops".'

   Practice item:

   Say, 'Try this one: "sausages, cheese".'

   If the learner responds correctly, proceed with examples below. (If not, give
   another example.)

Series	Response (backwards)
1. chicken, carrots 2. eggs, fish	
1. sugar, gravy, rice 2. cake, spaghetti, meat	
1. yogurt, cheese, tomatoes, peas 2. pizza, honey, cornflakes, melon	
1. strawberries, fish, peas, burgers, carrots 2. chips, cola, salad, milk, oranges	

2. Explain that you are going to do the same thing using numbers this time. Give a
   practice example: 5 – 2. Discontinue when learner has difficulties.

Series	Response (backwards)
3 – 7 8 – 2	
2 – 4 – 9 3 – 7 – 1	
5 – 3 – 4 – 2 7 – 3 – 6 – 4	
2 – 8 – 9 – 1 – 7 2 – 5 – 3 – 5 – 4	
9 – 2 – 7 – 8 – 3 – 5 4 – 9 – 4 – 3 – 1 – 6	
3 – 5 – 9 – 8 – 6 – 4 – 7 7 – 1 – 4 – 2 – 9 – 3 – 8	

For older learners, give only the digit span test.

Photocopiable

Assessment of Learners with Dyslexic-Type Difficulties © Sylvia Phillips, Kathleen Kelly and Liz Symes,
2013 (SAGE).

Appendix 2(e)   Visual sequential memory: test and record sheet

Name: **Date of assessment:**

Date of birth: **Chronological age:**

Pictures (for younger learners)

You will need two sets of identical pictures, each picture on a separate piece of card, e.g. a cat, a house, an apple, a book, a flower, a bird and a fish. (Shapes could be used.)

Practice item:

Give the learner one of the sets of six cards keeping one for yourself.

From your set, select two pictures and place them on the table/desk in front of the learner.

Say, 'Look at these pictures.'

Allow about 5 seconds for this.

Then cover them up and say, 'Look at your cards. Can you make the same pattern with some of your cards?'

The learner should select the same cards and arrange them in the same sequence. Show the correct sequence so the learner can self-check. If it is clear that the learner understands what to do, repeat the process using:

A. 2 sequences of 2

B. 2 sequences of 3

C. 2 sequences of 4

D. 2 sequences of 5

Build in a delay of 3–5 seconds before letting the learner put their cards down.

Write your sequence below, before testing. Stop when the learner gets **both** sequences wrong.

Sequence	Learner's response
1	
2	
1	
2	
1	
2	
1	
2	

Use the method below with both young and older learners.

Repeat the above activity using **letters** rather than pictures, using the sequences suggested below and making appropriate sets of cards.

Letters

Sequence 1

1. J   P
2. B   M

Sequence 2

1. Y   F   N
2. L   A   R

Sequence 3

1. X   F   M   G
2. S   D   A   U

Sequence 4

1. W   G   T   H   O
2. K   A   M   V   J

Notes: You can do this test using a set of wooden alphabet letters, having either the whole alphabet set or just the 21 used above.

For older learners, e.g. at secondary school, you can use **only** letters/numbers (i.e. not the pictures) and take the sequence up to 7 items.

Scoring/interpreting

In each case note the **ceiling**, i.e. how many items can be recalled correctly in sequence in **both** attempts. Note any particular difficulties (e.g. certain pictures/letters) and test behaviour, e.g. setting out their cards quickly; looking at you 'for clues'; hesitations etc.

Appendix 2(f) Assessment of alphabet knowledge: Record sheet

Name: **Date of assessment:**

Date of birth: **Chronological age:**

Grapheme–Phoneme Correspondence

Set 1: Lower case

Instructions:

1. Show the Test Card to the learner and ask him/her to go left to right across the page saying the **sound** each letter makes.
Circle the ones that are incorrect.

v	b	g	c	e	i
x	s	n	h	d	l
f	k	o	t	a	z
r	w	m	j	y	p
u	q				

2. Now ask the learner to look at them again and say the **name** of each letter.
Circle the ones that are incorrect using a different colour pen – or underlining.

Set 2: Upper case

Instructions

1. Ask the learner to look at Set 2 (capital letters) and ask him/her to say the **sound** each one makes.
Circle the ones that are incorrect.

B	G	O	H	X	Q
Z	L	Y	S	N	C
F	W	A	J	D	V
K	T	E	U	I	M
R	P				

2. Now ask the learner to look at them again and say the name of each letter.
Circle the ones that are incorrect using a different colour pen – or underlining.

Assessor's Notes:

Alphabet Sequencing

1. Ask the learner to tell you all the letters of the alphabet starting with A.

If the learner sings (but is correct) note that, and then ask him/her if he/she can say it **without** singing. If the learner gives sounds only, ask them to do it again saying **names**. Record any errors.

2. Give the learner a set of alphabet letters (or in the case of older learners, small cards (about 2.5 cm²) with an upper case letter on each) and ask them to set them out in alphabetical order. If incorrect, copy the sequence they make.

GRAPHEME–PHONEME CORRESPONDENCE CARD

Set 1   Lower case

v b g c e i

x s n h d l

f k o t a z

r w m j y p

u q

Set 2   Upper case

B G O H X Q

Z L Y S N C

F W A J D V

K T E U I M

R P

Photocopiable
Assessment of Learners with Dyslexic-Type Difficulties © Sylvia Phillips, Kathleen Kelly and Liz Symes, 2013 (SAGE).

GLOSSARY

Alphabetic principle: A letter (or letters) of the alphabet represents a sound, i.e. there is a relationship between a phoneme (sound) and the grapheme(s) (letter/s) which represent it.

Analytic phonics: An approach to teaching reading where learners are taught to recognise whole words and then analyse these into constituent units in order to identify letter–sound (grapheme–phoneme) correspondences. See also **synthetic phonics**.

Articulation: Production of speech depending on the position of the mouth, lips and teeth.

Assessment: The collection of information about an individual in order to make decisions about teaching. It may involve the use of a range of informal and formal approaches and evaluates an individual's knowledge/skills in an area.

Attention Deficit (Hyperactivity) Disorder (ADD/ADHD): A developmental, neurological disorder characterised by attention difficulties, impulsive behaviours and distractibility often accompanied by hyperactivity. This can be a co-existing condition with dyslexia.

Auditory Discrimination/Perception: The ability to identify similarities and differences when listening to sounds. This is now usually assessed as part of the assessment of phonological awareness/phonological processing.

Autistic Spectrum Conditions (ASC) often referred to as ASD (Disorders): A spectrum of behaviours characterised by difficulties in: social interaction, communication and understanding the views of 'others'. It is often accompanied by routine/ritualistic behaviours. There is a wide range of such behaviours, so that some may have very little speech and have severe learning difficulties whereas others may be very articulate and learn quickly. Autistic Spectrum Conditions are often **co-morbid** (co-exist) with dyslexia.

Automaticity: Ability to respond quickly, without attention or 'conscious' effort (thereby allowing effort/thinking to concentrate on comprehension or other aspects of a task). See also **speed of information processing** and **rapid automatised naming**.

Basal level of tests: The entry level/point of items at which testing should start. Test manuals provide details.

Blend: Two or more adjacent consonants whose sounds flow together but retain discrete sounds, e.g. 'sp' in 'spin' is an initial consonant blend and in 'lisp' is a final consonant blend.

Ceiling levels of tests: The point at which testing should be discontinued. Test manuals describe this. (The term 'ceiling' is also used to describe the upper age limit of a test.)

Cerebellum: The area of the brain integrating motor skills and balance (providing feedback on the position of the body in space). Neural pathways link the cerebellum to the motor cortex, sending information to the muscles, thereby causing them to move.

Cognition: Processes concerned with knowing, perceiving and thinking. Cognitive processing skills include the use of working memory, speed of information processing and phonological processing. Auditory and visual discrimination/perception may be considered separately *and* within these.

Cognitive ability/underlying ability: 'Cognitive ability' is sometimes used as a term to describe a general underlying ability to learn. It is recognised as multidimensional, consisting of many processing skills which, because many are so positively correlated, have given rise to a concept of 'general underlying ability'. Major tests of general cognitive ability offer a 'full score' to indicate overall ability. Often these comprise two parts: **non-verbal/fluid** and **verbal/crystallised**. Each of these two areas involves a number of processing skills and perceptions.

Co-morbidity: The co-existence of one or more disorders/difficulties in addition to a primary disorder. Some specific learning difficulties are commonly found to 'co-exist' with dyslexia, e.g. autistic spectrum conditions (ASC) – particularly Asperger's Syndrome; dyspraxia/Developmental Co-ordination Disorder (DCD); and Attention Deficit (Hyperactive) Disorder (ADD/ADHD).

Confidence band/confidence interval: The range of scores within which a 'true' score is likely to fall.

Construct/psychological construct: This is a term for a psychological concept, i.e. a hypothetical construct to describe a characteristic or notion which is not directly observable, e.g. intelligence, ability, motivation, self-esteem.

Correlation coefficient: A statistical technique is used to show the relationship between two variables. It is quoted as between +1.0 and −1.0. A correlation coefficient of 0.8 or 0.9 is therefore an indication of a strong positive relationship.

Criterion-referenced test: A test in which performance is measured in relation to a pre-determined set of standards of achievement, e.g. a test of phonic skills in reading.

Crystallised ability/crystallised intelligence: The ability to accumulate and use knowledge, skills and experiences in problem solving. It was originally considered a major factor of general ability; being the ability to reason using words and numbers. It is usually assessed by testing vocabulary and ability to reason verbally, drawing on knowledge and experiences.

Curriculum-based assessment: This usually means that items or areas to be assessed are taken from (or are very similar to those used in) a learner's classroom/lessons. The learner therefore will have experienced relevant teaching. In some texts about assessment, this term would be used to describe 'end-of-module' tests to assess, say, what they have learned in history. In this book we have occasionally used this term but more commonly have used 'teacher-made' assessment to denote informal assessment devised by a teacher, but which is related to the sort of activities with which a learner is familiar, e.g. reading a passage from a book, spelling words that have been taught, arithmetic tasks.

Decoding skills: The ability to pronounce a word by applying knowledge of grapheme–phoneme correspondence.

Developmental Co-ordination Disorder (DCD): See dyspraxia.

Developmental dyslexia: The characteristics of dyslexia develop naturally during childhood as opposed to being the result of, for example, an illness, accident or trauma as in acquired dyslexia, which might result from a stroke or accident.

Diagnostic assessment: Assessment conducted to discover what an individual knows/can do in relation to a given area and what requires further development, i.e. a learner's strengths and difficulties are explored in order to target areas for improvement. This can be based on formal or informal assessment procedures or a combination of both. (NB: 'Diagnosis' is a controversial term, see the discussion in this book.) It is often used as a form of assessment to decide whether a learner *is* dyslexic or has 'dyslexic-type' characteristics. A 'formal diagnosis' of dyslexia is currently required for students in FE/HE who may be eligible for a Disabled Student Allowance.

Digit span: A procedure used to assess short-term and working memory involving presenting a learner orally with a series of single digit numbers given randomly and asking him/her to recall them either in the order presented or in reverse order.

Digraph: Two adjacent consonants or two adjacent vowels in a syllable representing a single sound, e.g. 'th' in 'this' and 'oa' in 'boat'.

Directionality: The direction used in reading and writing. In English, this is left to right.

Discrimination: The process of recognising differences between stimuli. Both **auditory** and **visual** discrimination are important in literacy. (The assessment of auditory discrimination is often now conducted as part of the assessment of **phonological awareness**.)

Double deficit: A deficit in both phonological awareness and speed of processing/rapid naming.

Dynamic assessment: A form of interactive assessment whereby the assessor interacts with a learner during assessment in order to investigate a child's learning. The assessor can change/modify tasks to discover how the child learns best and how she/he approaches learning. It is popular with many educational psychologists and can provide very useful information for intervention. However, if standardised tests (or subtests) are used during this process, scores cannot be given, as the test is not administered according to the standardised procedure.

Dyscalculia: Difficulty in the conceptual understanding of number and quantity.

Dysgraphia: Very poor handwriting or the inability to produce the fine motor skills required for handwriting (considered to be a neurological dysfunction).

Dyspraxia (Developmental Co-ordination Disorder): Difficulty in controlling muscles and movement which can affect speech and/or balance and motor control.

Fine motor skills: Skills in controlling sets of small muscles and fingers such as in writing or grasping small objects. (It may also be applied to controlling other small muscles, e.g. controlling eye movements; producing speech.)

Fluency: (e.g. as in reading) The ability to read accurately and quickly, thereby facilitating understanding.

Fluid ability (fluid intelligence): Originally considered as a factor of general intelligence, it is the ability to solve non-verbal problems and think logically, independently of acquired knowledge. It is usually assessed using problems requiring visual-spatial understanding and performance in problem solving/reasoning (i.e. activities that do not require the testee to understand or use words).

Formal tests: Used in this book to describe standardised tests.

Formative assessment: The assessment that is on-going or takes place during a course or programme of study in order to improve learning. It provides important feedback to a teacher (e.g. in setting new targets for a learner; changing teaching methods) and to a learner (e.g. deciding which targets to attain in order to improve; opportunity to reflect on their own learning). Formative assessment is a major aspect of the teaching–learning cycle.

Grapheme–phoneme correspondence: The link between a grapheme (letter or letter cluster) and the phoneme (single speech sound) that it represents.

Group tests: An assessment procedure devised to be given to a group simultaneously. These usually (but not always) require some reading ability. They are often useful for **screening** purposes within a group and comparing with others of their age. However, they do not provide detailed information about an individual's performance or skills. They can be standardised, criterion-referenced or informal/teacher-made.

Hemisphere: The brain is divided into two parts (left and right hemisphere).

Individual Education Plan (IEP): The SEN Code of Practice (DfES, 2001) recommended that an IEP should be drawn up for children who are not making progress. This records what is 'additional' to or 'different from' a differentiated curriculum: Like an ILP, it will identify short-term target and specify review dates. However, it focuses on only three or four targets.

Individual Learning Plan (ILP): A plan devised for an individual learner to specify targets to be achieved within a specified time frame and to specified criteria of attainment.

The targets will form the basis of **direct teaching**. It may, therefore, contain more targets than an **Individual Education Plan (IEP)** and provide greater detail of both targets and methods/resources.

Individual tests: Tests that are administered to one person at a time. This means the behaviours during the test itself can be observed as well as the assessment results. They usually provide more detail about individual performance than group tests. They can be standardised, criterion-referenced or informal/teacher-made.

Informal tests: This term is used to describe non-standardised tests. They can include published materials and those that teachers devise. They are structured in order to obtain information about areas of strength and difficulties.

Invented spelling: The spellings of words where learners (particularly young children) are encouraged to apply their early knowledge of phonemes and letters to 'attempt' to spell a word. (A temporary 'stage' in learning to spell before normal orthography is achieved.)

Ipsative assessment: The term used when a comparison is made between current performance and that assessed previously, i.e. an individual's performance is compared with their prior performance, as when evaluating progress.

Irregular word: A word where the spelling contains an unusual (or infrequent) representation of a sound, e.g. said, one.

Lexical route: A system that relies on whole word processing.

Lexicon: A body of word knowledge, either written or spoken – a vocabulary.

Linguistic: Referring to language processing and language structure.

Long-term memory: The part of memory to which information is sent for permanent storage. It is seen as having an infinite capacity.

Magnocellular deficit: Difficulty in processing rapid moving information in either the auditory or visual pathways of the magnocellular system of the brain.

Miscue: An inaccurate response in reading which has been based on interpreting some of the 'cues' about the word provided by the context or syntax or by looking at similarities to other words containing some of the same graphemes.

Modality: A specific sensory pathway (e.g. visual, auditory, kinaesthetic, tactile).

Morphology: The study of how meaningful units are put together to form words (morpheme = a meaningful unit, which may be a word itself, such as 'find', or a group of letters, e.g. '-ing', which when added to a word, changes the meaning of that word).

Multi-sensory literacy programme: An approach to teaching literacy that involves the simultaneous use of at least two senses (visual/auditory/kinaesthetic/touch) and teaches listening, speaking, reading, writing and spelling together.

Neural pathway: Neurons are cells that make up the nervous system. Neurons are linked to each other (neural pathways) so that they can store and transmit information from one part of the body to another.

Non-lexical route: A system which breaks words down into grapheme–phoneme correspondence.

Non-verbal ability/reasoning tests: Non-verbal tests of reasoning involve the ability to analyse problems presented visually, requiring ability to see relationships and produce correlates. They may involve discovering patterns in a set of matrices, completing patterns, manipulating materials. They can be individual tests or group tests (which usually involve a basic use of pencil skills).

Non-word: A 'word' or grouping of letters which can be decoded phonically (i.e. the graphemes represent particular phonemes) but the word has no meaning in that language (English).

Norm-referenced test: Assessment of performance in relation to that of the normative group on which the test was standardised, e.g. a learner's score can be compared with that of learners of the same age in the cohort on which the test was standardised.

Occipital lobe: The rear part of the cerebral hemisphere processing visual information.

Onset: The initial consonant(s) in a word (e.g. 'c' in cat and 'scr' in scream). See also **rime**.

Orthography: The established spelling or representation of words in a written language.

Otitis media: Inflammation of the middle ear that can lead to a temporary hearing loss (sometimes permanent, particularly if untreated). In the case of very young children, it may impact on phonological awareness.

Percentile: The percentage of individuals in the standardisation sample scoring at or below a given score.

Phoneme: An individual unit of sound: the smallest unit of sound in speech.

Phonemic awareness: Awareness of the smallest units of sound and the ability to distinguish and manipulate individual sounds in words.

Phonics: The representation of an association between the printed form of letters and the sound(s) they represent.

Phonogram: A written symbol representing a phoneme (single unit of sound). It can also be called a phonograph.

Phonological: Relating to a speaker's knowledge about the sound systems in a language.

Phonological awareness: Knowledge of and sensitivity to the phonological properties of words in a language.

Phonological deficit: A difficulty in phonological processing, e.g. in segmenting or blending sounds or appreciating rhyme.

Phonological loop: Part of short-term memory that stores small bits of speech/sound information as they are being processed.

Phonology: The science or knowledge of the sound system of a language both segmental (e.g. phonemes) and non-segmental or supra-segmental (e.g. stress, pitch, volume). The latter is often described as prosodic features.

Polygenetic: More than one gene is responsible for a condition, e.g. dyslexia.

Prefix: A group of letters (forming a syllable) which is added at the beginning of a base or root word to change its meaning, e.g. 'mis' added to 'represent' to make 'misrepresent'.

Proprioception: The subconscious perception of movement, position and body/self in space coming from internal stimuli: sense of spatial orientation. (Often assessed by an occupational therapist.)

Pseudowords: Also known as a **non-words** or nonsense words.

Psychometrics: The science of psychological measurement. It is concerned with the theories and techniques used to measure psychological constructs, particularly through the use of **standardised tests.**

Rapid automatic naming: This is regarded as an important aspect of verbal ability and is concerned with how quickly an individual can name a series of printed objects/letters/colours/numbers presented randomly. It assesses **automaticity/speed of information processing**. It is often considered to be one aspect of phonological processing skills.

Recognition: Identifying a stimulus as the same as one experienced (learned) previously, e.g. word recognition; auditory recognition (listening for a particular sound in a word and picking it out by position).

Reliability: The extent to which a measure/score can be relied upon, i.e. that consistent measures/scores would be produced when given on different occasions or by different testers.

Rime: The written or spoken vowel and final consonant(s) in a word or syllable, e.g. 'at' in 'cat' and 'eam' in 'scream'.

Screening test: A procedure to identify individuals who may show characteristics indicating possible learning difficulties that may require further intervention. Screening tests are usually designed for use with large groups to identify those who need more detailed assessment.

Segmentation: Separating a word into units (such as onset and rime, syllables or individual units).

Semantic: Referring to the meaning of words.

Short-term memory: Refers to information presented verbally or visually that is stored for only a very short period of time.

Sight word: A word that is immediately recognised as a whole and does not require analysing. Some may be phonetically irregular, such as 'the', whereas others may be regular and originally have been decoded (but stored in memory through frequency of use and are then recalled as a 'whole word', e.g. 'sat').

Sound deletion: (phonemic deletion) The ability to delete a sound from a given word, e.g. to say 'dog' without the /d/.

Sound manipulation: The ability to omit (as in deletion) or change the 'order' of sounds in a word, e.g. say 'cat'; now change the position of /k/ and /t/.

Speed of information processing: This is concerned with the amount of time taken or rate at which information is received and organised/processed in order to respond to that information. It is often seen as a significant aspect of underlying cognitive ability.

Standard Deviation (SD): This shows the variation from the mean of a set of scores. In **standardised tests** this is based on an assumption of a normal distribution.

Standard Error of Measurement (SEM): This is an estimate of the error contained in a set of test scores and can be used to interpret the 'band' of scores in which a 'true' score is likely to be.

Standard Score: This is derived from the raw score in order to enable comparisons to be made between individuals. It is based on the scores of the standardisation sample (norm group).

Standardised test: A test that has been standardised in terms of administration and scoring.

Summative assessment: Assessment taking place at the end of a course/programme of study to measure a learner's knowledge/skills/understanding in relation to that course.

Syllable: A spoken or written unit that must have a vowel sound and can include preceding and/or following consonants. It is made by one impulse of the voice.

Syntax: The structures of grammar – the system governing how words must be ordered in phrases or sentences.

Synthetic phonics: Introducing letter–sound (grapheme–phoneme correspondences) and then blending/joining them to others to make meaningful units/words. See also **analytic phonics**.

Validity: The extent to which an assessment procedure/test measures what it claims to assess.

Variable: A term to describe a factor, characteristic or attribute in research and in psychometrics.

Variance: A measure of how factors (test scores in relation to assessment) are distributed in relation to the mean. 'Shared variance' is the amount that the variations of the two variables shown by a correlation coefficient tend to overlap. The percentage of shared variance is represented by the square of the correlation coefficient. An example is that if two tests (A and B) have a correlation of 0.8 then there is a 'shared variance' of 0.64. This implies that 64% of the variance in the scores in Test B is accounted for by factors in the scores of Test A. Where there is a correlation, e.g. reliability based on test–retest of 0.6, this suggests that 36% (0.6×0.6 expressed as a percentage) of the variance is a result of the same test materials/population tested, but 64% can be accounted for by other factors, e.g. individual differences such as tiredness, illness, motivation etc.

Verbal ability: This involves the ability to reason and solve problems using spoken (or written) language. This relies heavily on an individual's cultural and educational experiences and the way these have affected vocabulary and general knowledge. Verbal ability is often assessed by understanding and use of vocabulary, the ability to see and make verbal analogies and draw on verbal knowledge. It can be assessed by individual and group tests.

Visual discrimination/perception: The ability to identify similarities and differences in stimuli presented visually, e.g. letters, shapes, words etc. It can be easily assessed informally by teachers. Where there are other signs of visual difficulty there should be referral to an optician or optometrist.

Working memory: The part of short-term memory that holds on to information long enough to manipulate or use it, e.g. as in following an instruction or carrying out a mental calculation.

AUTHOR INDEX

SUBJECT INDEX

Readers are also advised to refer to the Appendices and Glossary